POWER AND
PLURALISM
IN AMERICAN CITIES

Recent Titles in
Contributions in Political Science
Series Editor: Bernard K. Johnpoll

POWER AND PLURALISM IN AMERICAN CITIES
Researching the Urban Laboratory

ROBERT J. WASTE

Contributions in Political Science, Number 165

GREENWOOD PRESS
New York • Westport, Connecticut • London

Library of Congress Cataloging-in-Publication Data

Waste, Robert J.
  Power and pluralism in American cities.

  (Contributions in political science, ISSN 0147-1066 ;
no. 165)
  Bibliography: p.
  Includes index.
  1. Municipal government—United States. 2. Elite
(Social sciences)—United States. 3. Pluralism
(Social sciences)—United States. 4. Community power.
I. Title. II. Series.
JS341.W38 1987   320.8'0973   86-19381
ISBN 0-313-25016-2 (lib. bdg. : alk. paper)

Library of Congress Catalog Card Number: 86-19381
ISBN: 0-313-25016-2
ISSN: 0147-1066

First published in 1987

Greenwood Press, Inc.
88 Post Road West, Westport, Connecticut 06881

Printed in the United States of America

The paper used in this book complies with the
Permanent Paper Standard issued by the National
Information Standards Organization (Z39.48-1984).

10 9 8 7 6 5 4 3 2 1

For Robert A. Dahl,
democrat, scholar, mentor, and friend

Contents

Figures and Tables

Preface

> We are, it appears, no closer today than in 1963 to the establishment of
> a firmly grounded set of empirical propositions about the world which
> command universal agreement, or indeed even a well articulated sense
> of what we know and what we do not know. Have we simply been
> pushing a rock uphill and watching it tumble back down again?
>
> Nelson W. Polsby, *Community Power and Political Theory*

Initially, this book grew out of a desire to provide an answer to questions
raised by students in my courses on urban politics. Students frequently
asked if a given community was democratic and, if so, how democratic. As
I suppose most urban scholars would do, I referred the students to Floyd
Hunter's "reputational elite," G. William Domhoff's "higher circles," and
Robert A. Dahl's "polyarchal" explanations of urban political life.[1] In so
doing, I found it necessary to clarify in my own mind exactly what claims
Dahl et al. were making when they claimed a polity was or was not a
polyarchy. Ironically, this was less easy to do than it may seem. Although
Dahl employed the term polyarchy consistently (despite some refinement
and modifications) since he and Lindblom introduced the concept in 1953,[2]
the vast secondary literature on polyarchy contains no less than four
different views of what Dahl meant by "polyarchy." So, one of the early
aims of the book became an effort to condense the polyarchal concept into a
set of basic claims or propositions and contrast this somewhat "mechanical
view" of polyarchy with the view(s) of polyarchy dominating the secondary
literature. In the course of doing this, I realized that my view of
polyarchy—although not different from Dahl's own view—was, in fact,
quite different from the view of polyarchy in the secondary literature. In
this respect, the reader may find the view of polyarchy described herein to
constitute a "revisionist" view of Dahl and polyarchy.

Secondly, the attempt to clarify the polyarchal concept led to a desire to provide a way to test it empirically. Currently, if two researchers argue over whether New Haven, for example, is or is not a polyarchy,[3] there is no good way to resolve the dispute. Arguments on both sides frequently appear to outsiders to be arguments based less on facts than on faith or ideology: Dahl asks who governs and gets governors; Domhoff asks who rules and gets rulers. While it will become abundantly clear to the reader that I am much closer to Dahl's perspective than that of Domhoff, I wanted to construct a way using prevailing social science practices to *prove* that New Haven, or any city, was or was not a polyarchy. Ergo, I designed the "empirical polyarchy method" described and tested in chapter 5. The empirical method not only provides a way to test municipal polyarchy empirically but also adds a further comparative and prescriptive dimension to polyarchal theory.

A third intent, perhaps less adequately realized in the present study, was to use the empirical polyarchy method to suggest a way out of the pluralist-elitist "impasse"[4] and to suggest a future research agenda for community power studies. For a more detailed treatment of these and related research concerns, the reader is directed to my earlier study entitled *Community Power: Directions for Future Research* (1986).[5]

A fourth intent was that the empirical polyarchy model contribute both to the emerging field of empirical democratic theory and help to rekindle a normative democratic inquiry of U.S. cities and governmental institutions, both municipal and national. Certainly, this moral or normative tone is the motive of writers such as Dahl, as well as Hunter and Domhoff. Increasingly though, it seems to me, the field of urban study is drifting away from such basic inquiry as: How democratic are U.S. cities? Is Atlanta *more democratic* than Chicago or San Diego? Why or why not? And what, if anything, can be done in the less democratic city to improve the democratic nature of its institutions and political life?[6] Increasingly, urban research is focusing on such specialized inquiry as the delivery of certain services, the politics of grantsmanship, the internecine intricacies of urban redevelopment, or inquiry into such substantive concerns as crime, transportation, budget know-how, and so on. Through such shifts in focus we gain much in the way of description but run the risk of losing our grasp of the "big picture" in American local and naitonal politics. Are we as a discipline (or, in the case of urban politics, it is more accurate to say a coalition of disciplines) providing Americans with the sort of information that enriches and enhances their political lives? To paraphrase the Socratic injunction, are we doing much these days to help the average citizen replace his or her *opinions* about the democratic polis with *knowledge* about the polis? Are we providing the grist for the mill that is necessary if citizens are to make an informed moral assessment about the adequacy of their purportedly democratic political culture? I think we could be doing a better job of it. This book is a step in that direction.

A fifth concern in writing the present volume was an intent (always healthy, one hopes) to raise the question of the standards of scholarship acceptable to the discipline. It seems to me that confusion surrounding the concept of polyarchy is the result of a far too casual reading of Dahl's theoretical writings on polyarchy. Good scholars—in some cases some of the finest in the field[7]—have sometimes done less than good work when it comes to analyzing Dahl and polyarchy. Frequently, Dahl and polyarchy have been used as strawmen (in some cases as punching bags) by authors intending to rail not against polyarchy or the polyarchal method per se, but against other more exotic (and, admittedly, more odious) ills such as the behavioral persuasion writ large, democratic-elitism, or a moral agnosticism which fails to address the so-called fact-value distinction.

The chapters which follow attempt to weave these themes into a coherent survey of Dahl and polyarchy. The first chapter traces the pluralist tradition in the United States, describes the place of Dahl's polyarchy within that tradition, and explains the basic concepts of the polyarchal theory. The second chapter examines the four views of Dahl prevalent in the secondary literature and describes the criticisms of Dahl and polyarchy advanced by representatives of these views. The third chapter addresses and dismisses a surprisingly popular—if incorrect—view of Dahl as an apologist for status quo American politics. The fourth chapter responds to various methodological criticisms raised against polyarchy and the pluralist method of examining community politics. The final chapter raises some further criticisms of polyarchy and attempts to meet some of these by presenting and testing the empirical model of polyarchy. It closes with a call for further research and a discussion of the prescriptive promise of the empirical polyarchal method. I have tried to present both a developmental study of Dahl's polyarchy and a preface to further polyarchal studies.

I am greatly indebted to several persons who have aided me in the course of this study. My heaviest debt is to Professor Larry L. Wade of the University of California at Davis and Professor Robert A. Dahl of Yale. Both men read earlier drafts and their comments and suggestions helped immeasurably. Larry Wade advised early and fortuitously on the scope of the project. Without his forceful hand, the study might have grown to unmanageable and quite possibly unintelligible proportions. Robert Dahl submitted good-naturedly to a barrage of interviews and brainstorming sessions. He read drafts and rewrites and never once showed a reluctance to follow a thought to its logical conclusion, whether that thought involved a criticism of my work or a criticism of his own thinking and writing. Without the contributions of Professors Wade and Dahl, this study of polyarchy would have been impossible.

I am indebted to a number of colleagues whose discussion and counsel has helped me to clarify my own ideas about polyarchy and community power studies. My debt to colleagues is extensive. It includes but is not limited to Fred Bergerson, Rufus Browning, Roger Cobb, G. William

Domhoff, Thomas Dye, Bob Grady, Pat Hanratty, Charles Hardin, Wood-row Jones, Jr., the late Jack Livingston, Charles Lockhart, Tim Lukes, Wiliam Lunch, Dale Rogers Marshall, William Neeley, Eric Nordlinger, Victor Profughi, Priscilla Regan, Glen W. Sparrow, Clarence N. Stone, Milburn Stone, David Tabb, Robert Thompson, and Marco Walshok.

I would also like to acknowledge my gratitude to the National Endow-ment for the Humanities, the Yale political science department, and Brown University for a summer fellowship at Harvard, a predoctoral fellowship, and computer assistance, respectively. The always gracious and expert advice of the manager of Brown's Social Science Data Service, Ms. Donna Souza, was especially helpful.

Finally, I wish to note my gratitude to Kathrine Lemke-Waste for many tasks and moments—ineffable to me now—but which I pray that time will give me the grace and the opportunity to express.

1

The Rise of American Pluralism

INTRODUCTION

It's been over twenty years since Robert Dahl asked who governed in New Haven. In this time the discipline has produced two answers and an argument. For Dahl, the leading adherent of the pluralist approach, New Haven was a "republic," a "pluralistic democracy."[8] However loose this description may seem to contemporary urban scholars, it was in the context of urban scholarship in the 1960s an attempt at craftsmanlike precision in the labeling of urban political regimes. Dahl sought to avoid describing New Haven politics as falling at either end of a continuum. He believed New Haven to be neither a hegemonic polity controlled by a cabal or "power elite"[9] nor a fully inclusive, participatory democracy. Dahl argued in *Who Governs?* that "leaders lead—and often are led. Citizens are very far indeed from exerting equal influence over the content, application, and development of the political consensus."[10] Even this description of New Haven was qualified. "In short," Dahl argued, "New Haven is a republic of unequal citizens—but for all that a republic."[11]

Thus, for Dahl, New Haven appeared as something of an enigma. It was neither an elite nor a democracy per se. In fact, in the context of Dahl's larger research on modern political regimes,[12] New Haven appears to be what Dahl would call a "polyarchy"; that is, a political regime in which "the democratic goal is still roughly and crudely approximated, in the sense that nonleaders exercise a relatively high degree of control over leaders."[13]

There are two problems with Dahl's characterization of power in American communities as polyarchal. First, the veracity of the polyarchal claim has been challenged. Scholars such as Floyd Hunter and G. William Domhoff, associated with various elitist approaches, claim that American cities in general and, for Domhoff, New Haven in particular, are elite political regimes. That is, both authors dispute Dahl's findings and argue that American cities are dominated by a "power structure"[14] comprised of members of a "ruling class."[15] Interestingly, in a recent study in which Dahl made available to Domhoff all the data and interviews from the classic 1961 study of New Haven, Domhoff concludes that Dahl's explanation is inaccurate. Rather, in *Who Really Rules?* Domhoff challenges Dahl's polyarchal view and asserts: "Wealthy businessmen are at the center of the social and upper class and are the rulers of New Haven and America."[16] Second, the substance, if not the veracity, of Dahl's claim has been called into question. What Dahl is claiming when he asserts that community x is a polyarchy is, at least in some quarters, manifestly unclear. In some respects polyarchy is a difficult concept if only because of the protean nature of its author. Dahl has written fifteen books and over fifty scholarly articles. Although first conceived by Dahl and Charles Lindblom in *Politics, Economics, and Welfare* (1953), the polyarchal concept has evolved, been tested, and refined in several of these subsequent studies. Thus, as shall be argued later in this chapter, polyarchy is not a static concept. What it is as a theory and what claims it is making when used as a label for a particular type of regime have shifted over time. Additionally, a formidable body of secondary literature has sprung up around the polyarchal concept. Unfortunately, rather than clarifying matters this has served only to muddy the waters further. As we shall make clear in the second chapter, the secondary literature on America's leading pluralist is itself extremely pluralistic. There are, in fact, four major schools of thought purporting to explain what the polyarchal approach to community politics is all about.

Thus, despite a small cottage industry of community power studies underscoring the veracity and substance or meaning of Dahl's New Haven description,[17] the meaning and the accuracy of Dahl's description of New Haven as "pluralistically democratic" (read: polyarchal) is still subject to question. Indeed, at least partially as a result of the confusion surrounding the polyarchal explanation of pluralism and because pluralists and elitists are at an "impasse"[18] as to which paradigm best explains community power, and because no solid way of testing the pluralist or elitist explanations currently exists,[19] the community power controversy has, in Clarence Stone's words, shown "no signs of abating after nearly three decades of controversy."[20] In fact, as Nelson Polsby noted in the preface to the 1980 edition of *Community Power and Political Theory*:

The literature on community power, no exemplar of clarity or intelligence when I first wrote this book [1963], has since its publication become even more dense with misunderstandings of all kinds, while burgeoning in nearly every direction—every direction that is, except toward the resolution of empirical problems about the shape and scope of power in American communities.[21]

This book is an attempt to rectify at least some of these misunderstandings. Relying heavily upon the earlier work of Dahl, Polsby, Raymond

Wolfinger, and David Ricci, this book will attempt first to clarify what is being claimed when Dahl or others assert that a community is a polyarchy and, second, to offer an empirical method for testing whether a given community is or is not a polyarchy[22] and in so doing to clear up the main misunderstandings revolving around both the veracity and substance of the polyarchal explanation of power in American communities.

HISTORICAL ANTECEDENTS: MADISON, TOCQUEVILLE, AND CALHOUN

Robert Dahl is the most recent in a lengthy tradition of American pluralist spokesmen. The pluralist legacy stretches back, at the least, to James Madison and Alexis de Tocqueville, and, in the longer view, pluralist tendencies exist in various theorists dating from the Italian Renaissance to the Scottish Enlightenment. Indeed, much could be made of the pluralist leanings in Machiavelli, Locke, Montesquieu, Rousseau, and Adam Smith.[23] Since the present study focuses on a more contemporary pluralist and because other studies of pluralist writers are readily available in the literature,[24] discussion here is confined to a brief description of the American school of pluralists and Dahl's place within that school.

Pluralism, the view that public policy in America is the result of a tug of war—often ending in a delicate balance or compromise—between various interest groups, has had several stages of development and expression by American spokesmen.[25] The early formulation of American pluralist thinking is best viewed in the writings of Madison and Tocqueville. In *Federalist* 10 and 51 (1787), Madison set forth the essence of what later became the pluralist orthodoxy.[26] Division or "faction" in political society (e.g., the division of society into owners, creditors, and debtors) is a given. The twin challenge of government is to be sufficiently powerful to manage such conflicting interests while not, at the same time, creating a government so strong that government itself becomes a dominant faction inflicting demands on the whole of society. Thus, in *Federalist* 10 the famous Madisonian view of pluralism emerges.[27] Madisonian pluralism envisaged a political solciety in which the multiple or plural interests in society (e.g., landed and nonlanded classes, moneyed and debtor classes, as well as manufacturing and mercantile classes) were used as "checks and balances" both against each other and, in combination, against a republican government—itself divided into a triangulation of counterbalanced elements.

TOCQUEVILLE AND THE "TYRANNY OF THE MAJORITY"

Alexis de Tocqueville's *Democracy in America* (1835, 1840) analyzed the early American experiment in republican government and expanded on Madison's account of pluralism.[28] Tocqueville saw the "tyranny of the majority" as a problem inherent in the Madisonian approach. A democratic government based on the majority rule principle could in its own way turn out to be as despotic as the older despotisms of the European monarchies. Tocqueville argued that America had few writers of note because such people were hampered by the role played by majority opinion in American society. Tocqueville argued that adherence to the wishes of the majority led to a leveling or commonality of opinion in both writers and legislators. This leveling of great writers and great statesmen, as well as the general lack of learning in the majority of citizens, might lead to a banality of literature and culture and, eventually, to a threat to the existence of free institutions themselves. Tocqueville concurs with Jefferson's argument that the "executive power in our government is not the only, perhaps not even the principal, object of my solicitude. The tyranny of the legislature is really the danger most to be feared, and will continue to be so for many years to come."[29]

For Tocqueville, although he was less sanguine in the second volume than in the first, the problem of tyranny of the majority was solvable, or, at the least, solvable in the American context. The resolution of the problem was fourfold. First, America did not appear to have a system of class dominance. Goods and resources were (then) widely dispersed. Second, there was not yet an institutional dominance in America. Institutions were decentralized and central power was checked by both national and regional counterparts. Further, these institutions were circumscribed in their actions by laws and a judiciary made the more pluralistic by the inclusion of a jury system.[30]

For Tocqueville, a third way to restrain the antipluralistic drives toward a tyranny of the majority was "Self Interest Rightly Understood." This was an extension of Madison's reasoning in *Federalist* 10.[31] Self-interest—"the only immutable point in the human heart"[32]—was to be used as a weapon to insure against political upheaval. Factions were to be made to see that their survival and interest depended upon the promotion of the interests of the whole. This was to be accomplished by what in modern times probably would be called the sociopsychological construction of a democratic worldview; that is, the construction of a society that encouraged pluralistic behavior on the part of its citizens. Earlier societies had used religion or a tradition of monarchy to unify citizens and avoid the dangers of faction. The American solution was to use three elements: good law (juries and the Constitution), patriotism (the vigor and pride of the citizens of the new republic), and the uniquely American freedom of association (the proliferation of clubs, organizations, groups, and social and political interests as well as a firmly entrenched religious pluralism) to chasten the American citizen.[33] The democratic "new man," or so Tocqueville hoped, would thus be inclined against faction because although inclined by nature to faction, he was constrained by a sociopolitical network of pluralistic beliefs and institutions that in their overlapping and aggregate effect would restrain and reshape the preferences of individual members of the polity.

CALHOUN AND THE "TYRANNY OF THE MINORITY"

If Madison and Tocqueville served as the early spokesmen for American pluralism, John C. Calhoun served as an early critic and revisionist. Calhoun's *Disquisition on Government* (1851) voiced a disquietude with the approach of Madison and Tocqueville to the problem of the tyranny of the majority.[34] Calhoun was a southerner concerned with tariff measures which advantaged northern manufacturers[35] and fearful that the South would be forced by an abolitionist faction in the North to give up the practice of slavery. He sought a safeguard against government by "artificial majority" —government control by the political party that is able to control government itself. Calhoun believed that a minority out of power should be able to protect its interests against a party or faction that was in power "by dividing and distributing the powers of government."[36] This doctrine of distributed powers or nullification was Calhoun's answer to the threat he called the "tyranny of the minority." The tyranny that Calhoun believed faced the South was the weak regional position of the southern Democrats vis-à-vis the national Democrats led by Jackson, the National Republicans, and the newly formed Whig party nominally led by Daniel Webster and Henry Clay.

Although the Constitution protected against the possibility of a tyranny of the majority via a republican form of government, checks and balances, and a Bill of Rights outlining minority rights, Calhoun believed that political parties unrepresentative of public opinion as a whole could (and *did*) translate their opinions into policy by winning election to national office. In this way a "tyranny of the minority" might arise.[37] A possibility for such control was already seen in instances like the heavy-handed use of the Alien and Sedition Acts by Federalists (1798-99), the imposition of a tariff on manufactured goods by northern manufacturing interests (1828-32), and an attempt by abolitionists to prevent slavery in the territories (1840-60).

Calhoun's remedy for this alleged defect in the governmental instrument was to propose an extension of *Federalist* 10's remedy for the "mischiefs of faction." In effect, Calhoun called for a "refounding" of the American republic.[38] He proposed a mechanistic system of government that (as did Madison) accepted "portions," "classes," "interests," "divisions," and "orders" as inevitable in political society and (extending Madison) seeks to check them so they are not at war. For Calhoun, Madison's republican conception led to government by an "artificial majority"—governmental control by the political party which is able to control government itself. True, *Federalist* 10 protects against a numerical majority usurping government, but Calhoun meant to improve on this by proposing universal suffrage as a protection against the artificial majority of party.

If universal suffrage is the first principle in his proposed remedy, "concurrent consent" or the "Negative" is his second principle. For Calhoun, the states needed a "Negative," an ability to veto major policy decisions made by the federal government. A concurrent resolution—involving a concurrent majority of the parts of the government (federal, state, and local)—would be required for all major policy decisions of government. Calhoun noted that the problem of infinite regress could be avoided by holding that at each level a numerical majority would rule. Thus, via the use of "concurrent consent," the influence of political parties could be overcome. The proposed new constitutionalism of Calhoun involved as much a limit to the powers of government as it did a limit to the conflict managed in society by government. It involved, in short, government policymaking in areas where unanimous agreement existed. Where it did not, it involved not the possibility of substantive policy but, rather, an agreement to disagree. In short, Calhoun proposed via the use of the concurrent consent device to render the constitutional order fully workable. The mischiefs of faction— both majority and minority—stood checked.

Although the question of the state legislatures exercising Calhoun's "Negative" was itself answered—at least partially—in the negative by the victory of Union forces in the Civil War, a not unsimilar argument was raised subsequently by such writers as Arthur Bentley, David Riesman, and David Truman.[39]

BENTLEY AND TRUMAN: THE ANALYTICAL PLURALISTS

Modern or orthodox pluralism begins with Arthur Bentley. In the *Process of Government* (1908), Bentley updated the theory of plural interest groups and became pluralism's most strident spokesman.[40] Combining the findings of (then) modern political science and traditional interest group theory, Bentley founded an approach to group politics described by Mancur Olson as "analytical pluralism." By analytical pluralists, Olson meant to group together a set of theorists who believed that "group interests are absolutely fundamental determinants of economic and political behavior."[41] As Bentley was to write in *The Process of Government*, groups—not individuals—are the proper focus of political study. "When groups are adequately stated, everything is stated. When I say everything I mean everything. The complete description will mean the complete science, in the study of social phenomena, as in any other field."[42] Individuals in the abstract were not important to Bentley. The "raw materials" of politics is "the action of men with or upon each other." Politics or political activity was, then, group activity.[43]

Bentley, then, concentrated on analyzing and describing the political activity of groups. Activity was either "manifest"—"external," evident, and "palpable"—or, "potential"—tendencies of activities, "nonpalpable activity."[44] Bentley sought vigorously to explain all social activity in terms of group as opposed to individual or ideational ("spook") activity. Although Bentley's major task (the development of a taxonomy of interest groups in political society) eluded him, his resultant theory of group politics and the variant of it popularized by David Truman are the core of what is today generally regarded as contemporary or orthodox pluralism. That Bentley had larger hopes is evident in his 1908 call for a taxonomy of groups. He wrote: "If we can get our social life stated in terms of activity, and of nothing else, we have not indeed succeeded in measuring it, but we have at least reached a foundation upon which a coherent system of measurements can be built up."[45]

The literature of the analytical pluralists is both extensive and complex, as is the accompanying litany of criticism that it has provoked. Necessarily, any attempt to present such arguments in terms of a brief sketch runs the risk of oversimplification. Such a risk is undertaken for two reasons. On the one hand, adequate and well-known accounts of Bentley and Truman are readily available to the reader who stands in need of a more complete account.[46] On the other hand it is necessary to sketch briefly the outlines of pluralist theory prior to Dahl in order to provide a context in which to discuss both Dahl and his critics.

Stanley Rothman has suggested that Bentley's "pluralism" can be viewed as a model composed of seven elements: four "concepts," two main or "supernumerary propositions," and one additional "middle range proposition"[47] (see Table 1.1). Bentley's primary "concept" was his focus on groups as the "raw materials of politics." Bentley's focus on groups was an attempt to move away from an institutional or legal formal approach to the study of politics which characterized American political science at the time of his writing. Bentley sought to get "underneath" this constitutional or institutional approach, to analyze the "raw materials" of political society.

Second, for Bentley, all groups were interest groups. "There is no group without its interest."[48] And the point is to trace the success or failure of these groups in pressing their interests. The study of politics becomes the study of factors that account for group effectiveness; for example, numbers, intensity, and techniques of group activities ("bribes, blows and allurements").[49]

Third, and of special importance for Bentley, was the category of not-yet-formed groups which he labeled "underlying groups." An underlying group was, as David Truman later noted, a potential group that lay on the fringe of political activity but might organize and act if its interests were threatened. Thus, in American politics it is possible to speak of a third political party which might arise if the major parties failed to articulate interests that were important to many citizens. Jacksonian Democrats, Lincoln and the Republicans, Roosevelt and the Bull Moose Progressives might all be viewed as underlying groups that eventually mobilized.

Equilibrium is the fourth basic concept of Bentley's pluralism. For Bentley, group activity and bargaining tends toward equilibrium since no group dominates all the other groups in society. There is, in Bentley's model, the suggestion that equilibrium or group balance is a good. In fact, Bentley does not speak of a "public" or "common good." The good implicit in the system is group harmony regardless of the ideational content of the policy that results from the group bargaining process.

Underpinning these concepts were several assumptions. First, Bentley believed that society can be viewed as a conglomeration of groups interacting with one another. Politics is essentially "brokerage politics,"[50] a process of group bargaining and competition for society's resources. Interestingly, for Bentley, groups were independent variables and government institutions were dependent variables.[51] The governmental institutions that prevailed in a given political culture were the result of the more basic activity of groups in society, rather than the reverse. To use Marxian terms, groups were the base of society, while governmental institutions were superstructural "reflections" of group activity. Bentley writes that no "social whole" exists, only the workings of group interests.[52] Further, "the society itself is nothing more than the complex of groups that compose it."[53]

A final assumption inherent in Bentley's pluralism is the presumed presence of factors leading to stability or equilibrium. Bentley argued that group interaction and the threat of intervention by underlying groups would promote equilibrium or harmony among groups. Group politics would result in moderate or harmonizing public policies.

Table 1.1
Rothman's Summary of Bentley's Pluralism

Concepts	Supernumerary Propositions	Subsidiary Proposition
1. group focus	1. Politics is group competition.	1. Underlying groups produce stability.
2. interest groups	2. Group interaction produces stability.	
3. underlying groups		
4. equilibrium model		

TRUMAN I: THE GOVERNMENTAL PROCESS

If Bentley founded modern pluralism and *The Process of Government* was its expression of orthodoxy, it remained for David Truman to popularize Bentley's theory and to bring Bentley's pluralism into line with the findings and thinking of American social scientists of the 1950s. In *The Governmental Process* (1951), Truman extended Bentley's theory of pluralism by introducing such concepts as "potential" and "overlapping" groups, "effective access" to the pluralist political arena, and "rules of the game."[54]

Building upon Bentley's earlier concepts of interest group and underlying group, Truman argued that the phrase interest group "refers to any group that, on the basis of one or more shared attitudes, makes certain claims upon other groups in society for the establishment, maintenance, or enhancement of forms of behavior that are implied by the shared attitudes."[55] "All groups are interest groups because they are all shared-attitude groups."[56] Truman noted that not all interest groups will have the same degree of "effective access" to governmental policy arenas. In fact, "the extent to which a group achieves effective access to the institutions of government is the result of a complex of interdependent factors." Groups may achieve effective access via one, or a combination of, three different means: (1) the group may possess a "strategic position in society" which it can use to good advantage, (2) the "internal characteristics of the group" (leadership, cohesion, membership size, or financial resources) may aid the group in pressing its claim, or (3) "factors peculiar to the governmental institutions themselves" (e.g., federalism, checks and balances, separation of powers) may aid an interest group in gaining effective access to the political arena.[57]

Truman held that not all groups will enjoy effective access to decisional arenas. Depending on the issue and resources available, some will have greater or lesser degrees of access. Additionally, modern pluralist society is characterized by a limited number, or class, of "chronic nonparticipants."[58] Truman differed with such writers as Pendleton Herring who argued that the nonvoting, nonparticipating citizens who occasionally are aroused to protest "unwonted activity" serve as a stabilizing counterweight to "the solid masses that constitute organized interest groups."[59] Admitting that this might be the case in rare times of genuine political crisis, Truman argued that pluralism was a stable political system not because a "solid and monolithic" set of organized interest groups were checked by "rarely aroused protests of chronic nonparticipants,"[60] but because organized interest groups were pluralistic rather than monolithic. Members of various groups frequently held memberships in multiple "overlapping" groups. Thus, a loyal Democratic voter could also belong to the Farm Bureau and the American Legion. Such overlapping membership tends to moderate the demands interest groups may make in the political arena.

Multiple membership in organized and overlapping groups is not the only explanation for stability in the American system. More important, for Truman, than overlapping memberships is the concept of "potential groups." Like Bentley's "underlying groups," potential groups are any combination of political actors sharing an attitude or mutual interest. Such groups, often not even needing to organize, exert a moderating influence on the already organized interest groups. Thus, an earlier observer could write that Delta planters in Mississippi "must speak for their Negroes in such programs as health and education," even though Delta blacks were not only not organized but systematically "denied the means of active political participation."[61]

Truman adds that potential groups have a systemic police-keeping role that goes beyond merely protecting their own self-interest. Potential groups keep the system honest. They defend what Truman calls the "rules of the game." Truman wrote of potential groups in their role as referee, noting: "More important for the present purposes than the groups representing separate minority elements are those interests or expectations that are so widely held in society and are so reflected in the behavior of almost all citizens that they are, so to speak, taken for granted. . . . These widely held but unorganized interests are what we have previously called 'rules of the game.' "[62]

For Truman the rules of the game in the American context include (but are not limited to) "the dignity of the individual human being," as expressed in the Bill of Rights; the necessity for "broad mass participation in the designation of leaders" and policies, as well as "semi-egalitarian notions of material welfare." Violations of the rules of the game weaken a group's cohesion, its community status, and its relative position vis-à-vis competing groups in the political arena.

DAVID RIESMAN: OTHER-DIRECTEDNESS
AND VETO GROUPS

David Riesman's *The Lonely Crowd* (1950) offered a further modification of modern pluralist theory. In *The Lonely Crowd*, Riesman argued that modern politics underwent a fundamental shift at or soon after the beginning of the twentieth century. Modern politics, argues Riesman, is pluralistic. Ruling class theories no longer apply to "contemporary America." Riesman notes that contemporary times were preceded by "two periods in American history in which a sharply defined ruling class emerged." These were the "Federalist leadership . . . landed gentry and mercantilist-money leadership" and the post-Civil War era of "Captains of Industry."[63] Riesman argues that no similar class or interest group hegemony exists in the post-1900 era. The captains of industry have been supplanted by "an entirely new type: The Captains of Nonindustry, of Consumption, of Leisure."[64] Actors, artists, and entertainers now share the public limelight with those who manage large industrial and financial concerns.

For Riesman, the rise of new and different influential groups in society has led to two developments: the shift in modern thinking from "inner-directedness" to "other-directedness." Given the plurality of groups in contemporary society—producers and consumers, organized business and organized labor, as well as multiple religious, regional, and ethnic groups—no single group or set of groups can dominate the political area. A multipolarity instead of a hegemony characterizes "contemporary America." In the struggle to effect government policy, these multiple groups check or "veto" each other. No one group has enough resources to dominate unilaterally the policy arena, although a temporary coalition of such groups (a "veto-power team") may occasionally "push a bill through a legislature."[65] Also, groups themselves may contain small veto groups within their own membership. As Riesman notes: "The best example of this is the individual farmer who, after one of the farm lobbies has made a deal for him, can still hold out for more. The farm lobby's concern for the reaction of other veto groups, such as the labor unions, cuts little ice with the individual farmer."[66]

Riesman suggests that in earlier times group leaders were attitudinally "inner-directed"; they were people who aimed their achievements at clear-cut goals and possessed the discretion and authority to accomplish these goals. In contrast to this earlier orientation, modern group leaders and members are necessarily "other-directed." Faced with both the multiple demands ("cues") and potential "veto" power of other groups in society, modern groups and leaders exhibit a greater uncertainty about their goals and their capacity to realize them. They have, in Riesman's words, become less inner- and more other-directed.

Riesman, in an argument that parallels Truman's "rules of the game," argues that groups are not checked in their competitive struggle for policy outcomes only by such considerations as "other-directedness" and "veto" groups. "Piety or decency" also plays a part. A general belief by Americans in "piety and decency" and "rules of fairness and fellowship" bridles all groups equally.[67] For Riesman, these considerations provide an ambiguous but functional ideational framework within which pluralist actors must remain. Riesman writes: "Piety or decency protects some minority groups that have no lobbies. . . . [R]ules of fairness and fellowship dictate how far one can go."[68]

Ten years after the publication of Riesman's *Lonely Crowd*, Truman had occasion to reassess his own view of how the "rules of the game" operate in pluralist politics.

TRUMAN II: THE DECLINE OF POTENTIAL GROUPS

In a new introduction to the second edition of *The Governmental Process* (1971),[69] Truman restated his concept of "rules of the game" and modified his explanation of how such rules are protected under pluralism.[70] The rules of the game are (1) an acceptance of the rule of law over a resort to violence, (2) the guarantees of the Bill of Rights, and (3) effective modes of mass participation both in institutions of government and in the organized groups in society—"a measure of access to the fruits of social enterprise."[71]

Modifying his earlier depiction of the role of potential and overlapping groups in upholding such "rules," Truman notes that the rules of the game are less strongly held by the mass electorate than by political actives (what Robert Dahl will later call the "political stratum") or elites. With some irony, Truman notes that perhaps even a majority of the population does not agree upon the rules of the game; although he adds that it is at the level of specifics rather than generalities (e.g., "freedom of speech") that elites and the mass electorate differ.[72] Echoing an argument suggested by Joseph Schumpeter in 1942, Truman argues that competing political elites provide the underpinning for the rules of the game in pluralism.[73]

Truman had earlier argued that federalism, with its "multiple points of access" to the governmental arena, acted as a resource to groups in a pluralist system. Groups lacking a national or state political base might still be effective at the local level. In the second edition, Truman notes that such a system also has a bias. Admitting that "any system, of course, tends to discriminate in favor of established groups and interests," Truman suggests that the American system with its "multiplicity of coordinate or nearly coordinate points of access to governmental decisions" affords unique opportunities both to groups seeking to change and those seeking to defend existing governmental policies."[74]

Thus, in writing of the role of elites and the multiple points of access, Truman modified in later writings various elements of both his description and defense of pluralist politics in the United States.

Figure 1.1
The Interest Group Politics Model (Bentley-Truman)

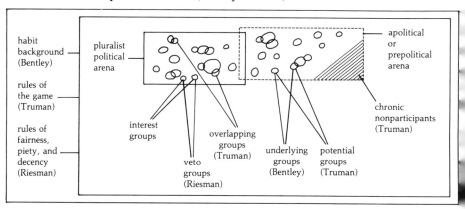

BENTLEY AND TRUMAN: A SCHEMATIC SUMMARY

What follows is a schematic representation (Figure 1.1) and a brief summary of the pluralist model of politics as presented in Bentley and Truman.

For both Bentley and Truman, politics was the result of interaction between interest groups in the political arena. Such groups may combine or act separately to effect the outcome of the public policy process. Frequently, membership in one group (the National Association of Manufacturers, for example) might also overlap with membership in one or more other interest groups (e.g., the U.S. Chamber of Commerce, the Republican party, the American Legion). For Bentley and Truman, overlapping membership, the possibility of a veto by other groups active in the political arena, the marginal possibility of clamorous and possibly violent activity by the chronic nonparticipants in society, as well as the general adherence of all active groups to widely shared standards of conduct and process all serve to produce a relatively stable and representative system of pluralist politics.

THE CRITIQUE OF THE ANALYTICAL PLURALISTS

The analytical pluralists have been assailed both for their formulation of such concepts as "groups," "interest groups," and "potential groups," and for the supernumerary propositions which underpin pluralist theory. As Stanley Rothman points out, Bentley and Truman used rather casual formulations of the concept of "group."[75] There is, for example, no distinction made between primary and secondary groups, although the importance of this had presumably been known to Truman since the publication of *The People's Choice* by Lazarsfeld, Berelson, and Gaudet in 1944.[76] Mancur Olson notes that the analytical pluralists do not take into account the difference between market and nonmarket—or of large and small groups—which Olson alleges operate quite differently.[77] Edward Banfield and James Q. Wilson have pointed to important differences also existing between ad hoc and formal, as well as voluntary and ideological, groups.[78]

Second, several critics have attacked the concept of "interest group" as presented in Bentley and Truman. Olson criticized the "anarchistic fallacy" inherent in Truman and Bentley. Interest groups do not automatically form, and stay formed, around a common interest. Many groups do form and take action in the pluralist arena, but this action is a by-product of group formation. Groups are formed by the use of "selective incentives" ("the carrot and the stick"). Participation in the political arena is secondary. Thus, the leadership of the American Medical Association, which gathers a large membership via the use of selective incentives (group rates on malpractice and life insurance, a reputable professional journal and—in some cases—professional certification to practice medicine), can use the organizational resources generated by such incentives to fund a political action committee to lobby against national health insurance.[79] Additionally, Robert Michels has argued that an "iron law of oligarchy" exists for all organizations. Interest group leaders and members will inevitably develop a separate set of interests. Michels argues that membership and leadership of interest groups, even in the most democratically inclined of organizations, will invariably be at odds.[80]

Third, as Truman admits in his 1971 introduction, the concept of "potential group" is faulty. Simply stated, potential groups do not do what Truman said they would. Far from underwriting the rules of the game, would-be potential groups either fail to form or are systematically prevented from forming, or, if formed, are often prevented from gaining "effective access" to the political arena. As Grant McConnell has noted, even such large groups as the American Farm Bureau, the U.S. Chamber of Commerce, and various units of organized labor were not formed spontaneously but as the result of governmental incentives and action.[81] Further, Theodore Lowi has argued that it has proved impossible in the recent past for some groups, especially low resource and minority ethnic groups, to enter the political arena (even to the extent of voting) without the assistance of state or private coercion.[82] Thus, the reliance of Bentley and Truman prior to 1971 upon underlying or potential groups to uphold the rules of the game is misplaced.

Finally, the two main or supernumerary propositions of the analytical pluralists involve problematic assertions. Many critics argue that political society is more than a "mere conglomeration of interacting groups."[83] There are important variables that seem to point beyond the simple aggregated groups model of the analytical pluralists. Olson has suggested that the groups explanation deprecates the role of formal political institutions. In addition, the theory does not explain the nonjoiner, in Mancur Olson's terminology a "free-rider" who refuses to join an interest group and whose refusal is based on a rational cost-benefit calculation. Why should I participate in a Friends of the Library fund drive (or donate to the United Way) if later the services will be available at no cost to the entire community? It is partially to prevent the problem of the free-rider that, as Olson argues, organizations avail themselves of carrot-and-stick-type selective incentives.[84]

A further problem is the origin of the rules of the game. Truman, Bentley, and Riesman all have versions of rules of the game, yet the origin of such rules is dimly explained. Bentley argues that such precepts spring from a "habit background" which surrounds and supports group culture. Two difficulties ensue for the analytical pluralists at this juncture. How did the rules arise in the first place? How are we to explain the differences in intensity with which various groups within the political culture adhere to these norms? A final difficulty is raised by the troubling question of what criteria are to be used in assessing any proposed changes in the rules. What is the process for the legitimation of rule changes?

The second major assumption of the analytical pluralists, that "interest group activity will result in equilibrium," is also problematic. Why not disequilibrium as readily as equilibrium? The equilibrium assumption entails what Lowi calls the "myth of the automatic society"[85]—a view of political society implying that group balance will result from group interaction. To this, Grant McConnell has argued that the implied "invisible hand" does not always operate, especially in the arenas of agricultural and business policymaking and regulation wherein private interest groups have locked up or "privatized" a previously public policymaking process.[86] And, even when the "invisible hand" does work, critics such as John Kenneth Galbraith have denounced its workings as "perverse."[87] Policy resulting from a compromise between the leading dominant groups may not be desirable. It may result in brokerage or "interest group liberalism"—policies that some observers believe to be normatively undesirable (e.g., tobacco subsidies which are not in the larger public interest but serve the interests of a small but powerful agribusiness elite). Both Lowi and McConnell (as well as Truman in his 1971 introduction) have charged that such a system has a bias toward conservatism. Noting this bias, one famous critic of orthodox pluralism felt justified in charging that "the flaw in the pluralist heaven is that the heavenly chorus sings with a strong upper-class accent."[88]

THE DEFENSE OF ORTHODOXY

Pluralist orthodoxy was not without its defenders. The most prominent of these were two Harvard professors, Talcott Parsons and John Kenneth Galbraith. Galbraith, in an argument he subsequently rejected in 1967, argued in *American Capitalism* (1952) along lines similar to that of Riesman's later "veto power argument."[89] Groups in society were checked by other groups. No one group could dominate the policy arena because of "power from across the market"—the "countervailing power" of other groups that sought to violate the rules of the game, or sought private benefits at the expense of the other players in the pluralist arena.

Parsons was more oblique in his defense. Rather than mount a vigorous defense of pluralist orthodoxy, Parsons attacked the rival power elite paradigm of C. Wright Mills. Parsons' criticism and Suzanne Keller's later criticism in *Beyond the Ruling Class* (1963), while not sufficient to rehabilitate orthodox pluralism, raised serious doubts about conventional "power elite" methodology and assumptions.[90] With both orthodox pluralism and power elite approaches the subject of serious criticisms, the need for a revision of one or both approaches to the study of group influence seemed readily apparent.

DAHL, LINDBLOM, AND SARTORI: THE INSTITUTIONAL PLURALISTS

The 1950s saw the rise of a school of theorists which shall be labeled "institutional pluralists."[91] Acknowledging the importance of interest group activity, the institutional pluralists pushed beyond the vague description of interest group activity found in pluralist orthodoxy. Rejecting Bentley's maxim that "when groups are adequately stated everything is stated," Dahl,

Charles Lindblom, and Giovanni Sartori expanded pluralist theory to include a description of governmental institutions that are crucial to democratic societies and through which groups contend with each other to achieve their aims. The institutional pluralists, then, focused on both interest groups *and* the institutional matrix in which these engage in political activity. These institutions include secret ballot elections, freedom of speech, assembly and the press, the right of "out" groups to compete electorally with the prevailing politically dominant group(s), and the orderly installation of a duly elected government.[92] Dahl and Lindblom coined the term[93] "polyarchy" to describe the institutions which, by 1953, had come to characterize modern pluralist regimes. Building on this, Sartori described the governmental structure of postwar Italy as an "elective polyarchy."[94]

The reasons for the rise of institutional pluralism appear to be threefold. First, the criticisms of orthodox pluralism à la Bentley and Truman were, at least in part, persuasive. Describing groups was not the same thing as describing all political activity. Groups needed a context, an environment, and this environment needed a better explanation than that provided by Bentley, Truman, or Riesman. Group activity unfolds within a context of governmental and economic institutions (e.g., Italian politics, Boston or New Haven politics, or, alternately, market capitalism or nonmarket economic activity). Institutional pluralism arose as an attempt to fill the descriptive gap inherent in orthodox pluralism—to present a more adequate picture of the context of interest group activity.

Second, in terms of the level of analysis, the institutionalists wanted to move pluralism from the general to the specific. Orthodox pluralist theory described a general pattern of interaction. It did not, however—except in the most general of terms—describe Western European or American politics. As Sartori was to complain in 1958: "It is not my purpose to talk about something that does not exist, and that I am unable to judge . . . [if it] exists by using a yardstick which in turn does not exist."[95] Or, as Dahl and Lindblom wrote in 1953, their goal was to describe "the something, the concrete institutions that currently exist" in the West.[96] In this, the institutional pluralists mirrored a "behavioral" trend in political science of the 1950s, a trend away from strictly theoretical concerns to empirically verifiable propositions and claims.[97]

A third reason for the rise of institutional pluralism had to do with the specific research interest of each of the institutional pluralists. Dahl was interested in community politics, American national politics, and Western European politics. His coauthor, Charles Lindblom, was interested in analyzing relations and activity among the market forces of the United States and Western Europe and the demand economy of Eastern Europe. Sartori, in turn, was interested in studying the governments of Western Europe in general and post-World War II Italy in particular. Thus, each had a reason to develop a model that was more specific in nature than the general orthodox pluralist model. Combining forces, Dahl and Lindblom developed the "polyarchal" model in *Politics, Economics, and Welfare*, their 1953 study of the socio-political control processes then prevalent in post-World War II societies. *Democrazia e definizione*, Sartori's 1958 study of democratic theory and postwar Italy, sought to study the conditions then present in Italy and Western political societies in general. As coinventor of the term "polyarchy," and its most prolific spokesman, Dahl eventually emerged as the primary figure among the "polyarchal" or institutional pluralism movement. Indeed, in a series of subsequent studies, Dahl refined the concept of polyarchy and sought to use the theory to classify and comment upon modern political regimes and oppositions. As a result of this work and its subsequent prominence and controversy, Dahl and polyarchy have emerged, respectively, as the leading pluralist and pluralist variant in contemporary social science. As David Ricci has observed: "Although Truman's group theory was realistic and persuasive to many, some felt instead that it was misleading and overly optimistic. The criticisms advanced . . . were valid enough so that with time Truman's group theory was gradually abandoned by political scientists in favor of the more complex understandings of groups offered by the pluralist theory of Robert Dahl in the late 1950's and early 1960's."[98]

POLYARCHY: AN INTRODUCTION

Polyarchy is a label developed to describe the largely democratic societies (predominantly but not exclusively in Western Europe and North America) that share basic institutions crucial to democratic regimes, including the freedom to vote in secret ballot elections in which the vote of each member has about the same weight, the freedoms of speech and assembly, the right to petition and redress grievances, the right to expect that duly elected officials will be allowed to assume office following their election, the right to alternative sources of information including sources not under the unilateral control of the government, the right to offer rival policies from those that are offered by the prevailing governmental officials, and the right to seek office based on the presentation of those rival policies and rival candidacies. The theory of polyarchy is, then, remarkably straightforward. It is what it purports to be—a description of most modern Western political societies. In addition, polyarchal theory as developed first by Dahl and Lindblom and later as it was expanded by Dahl, also contained a set of institutions and characteristics that were not meant to be descriptive but prescriptive. Occasionally, Dahl or Lindblom used polyarchy in this normative or ideal sense—for example, to describe a strongly democratic state, a state that Dahl later characterized as "egalitarian polyarchies," regimes "at the limits of human realization." Polyarchy is, to steal a phrase from the so-called harder sciences, a compound element. It has a basic descriptive element used to describe the "going concern" or usual structure of modern political society in the West, and it has an idealized or rarified element which is frequently held up to measure the performance of the institutions described in the earlier element. Thus, the first element of polyarchal theory (the basic set of institutions that are held to characterize the fairly democratic societies of the West) appears to be purely descriptive, while the second set is—almost by definition since it is admittedly "idealized"—a normative benchmark against which to measure various actual regimes ("going concerns").

It should be noted that even the straight set of institutions contained in the first element of polyarchal theory is descriptive *and* normative . The basic institutional set is descriptive in two senses. First, the authors clearly prefer the more democratic regimes of the West to the more authoritarian regimes of the East, and they say so clearly and frequently. Thus, for example, Dahl and Lindblom refer to themselves as "noncommunist, antifascists" and "democrats." Second, the authors in *Politics, Economics, and Welfare* do not resort to the concept of "egalitarian polyarchy" which Dahl develops at some length later in *A Preface to Democratic Theory* (1956) to criticize the United States. They do not need to resort to the idealized concept of polyarchy in criticizing the United States because, on several counts—including the status of American blacks in the South, the status of American women prior to the extension of the vote to women, and the watering down of voting weights for individuals attributable to the fact that each American state regardless of population size is entitled to two U.S. Senators—the United States performs poorly when compared to the "average" of all the other polyarchal states in the West. Thus, the essence of polyarchy, from its early inception in 1953 to the present, has been a basic set of institutions that characterize the more democratic regimes in the West and a secondary set of institutions used, alternately, to suggest patterns in which it may be anticipated that the states may evolve as they strengthen democratic institutions and practices and to suggest the shape(s) that truly democratic government—government at the limits of human realization—might eventually take. Because the distinction between these uses of the term polyarchy—for example, polyarchy as a description of the "average" political regime in the West, and polyarchy (read "egalitarian polyarchy") as a normative measure of what the democratic regimes in the West *ought* to look like—is confusing to read, and because it was (arguably) misread by several of the major critics of polyarchy, the secondary literature that surrounds Dahl and the polyarchal concept is somewhat akin to an intellectual minefield. At a minimum, it is both confusing and confused. As we shall argue in the next chapter, substantial dispute exists about what polyarchy is and what its author intends. The purpose of the final section in this chapter is to clarify Dahl's use of the term and, by so doing, to facilitate an understanding of his theoretical model of polyarchy. While it is possible that the existence of a clarified model will not blunt the criticism of Dahl reviewed in the next chapter, it should provide such critics with a unified and accurate target to attack. The basic argument of this and the next chapter is that Dahl's critics have directed their criticisms somewhat wide of the mark.

As noted earlier, Dahl and Lindblom did not set out to write on democracy per se. Rather, they attempted in *Politics, Economics, and Welfare* to describe "the something, the concrete institutions that currently exist"[99] in the West. Following up this theme, Christian Bay and other critics would later argue that Dahl not only described the "going system" in theoretical terms but, further, that he elevated this description of current reality (read: "polyarchy") into a normative measure for contemporary politics.[100] Thus, for Bay, Jack Walker, Henry Kariel, and others, Dahl had devised a measure that presented contemporary politics in the best possible light.[101] What regime could fail to look attractive if the normative expectations built into the system were the current conditions under which the system operates? While not entirely without merit, the Bay-Kariel criticism of polyarchy depends on a casual reading of Dahl, a reading unsupported by a closer examination of the origins and substance of the polyarchal theory of politics.

POLYARCHY: A DEVELOPMENTAL MODEL

In *PEW*, Dahl and Lindblom present polyarchy as one of four "politico-economic techniques whereby nations and smaller groups attempt to maximize attainment of their goals."[102] Polyarchy is contrasted with bargaining, hierarchy, and the price system as a means of social control available to modern regimes. In an argument which paralleled similar "end of ideology" arguments by Daniel Bell, the authors suggested that successful modern governments will avail themselves of all four means of control. Rather than persisting with one approach due to reasons of ideology or traditional practice, situations may dictate that regimes, which have traditionally used one form of control to the exclusion of the other three, may wish to be more pragmatic in the future. Thus, modern Western and Eastern bloc states may increasingly come to choose pragmatically among price system ("control of and by leaders"), hierarchy ("control by leaders"), polyarchy ("control of leaders"), or bargaining ("control among leaders").

In *PEW*, the authors argued that all four control mechanisms contain both promise and problems. Of the four, polyarchy is the most novel—in its attempt to explain current governmental practices in the West and to provide direction to that practice—and for that reason is the least developed member of the fourfold control typology. Polyarchy is incomplete and, as the authors admit, is a "crude" descriptive and prescriptive device in its early formulation. Importantly, even at this early stage, polyarchy was as much an ideal type in the Weberian sense as it was a practical description of modern politics. Dahl and Lindblom sought to provide "solutions" to modern political problems. This is evident in the first formulation of polyarchy, when they wrote:

In some societies the democratic goal is still roughly and crudely approximated, in the sense that nonleaders exercise a relatively high degree of control over leaders. The constellation of social processes that makes this possible we call polyarchy. Polyarchy, not democracy is the actual solution to the First problem of politics. Like most actual solutions to difficult problems it is untidy and highly imperfect.[103]

In *PEW*, the reader is given a brief definition of polyarchy—"a high degree of control over leaders by nonleaders." In addition to this, the authors attempt to operationalize polyarchy by providing a more expanded view of what polyarchy is and what the preconditions to polyarchy might be. All but the most casual of readers will note that the early attempts at operationalization ignored some serious difficulties, or, worse yet, assumed that these problems were either resolved or simply absent. The most pressing of these problems was the problem of determining whether a given polity is or is not a polyarchy. What, in theoretical terms, are the empirical criteria which are to be used to determine if nonleaders in a particular country exercise a "high degree of control" over leaders? The answer provided by the authors is problematic. The criteria provided are judgmental and subjective. Although Dahl wrestled with this in *Preface to Democratic Theory* (1956), it is a problem that continues to haunt polyarchal theory. We are urged to note if the country in question has six (in *Preface* the list grew to eight) institutional "characteristics." If so, it is a polyarchy. In fact, in operational terms, any country which can be said to have all six characteristics is a polyarchy. These characteristics are:

1. Most adults in the organization have the opportunity to vote in elections with no significant rewards and penalties directly attached either to the act of voting or to the choice among candidates.

2. In the elections the vote of each member has about the same weight.

3. Nonelected officials are subordinate to elected officials in making organizational policy. That is, when they so wish, elected leaders can have the last word on policy with nonelected officials.

4. Elected leaders are in turn subordinate to nonleaders in the sense that those in office will be displaced by alternative leaders in a peaceful and relatively prompt manner whenever a greater number of voters cast their votes for alternative leaders than those in office.

5. Adults in the organization have available to them several alternative sources of information, including some that are not under significant control by government leaders. "Available" in this context means only that members who wish to do so can utilize these sources without incurring penalties initiated by government leaders or their subordinates.

6. Members of the organization who accept these rules have an opportunity, either directly or through delegates, to offer rival policies and candidates without severe penalties for their doing so.[104]

"Admittedly," note Dahl and Lindblom, "one could debate many of the terms in each of these criteria. Political theorists do so endlessly."[105] Many of their criteria are judgmental and are not universally acceptable. They raise such questions themselves and provide what they hope to be a convincing answer:

How many adults is "most"? What are "severe" penalties? How equally weighted must votes be to have "about the same weight"? For example, does the federal system in the United States permit this country to qualify fully as a polyarchy? How soon is "relatively prompt"? Just how subordinate must non-elected officials be? No doubt further operational criteria could be set up for each of these short hand symbols, but the important quarrels over the application of the criteria arise over factual disputes, not over definitional questions. If the authors' view of the facts—a view shared by most noncommunist antifascists—is correct, then clearly the Soviet Union and Spain lack all the characteristics of polyarchy; so do most large American corporations, and many trade unions and some boss-ridden municipalities lack several important ones.

Each of the criteria can therefore be expressed in terms of a continuum. For example, because the voters of Nevada elect the same number of Senators as all the voters of New York State, the American national government meets the second criterion of polyarchy less fully than does, say, Great Britain. Moreover, a process is polyarchal only with respect to a given membership. Before women were permitted to vote in France, French national government was a polyarchy for men only. In the United States, the South as a whole has never been a polyarchy for Negroes or indeed even for many poor whites. But for registered Democrats in the South, the process is a polyarchal process.[106]

Thus for Dahl and Lindblom "it is very easy to say that the USSR is not a polyarchy and that the United States, Great Britain, Canada, New Zealand, Australia, France, Norway, Sweden, Denmark, Mexico and Israel are. For it is correct to say that in these latter countries non-leaders exercise a high degree of control over governmental leaders and in the USSR they do not."[107]

It is this remark and similar ones in other works that have precipitated a host of critical comment. Actually, the criticism focuses in on one of the least interesting aspects of the remark, and one that quickly becomes a nonissue. Dahl has been criticized for labeling the United States a polyarchy. Such a label appears to be a judgment call, one that can be disputed either by questioning the interpretation (as Dahl and Lindblom note) of the operational terms used as criteria for polyarchy, or by questioning the judgment on empirical terms. One may charge, for example, that the authors do not present sufficient data to support their assertion that the United States meets each of the six criteria. It may be objected that Dahl and Lindblom use their own model somewhat atheoretically; they simply assume that the United States is a polyarchy. All of these are serious charges with which Dahl has tried to cope. Interestingly, few of them are charges advanced by Bay, Walker, Kariel, or Connolly et al. Instead, for such critics, it is enough to say that Dahl has identified the United States with polyarchy. Since polyarchy is more or less an abstracted version of the status quo, Dahl has idealized the "going system" of American politics as the best possible—most polyarchal, most democratic—system attainable.

He has glorified the status quo and in so doing becomes an apologist instead of a critic of current American political practices. The problem with this argument is that it fundamentally misunderstands what Dahl means by polyarchy and what qualifications Dahl has appended to his observation that the United States is a polyarchy. Polyarchy, for the critics, means the arena theory of polyarchy as set forth by William Connolly (see the discussion of Connolly and the arena theory of pluralism in chapter 2). For Dahl, polyarchy means something quite different; something spelled out quite clearly in *PEW* and subsequently amended in *Preface* and *Polyarchy*.

We turn now to a further explanation of the early model of polyarchy presented in *PEW*, followed by a highly condensed presentation of the model as it currently stands. In so doing, we mean to suggest that the polyarchal model is: (1) developmental in its orientation—that it encompasses a progression in normative terms from prepolyarchal states to polyarchies; (2) that Dahl has used the term polyarchy in several senses—a fact glossed over by all of Dahl's critics; and (3) that Dahl's theory of polyarchy is not static but has changed and modified over time. Although the heart of the theory remains the same, Dahl has added important modifications in both substance and in tone since its inception in 1953.

In the present section, the substantive changes in polyarchy since the publication of *Politics, Economics, and Welfare* (1953) are considered. In chapter 3, changes in tone and emphasis are addressed.

THE PRECONDITIONS OF POLYARCHY

In *PEW*, Dahl and Lindblom set out six (eight in *Polyarchy*) preconditions for polyarchy. These are social indoctrination, a basic societal agreement, social pluralism, a high degree of political activity, the circulation of political leadership, and a final precondition which might be labeled the "sociopsychological variable." While perhaps not an exhaustive or causal list, it seeks to fill an important theoretical gap. How, in fact, do polyarchies arise? Under what circumstances and conditions? What must occur if nonpolyarchies or "near-polyarchies" (a label Dahl uses in *Polyarchy*) are to make the transition to polyarchy? Collectively, these six conditions lead to a condition of equality of control (dispersed or popular control) in a given polity. Granting the existence of Michels' "iron law of oligarchy," the authors argue that social systems have two conflicting tendencies. One is the tendency toward oligarchy and inequality noted by Michels and Mosca. The second is "a tendency away from purely unilateral control which we might call the 'countervailing law of reciprocity.' "[108] Collectively, the six conditions listed as preconditions of polyarchy "counteract the tendencies toward inequality of control and strengthen reciprocity."[109]

All six of the preconditions to polyarchy are interdependent. Of these, social indoctrination—an infelicitous phrase which would probably be supplanted with "political socialization" were *PEW* being rewritten today—is necessary because it impacts political leaders in three ways. "It inhibits certain types of behavior, and even certain 'evil thoughts.' " A president, even one "hounded" into resignation, may not "even in his moments of bitterest struggle with Congress . . . [give] an instant's conscious thought to, say, military repression of the Congress." Rather, social indoctrination "permits certain approved substitute behavior. The President whose unconscious wish might be to shoot all Congressmen is left free to slay them over the microphone, or by manipulating patronage." Finally, "social indoctrination teaches political leaders to expect punishment if they seriously violate the norms of polyarchy."[110]

A second catalyst to and precondition of polyarchy is a societal "agreement on those basic issues and methods that facilitate peaceful competition and the opportunity for nonleaders to switch their support to rival leaders."[111] Further,

There must be agreement that political leaders can legitimately acquire office only by winning a plurality of votes following an election campaign, and that they must peaceably leave office when they have lost an election. . . . Second, there must be agreement that most adults have a legal right to participate in elections without expectation of rewards or penalties administered for the mere act of voting or choice of candidate. . . . Thirdly, there must be agreement that rival politicians should have a legally enforceable opportunity to organize themselves compactly for the purpose of winning votes; which is to say, an opportunity to criticize the government.[112]

Social pluralism is the third precondition of polyarchy. The authors note, "Polyarchy requires a considerable degree of social pluralism—that is a diversity of social organizations with a large measure of autonomy with respect to one another."[113] Social pluralism buttresses polyarchy by offering citizens a multiplicity of groups which can speak for and support their particular policy preferences. Pluralism also spurs competition within a polity and facilitates political opposition to established policies and leadership "and facilitiates the rise of political leaders whose main skill is negotiating settlements among conflicting social organizations. Thus, the whole cast of the political elites is modified by pluralism; the fanatic, the

Messianic type, the leader whose aim is to consolidate the supremacy of some group tend to trip themselves up on the barrier of groups and group loyalties."[114]

Building on an argument raised earlier in Madison, Tocqueville, Bentley, Truman, and Riesman, the authors argue that "social pluralism increases the probability that one is simultaneously a member of more than one social organization; hence, action by a leader against what seems to be an enemy organization may in fact strike against his own alliance."[115]

A final salutory effect of social pluralism is that it often produces diverse sources of information and communication among citizens. The efficacy of this diversity is partially undercut, however, by the tendency of modern citizens to use information to reinforce preexisting patterns of belief. Diversity of information is at least partially blunted by such factors as opinion leaders and opinion followers, noncognitive or affective opinion processes and such phenomena as selective attention, perception, and retention.

For Dahl and Lindblom, political activity and circulation are necessary preconditions for polyarchy. The level of political activity must be such that "enough people must participate in the governmental process so that political leaders compete for the support of a large and more or less representative cross section of the population." As Dahl and Lindblom admit, their description of political activity is a rather "imprecise formulation."[116]

It is true that "the opportunity to exert control through elections and other forms of political activity . . . is never equally distributed . . . [and] that higher-income people, and the better educated more than the poorly educated . . . [and, further] because campaigns are exceedingly costly, the wealthier a person is, the more strategic his position for bringing his position to bear on politicians." Nevertheless, "the problem is not one so much of insuring that all citizens have approximately equal opportunity to act, using 'opportunity' in a realistic rather than legalistic sense."[117]

For Dahl and Lindblom, legal bars to political activity would include inegalitarian election laws. "Realistic" impediments to polyarchal political activity would include attitudinal factors which may be beyond the control of a democratic state and socioeconomic factors which the modern state could or ought to address. While admitting traits such as personality, optimism, and "willingness to act" may be beyond the purview of the state, Dahl and Lindblom suggest that the state can do much to equalize socioeconomic factors such as income, wealth, and education. Noting that "political activity and control are closely correlated with income, education and status," the authors argue that "a high degree of income equality is a prerequisite for a high degree of political activity."[118]

Additionally, it should be noted that, unlike Schumpeter's model of democracy in which the shifting elites compete for mass electoral support, PEW calls for a two-stage electoral model. For Dahl and Lindblom, "a polyarchy would possess in effect two stages of indirect representation; through the prescribed elections to public office and, below these, through the operating official 'elections' for members of the political active."[119]

A fifth precondition for polyarchy is elite "circulation." By this, the authors mean that alternative political leaders must exist and their governing leaders must yield if they are successfully challenged at an election. Further, political actives need freely to admit new members into their ranks. Dahl and Lindblom argue that widespread public education and universal suffrage facilitate such circulation. Political circulation does, however, present problems of regime stability. Placed on a continuum, regimes with little or no circulation should be labeled as authoritarian states while those with extremely high degrees of circulation might justifiably be labeled anarchal. Seeking to resolve this dilemma, the authors argue: "One cannot reduce the matter to a qualitative proposition but the general rule is clear: Circulation must be rapid enough to prevent the exclusion of any people with significant control outside government; it must be gradual enough so that the existing leadership is not swamped and therefore incapable of transmitting the habits of polyarchal control."[120]

The final precondition for polyarchy set forth in *PEW* is actually a "basket" or collection of variables including psychological security, limited disparity of wealth and income, and widespread education. Because they are partially assumed in the earlier discussion and because "these are not conditions that can be easily converted into satisfactory operational criteria," Dahl and Lindblom declined to elaborate on these criteria. They assumed that their use of this prerequisite is uncontroversial. They note:

Hardly anyone today denies this fact, even conservative American Republicans . . . [that] differences in wealth generate differences in control outside of government and therefore in it; advantages in wealth buy advantages of education, organization, and hence advantages of control. . . . [D]oubtless few of our readers will quarrel with the proposition that widespread illiteracy and ignorance immeasurably increase the possibilities that polyarchy will fail to survive in any modern, complex, industrialized society.[121]

POLITICS, ECONOMICS AND WELFARE: A SUMMARY

In *PEW*, polyarchy emerges as one of four methods of sociopolitical control. It is a form of majority rule—control of leaders by nonleaders— and has six definitional characteristics. It arises as a result of six preconditions or prerequisites and, in both a normative and descriptive sense, a polyarchy would be completely developed were it to meet all six of the definitional characteristics. Any polity that could meet all six characteristics or criteria would be a fully developed polyarchy, an ideal polyarchy. In *Preface*, Dahl will call these "egalitarian polyarchies." Not in *PEW* or in any other work does Dahl state that this ideal has ever been achieved.[122] The United States, Great Britain, Canada, Sweden, France, and West Germany may be more developed as polyarchies than some other states but they are not fully developed; they are not ideal polyarchies. It is clear in *PEW* that polyarchy is used in two senses: first, to describe an ideal democratic state which is realizable in modern society but which is ideal because it represents criteria for a democratic process "at the limits of human realization"; and, second, polyarchy as a label to identify those modern polities which have experienced preconditions favoring polyarchy and more closely approximate the ideal. In *PEW*, then, several countries that have institutions and societal guarantees that approximate the ideal characteristics are called polyarchies by the authors. This dual use of polyarchy as a label to designate at times an ideal regime and at other times a modern polity approximating this ideal has precipitated some confusion in those who have sought to assess the model. Extreme examples of this confusion can be seen in such writers as Bay and Walker who misunderstood Dahl's use of the model. Taking Dahl's two primary assertions, they confused them. True, Dahl asserts that the United States is a polyarchy. True, also, Dahl asserts that polyarchy is an ideal, an ideally democratic modern regime. What is important to note, a fact continually overlooked by most critics of Dahl, is that he is using polyarchy differently in each of these two assertions. The first one refers to a functioning but hardly ideal state, the second to a democratic state "at the limits of human realization."[123] Twice Dahl has attempted to clarify his protean use of "polyarchy" as a term; twice he has succeeded. Nevertheless, critics of Dahl still argue that he confuses practices with preferences; that he regards the going concern in the United States as an ideal polyarchy. The most charitable thing that can be said about such a reading of Dahl is that such readers have been confused by the ideal notion of polyarchy in *PEW*. Critics who continue in their confusion after reading *A Preface to Democratic Theory* or *Polyarchy* have simply misread (or not read at all) Dahl's various treatments of polyarchy.[124]

THE MECHANICAL MODEL: *PREFACE* AND *POLYARCHY*

Although polyarchy as a theoretical model remains today essentially as it was when first presented in *PEW*, Dahl has twice amended it in efforts at clarification and empirical testing. In *Preface* and *Polyarchy*, Dahl extended polyarchal theory to include points not previously raised or raised ambiguously in *PEW*. What follows is a rather simplistic and mechanical presentation of polyarchy which incorporates these changes and portrays Dahl's polyarchal theory as it currently stands.

Dahl uses the term polyarchy developmentally. Accordingly, for Dahl, polities may be placed along a continuum ranging from fully democratic to authoritarian regimes. Thus, depending on its degree of democratization, a state could be in ascending order: a hegemony, a near-hegemony or competitive oligarchy, a mixed regime, a near-polyarchy, a polyarchy, or a fully democratized ideal democracy (an "egalitarian polyarchy").[125] Countries are placed along this continuum after a determination is made as to how closely they approximate each of eight definitional characteristics of an ideal procedural democracy.

In *PEW* and *Preface*, Dahl argued that to be a polyarchy in the ideal sense it was necessary and sufficient for a majority rule state to meet each of six definitional characteristics. Since, as Dahl admits, no state fully meets all six (expanded in *Polyarchy* to eight) criteria—although he holds that the United States and Great Britain come closer than any other existing states—we are left to regard the United States and Great Britain as simply polyarchies, or polyarchies per se—as opposed to egalitarian polyarchies. (Dahl later substituted the term "ideal democracy" or "procedural democracy" for egalitarian polyarchy—this is, in part, an effort to end some of the terminological confusion involved in distinguishing such polities from ordinary or "working" polyarchies.)

In *Polyarchy* (1971), Dahl set forth a list of "institutional guarantees" that are necessary and sufficient conditions for a working or ordinary polyarchy. To be a polyarchy, a modern state must have a majoritarian form of rule and extend all eight of the following institutional guarantees to its members:

1. Freedom to form and join organizations.
2. Freedom of expression.
3. Right to vote.
3. Eligibility for public office.
5. Right of political leaders to compete for support.
   5a. Right of political leaders to compete for votes.
6. Alternative sources of information.
7. Free and fair elections.
8. Institutions for making governmental policies depend on votes and other expressions of preferences.[126]

If the conditions listed above are necessary and sufficient to classify a state as a polyarchy, they are buttressed in *Polyarchy* with a list of necessary but insufficient conditions—conditions that favor polyarchy and tend to promote it. These nurturing or prerequisite sociopolitical conditions, along with a comparable list of conditions "least favorable to polyarchy," are listed in Table 1.2.

The nurturing conditions listed in Table 1.2 are attempts by Dahl to elaborate upon and, in one case, to quantify preconditions for polyarchy

Table 1.2
Conditions Favoring Polyarchy

	Most favorable to polyarchy	Least favorable to polyarchy
I. Historical sequences	Competition precedes inclusiveness	Inclusiveness precedes competition
II. The socioeconomic order:		
A. Access to		
1. Violence	Dispersed or neutralized	Monopolized
2. Socioeconomic sanctions	Dispersed or neutralized	Monopolized
B. Type of economy		
1. Agrarian	Free farmers	Traditional peasant
2. Commercial-Industrial	Decentralized direction	Centralized direction
III. The level of socioeconomic development	High: GNP per capita over about $700-800	Low: GNP per capita under about $100-200
IV. Equalities and Inequalities		
1. Objective	Low or decreasing	High: Cumulative
2. Subjective: relative deprivation	Low or decreasing	High or increasing

V. Subcultural pluralism		
1. Amount	Low	High
2. If marked or high	None a majority	One a majority
	None regional	Some regional
	None indefinitely out of government	Some permanently in opposition
	Mutual guarantees	No mutual guarantees
VI. Domination by a foreign power	Weak or temporary	Strong and persistent
VII. Beliefs of political activitists		
1. Institutions of polyarchy are legitimate	yes	no
2. Only unilateral authority is legitimate	no	yes
3. Polyarchy is effective in solving major problems	yes	no
4. Trust in others	high	low
5. Political relationships are:		
strictly competitive	no	yes
strictly cooperative	no	yes
cooperative-competitive	yes	no
6. Compromise necessary and desirable	yes	no

Source: "Table 10.1. Conditions Favoring Polyarchy," Robert A. Dahl, *Polyarchy: Participation and Opposition* (New Haven: Yale University Press, 1971), p. 203.

first set forth in *PEW*. It should be noted that four preconditional variables used in *PEW* and assumed by Dahl to be preconditions tending to favor and promote are not included in the 1971 list. These are: social pluralism, high levels of political activity, political circulation and the sociopsychological variable—psychological security, relative income disparity, and widespread education. Dahl did not add these four variables to the 1971 list because they did not lend themselves to the measurable or empirical catalog which the list was designed to create. Dahl regarded (and still regards) the four variables as necessary preconditions for polyarchy. The 1971 list was not meant to be exhaustive but suggestive and helpful for empirical work. Thus, a per capita GNP figure is included as a means of measuring the "limited disparities in wealth and income" discussed in *PEW*. In a similar manner, Dahl means to heighten an important nuance by adding a discussion of subcultural pluralism to contrast with his remarks on cultural pluralism in *PEW*. As his discussion of subcultural pluralism is meant to indicate, cultural pluralism is a necessary precondition for polyarchy. Nevertheless, it is possible for a political system to be excessively pluralistic—to be, in effect, Balkanized, stalemated, or "excessively" conflictual.

In addition to amending the earlier discussion of nurturing conditions, *Polyarchy* includes speculation by Dahl on the general historical circumstances or "sequences" which favor (see Table 1.2) the emergence of a polyarchal regime. The key to Dahl's discussion at this point is his insistence that, in order for polyarchy to be stable, competition must precede inclusiveness. By this Dahl means that hegemonic regimes that undergo rapid transformations to a much more participatory, more inclusive polyarchal framework via a revolution or a sudden upheaval, are inherently less stable than are regimes in which a lengthy period of elite competition preceded the eventual change to polyarchy. In the latter case, these regimes can be said to be more favorable to polyarchy, more favorable to the stable maintenance of a polyarchal order because the period of elite competition generally produces norms which are of help in maintaining a polyarchal regime. In such cases, norms such as toleration of opposition, adherence to a common rule of law, a belief in the legitimacy of rules and elections have been accepted by members of the competing elites. Since such norms already exist in the political culture of the polity prior to the emergence of a polyarchal state, Dahl argues that Western European experience suggests that these norms are more readily learned and more permanently embedded in the political culture of polyarchies which came by these norms slowly. This is not to say that a revolutionary order could not transform a hegemonic state into a polyarchy overnight. Rather, the point is that relatively few polyarchies which have been rapidly inclusive in terms of participation, membership, and decision-making have long endured.

In *A Preface to Democratic Theory*, Dahl clarified the wording of six

Table 1.3
The Definitional Characteristics of an Egalitarian Polyarchy

Polyarchy is defined loosely as a political system in which the following conditions exist to a relatively high degree:

During the voting period:
1. Every member of the organization performs the acts we assume to constitute an expression of preference among the scheduled alternatives, e.g., voting.
2. In tabulating these expressions (votes), the weight assigned to the choice of each individual is identical.
3. The alternative with the greatest number of votes is declared the winning choice.

During the prevoting period:
4. Any member who perceives a set of alternatives, at least one in which he regards as preferable to any of the alternatives presently scheduled, can insert his preferred alternative(s) among those scheduled for voting.
5. All individuals possess identical information about the alternatives.

During the postvoting period:
6. Alternatives (leaders or policies) with the greatest number of votes displace any alternatives (leaders or policies) with fewer votes.
7. The orders of elected officials are executed.

During the interelection stage:
8.1. Either all interelection decisions are subordinate or executory to those arrived at during the election stage, i.e., elections are in a sense controlling.
8.2. Or new decisions during the interelection period are governed by the preceding seven conditions, operating, however, under rather different institutional circumstances.
8.3. Or both.

Source: Robert A. Dahl, *A Preface to Democratic Theory* (Chicago: University of Chicago Press, 1956), p. 84.

definitional characteristics of ideal or egalitarian polyarchy first developed in *PEW*. Although Dahl has called the regime thus designated by different names over the years—ranging from egalitarian polyarchy to procedural or ideal democracy—the criteria for such a regime have remained much the same. In *Preface* Dahl clarified the wording and added two additional "interelection stage" criteria (see points 8.1-8.3 in Table 1.3). These necessary and sufficient criteria for an ideal polyarchy—a "democracy at the limits of human realization"—have remained constant in the polyarchal model since their clarification in *Preface*. The list as presented in *Preface* is given in Table 1.3.

THE MECHANICAL MODEL: A SUMMARY

In *Preface* and *Polyarchy* Dahl clarified and extended the polyarchal theory of politics first developed in *PEW*. The model as it currently stands includes four sets of variables. These are: (A) a requirement that the state in question be governed by a majority-rule principle; (B) a set of definitional characteristics that are necessary and sufficient for an "egalitarian poly-archy" or ideal democracy—a democracy at the limits of human realization; (C) a third set including lesser institutions and guarantees that are necessary and sufficient for a polyarchal state—which, in fact, collectively define polyarchy. In the developmental sense, these are intermediate institutions that fall between the conditions of ideal democracy or egalitarian polyarchy and the conditions that give rise to or favor polyarchy; (D) a final element in the polyarchal model is the set of preconditions that favor or promote the establishment of a polyarchal state. These preconditions, although necessary to the establishment of a modern polyarchal state, are insufficient indicators of the existence of such a state. A schematic summary of Robert Dahl's fourfold model is given in Table 1.4.

Dahl's theory of polyarchy is based on the developmental schema illustrated above. The complete developmental model encompasses all four sets of variables (A, B, C, and D). When Dahl speaks of whether a given polity is a polyarchy, he is employing only parts A and C of the model illustrated. Frequently, Dahl has asked if a given polity is a complete polyarchy—if it is a fully developed polyarchy. In such cases, Dahl is referring to parts A and B of the polyarchal model. For Dahl, states that can be designated as polyarchies (C) are normatively preferable to those that are not. However, even polyarchies are less preferable than those states that have institutionalized democracy to "the limits of human realization" (B). This is the case for Dahl despite the fact that, as it currently stands, egalitarian polyarchy (part B of the model) is, in empirical terms, an empty set. Dahl has never suggested that any state has realized this ideal norm. Dahl has frequently suggested that, with some reservations, the United States is a polyarchy (C). What Dahl has never said nor implied is that the United States is an egalitarian polyarchy—an ideal democracy (B). Yet, as has been argued earlier and shall continue to be examined in the next two chapters, this is exactly what some critics of Dahl assert that he has said.

In the present chapter we have traced the major spokesmen and variants of American pluralism. In so doing, we have noted the emergence of poly-archy as the leading—if controversial—contemporary expression of American pluralist thought. We turn now to a more detailed survey of the criticisms and critics of the polyarchal theory.

Table 1.4
Robert A. Dahl's Theory of Polyarchy

Egalitarian Polyarchy/Ideal Democracy

During the voting period:
1. Every member votes.
2. The weight assigned to each vote is identical.
3. The alternative with the greatest number of votes wins.

During the prevoting period:
4. Alternative policies to those presently scheduled can be scheduled for voting by interested parties.
5. All individuals possess identical information about the alternatives.

During the postvoting period:
6. Alternatives (leaders or policies) with the greatest number of votes displace alternatives with fewer votes.
7. The orders of elected officials are executed

During the interelection state:
8.1 All decisions arrived at are subordinate to those arrived at during the election stage, i.e., elections are controlling.
8.2 Or new decisions during this stage are governed by the preceding seven conditions, operating, however, under rather different institutional circumstances.
8.3 Or both.

(B)

Polyarchy

1. Freedom to form and join organizations.
2. Freedom of expression.
3. Right to vote.
4. Eligibility for public office.
5. Right of political leaders to compete for support.
   5a. Right of political leaders to compete for votes.
6. Alternative sources of information.
7. Free and fair elections.
8. Institutions for making government policies depend on votes and other expressions of preference.

(C)

MAJORITY RULE PRINCIPLE

(A)

Table 1.4 *(continued)*

Conditions Favoring Polyarchy

1. Historical variable: Competition precedes inclusiveness.
2. High level of socioeconomic development (GNP $700+).
3. Low level of dispersed inequalities.
4. Low level of subcultural pluralism.
5. Weak or temporary domination by any foreign power.
6. Political activists believe in legitimacy of polyarchal institutions, illegitimacy of uniliateral authority, polyarchy effective in solving major problems, other members trustworthy, compromise as necessary and desirable in political relationships.
7. Social pluralism present.
8. High degree of political activity.
9. Circulation of political leadership.
10. Sociopolitical variable present—psychological security, limited disparities in wealth and income, and widespread education.

(D)

Source: Abstracted from tables and text of Robert A. Dahl and Charles E. Lindblom, *Politics, Economics, and Welfare* (Chicago: University of Chicago Press, 1953), 227-324; and Robert A. Dahl, *A Preface to Democratic Theory* (Chicago: University of Chicago Press, 1956), 84 ff., and *Polyarchy* (New Haven: Yale University Press, 1971), 3, 203 ff.

2
The Critique of American Pluralism

One of the difficulties in assessing Robert Dahl's immensely influential explanation of American politics is that not all the commentators agree on a common definition of "polyarchy," the keystone of both his theoretical and empirical work. Thus, Dahl's explanation stands somewhat paradoxically, in need of explanation itself. Further clouding the issue is the fact that bibliographic studies of Dahl often produce radically different—in some cases contradictory—explanations of Dahl's ideological or methodological perspective. In the four main bibliographic studies to date, Dahl has been characterized alternately as a committed student of modern democracy, an apologist for an undemocratic and inegalitarian status quo, a scholar seeking to "eclipse" older notions of democracy with a new theory of democratic-elitism, or, finally, as a "value-free" behavioral scientist unconcerned with the normative implications of his study of modern political regimes.[127]

Not all of these views are accurate, and even those which are require some qualification. As such it is our hope in the present study to unravel some of the ambiguity currently surrounding the work of Robert Dahl and the polyarchal theory of politics.

DAHL AS DEMOCRAT

In a perceptive essay, George Von Der Muhll argued in 1977 that the central element in Dahl's work is the "democratic question." For Von Der Muhll, Dahl's writing, spanning more than three decades and including fifteen books and over thirty published articles, constitutes a study of "contemporary democracy." As Von Der Muhll notes:

Dahl's focus on modern, large-scale democratic government has remained unwavering . . . [despite] marked discontinuities of content, scope and level of abstraction over the years. . . . For more than a quarter of a century, Dahl has sought to analyze modern democratic government—its operation, the conditions that encourage or threaten it, the logical status of the propositions in terms of which it is discussed and evaluated.[128]

Von Der Muhll's contention is apt; however, more might be added. Dahl has approached the study of modern regimes along two dimensions. While it is true that Dahl has kept the democratic theme uppermost in his studies, the studies themselves are of two sorts. They are characterized either by a concern with democracy and locale, or with democracy and modernity. Second, Dahl has alternated between studies that emphasized primarily theoretical concerns and those that are more in the realm of practical inquiry or empirical studies.

LOCALE AND MODERNITY

Although none of Dahl's works deals exclusively with democracy in a given locale or, alternatively, exclusively with the problems of realizing democratic rule in modern, usually Western circumstances, these concerns are evident in all but one of Dahl's books. Imposing this admittedly artificial construct on Dahl's basic works—what Von Der Muhll has aptly labeled "the essential Dahl"—facilitates an interesting line of inquiry.[129]

If one adopts the locale/modernity distinction to introduce the main works within the "essential Dahl," Von Der Muhll's "democratic focus" argument can be extended to suggest that Dahl has focused alternately upon considerations of democracy and locale or of democracy and modernity. Thus, Dahl's work may be seen as a series of inquiries about the character and shape of the policy process in various locales. He has asked if congressional decision-making in foreign policy is democratic,[130] if government and politics in New Haven are democratic,[131] if the United States is a pluralist democracy,[132] and to what degree the same may be said of regimes and oppositions in Western Europe.[133]

Dahl has coupled the inquiry into democracy and locale with a parallel inquiry into various aspects of modern political life. Thus, in a survey of politics in industrialized Western society, Dahl asked about the impact of secrecy,[134] of new market techniques and corporate influence,[135] of changing times and the increasing role of technocrats,[136] and of the impact of size[137] and scale of modern populations upon democratic theory and institutions.[138]

Although Dahl's democratic focus can be subdivided into a concern with locale or with the conditions of modernity, such distinctions have an important failing. They point to Dahl's focus without providing an explanation for it. To be sure, the motivation of a scholar for selecting a given perspective is not always a relevant question, unless, of course, the author has insisted otherwise. In Dahl's case, he has. Dahl is, as Stanley W. Moore puts it, a man with a "task."[139] Dahl has been quite clear about what his task is, and his explanation helps to clarify his democratic focus. Thus, while a discussion of Dahl's focus is useful, it tells us little about Dahl's underlying research task or the theory of polyarchy which grows out of it.

DAHL'S TASK

Dahl's task, simply put, has been a career-long attempt to replace an "older" conception of democratic theory with a new theory; one that "roughly and crudely approximates . . . [the earlier one] in the sense that non-leaders exercise a relatively high degree of control over leaders."[140] The new theory, albeit an "untidy and highly imperfect"[141] one, is "polyarchy."

Dahl's task arises from a problem with the relationship between democratic theory and, as he sees it, the "real world." In *Politics, Economics, and Welfare,* Dahl and Lindblom argue: "If governments were placed on a continuum running from full achievement of democracy to an exclusively unilateral dictatorship, no real world instance would fit either end of the continuum."[142]

The problem, then, becomes one of praxis; the linking of theory and practice. This dichotomy, of attempting both to develop a new theory and to test it, to create it and to see if it works in practice, is a theme throughout Dahl's corpus. This twofold emphasis in Dahl has led to a dichotomy in his work; an emphasis, at times, on primarily theoretical projects and, at other times, on practical or empirical inquiry.

Dahl has written of the reasons that provoked him to undertake the construction and testing of a new theory of democracy. The "older" theory has great problems. In a study of the problems that atomic energy poses for a democratic polity, Dahl noted that "as a plain statement of fact, the proposition is scarcely debatable; the political processes of democracy do not operate efficiently with respect to atomic energy policy."[143] The problem, then, is about the impossibility of a possible reconciliation of modern life with "classical democratic theory" and about the possibility of constructing a wholly adequate new theory. He writes, "If classical theory is demonstrably invalid in some crucial respects, it is not clear how we are to go about constructing theoretical models to replace the older ones."[144] Nevertheless, Dahl attempted just such a replacement. In a treatise regarded as a significant ground-breaking effort by scholars as diverse as Giovanni Sartori and Amitai Etzioni,[145] Dahl and his coauthor, Charles Lindblom, set forth their "untidy and highly imperfect" theory of polyarchy.

It should be noted, however, that by suggesting Dahl sought to replace an older theory with a new one, we have oversimplified the case. There was a problem that Dahl encountered in attempting to replace "older" theory which is analogous to a problem encountered by a careful reader of Dahl's own theory. Dahl noted in *A Preface to Democratic Theory*: "One of the difficulties one must face at the outset is that there is no democratic theory—there are only democratic theories."[146] To a lesser degree, the same might be said of polyarchy. There are several versions of what Dahl means by the term polyarchy.

DAHL AS DEMOCRAT: SUMMARY

Von Der Muhll, Sartori, and Etzioni[147] have emphasized the democratic concerns and commitments underlying Dahl's writings. For such readers, Dahl's work can be viewed as an attempt to fashion a modern democratic theory coupled with various attempts to validate empirically the new theory. Again, as with the earlier locale/modernity dichotomy, it is necessary to insist that the theory/practical inquiry dichotomy is somewhat artificial given Dahl's sensitivity to the requirements of both theory and evidence. Nevertheless, a prescriptive/descriptive or theory/empirical-testing distinction is productive in categorizing Dahl's work. While none of Dahl's works is a pure example of either type, all of the studies—except *Polyarchy*—emphasize the development of the new theory or attempt to test it.[148] The practical and the theoretical inquiry have remained ongoing in Dahl's research. Neither the theory nor its empirical testing has reached a point of final resolution; both Dahl's conception of polyarchy and his attempts to validate it are still under way. Both the theory of polyarchy and the method Dahl has used to test it have undergone changes since the inception of the concept of "polyarchy" in 1953. Possibly, more modifications are yet to come.

A major contention of the present study is that neither Dahl's theory nor his methodology has been static. Each can and has changed over time. Such an argument is not universally acceptable. A number of critics have treated Dahl's theory of polyarchy and his methodology as a finished product. This has led to two sets of problems. On the one hand, early formulations of theory or method—typically abstracted from *PEW* (1953) or *Who Governs?* (1961)—have been severely criticized in the literature. On the other hand, having once criticized the early (pre-1967) Dahl on both methodological and theoretical grounds, the critical dialogue on Dahl and polyarchy has all but disappeared from the literature of political science.[149]

There are several reasons that might justify the one-shot approach described above. It might be argued that (1) the critics were right; they were scrupulously fair both in their characterization of Dahl and their description of his model of polyarchy; (2) the critics were right in another sense, that is, in their criticisms of the model of polyarchy which they have correctly described in step (1) above; (3) it might be correct to cut short a critical dialogue on Dahl if the critics were not only right but exhaustively so—that is to say, if they have covered all the ground that will prove productive to examine; (4) finally, an abbreviated critical dialogue is justified if the theory remains static; if it does not undergo change or modification and if the three criteria listed above are also fulfilled. Conversely, should any of these three criteria be unmet or inadequately met, a reexamination of Dahl would seem in order. Unhappily—except in terms of symmetry—the critical literature on Dahl fails on each of the four points listed above. We turn now to a case in point—the theoretical critique of Robert Dahl.

DAHL AS APOLOGIST: THE "CRITIQUE OF TOLERANCE"

The theoretical critics make two major allegations: First, polyarchy is "biased" in favor—or overly tolerant of—the status quo in American politics. Second, polyarchy, far from being a democratic theory, is actually democratic-revisionism; it is yet another reformulation of Joseph Schumpeter's "elitist theory of democracy."[150] We shall explore each allegation in turn.

In a 1971 study, Ricci divided Dahl's critics into two camps: the "critique of tolerance" and the "critique of method."[151] While we will broaden the scope to include material not discussed by Ricci, the distinction is a useful one. The "tolerance" critics make three charges: (1) Dahl has a status quo focus or "bias"; (2) Dahl cares little about current high levels of citizen apathy and low levels of political participation; or (3) Dahl lacks concern for low-resource groups—groups which some commentators suggest have become "permanent minorities" within American politics.[152]

THE ARGUMENTS USED: THE STATUS QUO BIAS

William Connolly, Henry Kariel, Theodore Lowi, and David Ricci argue that polyarchy has a "bias" in favor of the status quo.[153] To such critics, polyarchy all too often boils down to a theoretical justification for the brokerage politics inherent in "interest group liberalism."[154] Connolly et al. concede that polyarchy loosely describes the actual workings of American politics but insist it does not and should not describe the ideal workings of a polity. Polyarchy may explain American politics but it does little to improve political conditions. As a system, polyarchy is tolerant of—even conducive to—low levels of citizen participation, high levels of citizen apathy, and a host of social ills including but not limited to

racial discrimination, air and water pollution, violence, crime, suppression of political dissent, urban decay, inequitable tax structures, the deterioration of mass transportation, the widespread use of drugs, the plight of American Indians, the Vietnam atrocities, the conditions of the poor, consumer fraud, planned obsolence [and] the inferior status of women.[155]

In a nutshell, for the tolerance critics polyarchy provides a descriptive but certainly not a prescriptive model of American democracy.

There are many subcurrents within the tolerance school. As Ricci notes: "It is extremely difficult to abstract a pattern, to systematically analyze the critique of tolerance, because its sources and elements are too disparate."[156] Nevertheless, there is one commonality among members of this school; they appear to accept (although to varying degrees) the explanatory power of Dahl's theory of polyarchy. It is the prescriptive implications of polyarchy that trouble such critics. Dahl, they argue, confuses political is with political ought.

APATHY AND POLITICAL PARTICIPATION

For Ricci, Dahl and the tolerance critics do not really disagree about "who may participate, who does participate, and who actually makes political decisions; they differ only in their interpretation of the significance of those facts."[157] Critics argue that Dahl accepts current levels of political participation and voter apathy as acceptable and, perhaps, inevitable. Further, Dahl has factored this lack of participation into his "new" democratic theory. The critics take Dahl's argument to be something like the following: Modern, complex democratic society provides citizens with a multiplicity of opportunities and choices. Many of these opportunities—of which political participation is but one—require large expenditures of time, energy, effort, and, often, monetary resources. Most citizens will choose not to enter the political arena. They may occasionally vote but in other respects they shun politics for more private pursuits. This largely apolitical man, *homo civicus*, seeks satisfaction in his private life. Nevertheless, *homo civicus* has an indirect impact upon the political arena—such actors occasionally vote on officeholders and various tax and policy referenda.

In contrast to *homo civicus, homo politicus* is inclined to political participation. Such individuals enter the political arena, join or form coalitions, run for political office, and broker with other groups to affect public policy. Thus, Dahl presents a picture of society divided into politically active and apolitical strata. If modern times do not produce large numbers of political actives, town meetings, and conventioneering, we are told not to worry. Beyond some minimal threshold, the levels of numbers of citizens acting politically is not what is crucial to democracy. What is crucial is not the substance of nearly universal participation but the existence of a process that guarantees the legal right of participation to all citizens, a process that prohibits the small numbers who do participate from disenfranchising those who do not. Further, the political stratum is constrained in what it can and cannot do. Since he or she tends to be more accepting than *homo civicus* of Constitutional protections insuring minority rights, *homo politicus* is partially self-restrained. The political structure also restrains the political stratum. *Homo civicus* can restrain the political actives by electoral and other avenues of interest articulation as well as, infrequently, resorts to extralegal acts of violence and dissent. Thus, democratic and representative policies are guaranteed not by high levels of participation but by the processes of modern polyarchy.

This description is criticized on two fronts. It "tolerates" high levels of citizen apathy and nonparticipation and, second, it focuses on the process or "the forms of democracy—our rights and our frequent elections"—but not on the "substance of democracy."[158]

Lane Davis, Graeme Duncan, Henry Kariel, and Robert Pranger argue that Dahl's emphasis on democratic process is misplaced. In order to be genuinely healthy, a substantive base of politically active citizens must underlie the allegedly democratic procedural superstructure of democracy. To condone less is to tolerate a "new democracy" which does not encourage active citizenship but "eclipses" it. Dahl's new theory more or less adequately describes the status quo but it does little to change it. Davis insists that the "cost of realism" is the replacement of older notions of democracy with an inferior coin of the realm. Substantive democracy is supplanted by procedural polyarchy. In its strongest formulation, the "participation critics" have—admittedly, in some cases by implication—charged Dahl with not seeking to encourage maximum citizen participation and in so doing ignoring the "one essential condition of a decent society . . . [and] the good life."[159]

Democratic "substance" and participation critics argue not only that Dahl accepts current levels of political participation but that polyarchy elevates this descriptive account into a prescriptive norm. In effect, Dahl is charged with being an apologist for the status quo. *Homo civicus* and the apolitical stratum are seen as both an explanation and a justification for the brokerage politics that characterize the political stratum.

PERMANENT MINORITIES AND THE ARENA THEORY

Several of the critics described above accept polyarchy as an adequate descriptive model of American politics. Their objections turn on a rejection of polyarchy's normative implications. We turn now to an examination of the view of pluralism that underpins such criticism and to two types of critics who reject this view.

The model of polyarchy assumed by the first subset of status quo critics has been described by William Connolly as the "arena theory" of pluralism. In this view, political society is divided into two camps: the political arena populated by *homo politicus* and the apolitical arena populated by *homo civicus*. The apolitical arena is subdivided into actors who are inclined occasionally to vote and to donate limited amounts of time or money to campaigns, and those not so inclined. Policy issues are resolved in the political arena as the result of bargaining among politically active groups. Finally, the political arena is constrained in what action it may take due to the potential for electoral or interest group activity by actors within the apolitical arena. Figure 2.1 is a schematic representation of the arena theory of polyarchy.

Connolly has described the arena theory in the following terms:

Figure 2.1
Polyarchy Model: The Arena Theory Variant

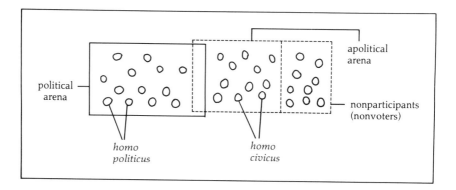

There is no ruling class or power elite which dominates government over a wide range of issues. Rather, there are numerous bases for political power in American society—wealth, prestige, strategic position, voting power—and while each resource is distributed unequally, most identifiable groups in the system have and make use of advantages in one or more of these areas. The competitive party system plays a major role in maintaining the system of pluralism. Since the "in" party's voting coalition is always threatened by the "out" party's voting attempts to create new issues which will shift marginal voters to its side, both parties constantly strive to increase their support among the major social and sectional groupings in the country. The result is a broad range of minorities whose preferences must be taken into account by leaders in making policy choices. Any "active" and "legitimate" group can usually "make itself heard at some crucial stage in the process of decision."[160]

Several of Dahl's early passages (pre-1968) would seem to support the arena view of polyarchy. In 1961, Dahl expressed the opinion that "very few individuals or groups in New Haven, and I believe this to be true in the United States, are totally lacking in political resources of some kind."[161] In his textbook, *Pluralist Democracy in the United States* (1967), Dahl reiterated essentially the same point: "Few groups in the United States who are determined to influence the government—certainly few if any groups who are organized, active and persistent—lack the capacity and opportunity to influence some officials somewhere in the political system in order to obtain at least some of their goals."[162] In *Who Governs?* Dahl appears to present a similar account of ethnic group politics in America. New Haven politics presents difficulties to out-group ethnic minorities which are eventually able to organize and achieve influence, at times dominance, within the political arena. Thus, in the second chapter, Dahl presents what amounts to an "ethnic stepladder" or "wave theory" depiction of New Haven politics. Early New Haven politics was dominated by wealthy community "patricians," who in turn were replaced by succeeding waves of "entrepreneurs," "explebians," and immigrant ethnic "new men." No minority group is ever permanently frozen out of the political arena. They need only organize, be active and persistent and they will eventually be successful in their attempts to "influence some officials somewhere in the political system . . . [and] obtain at least some of their goals." The implication for nonwhite, low-resource groups seems clear. They will succeed in much the same way as other entering groups—notably, Italian and Irish immigrants—did before them.[163]

Several critics have taken issue with Dahl's "arena theory" of polyarchy. Arena theory misrepresents the current plight of the poor and nonwhite in political society.[164] Far from acting as a check on or entering the political arena, low-resource minorities have become "permanent minorities" in American politics. Not presently active in politics, such groups lack the necessary resources (leadership skills, education, financial resources, strategic position in society, internal organization) to be "active," "organized," or "persistent" in the foreseeable future. Lacking such resources and—as Michael Harrington has noted[165]—lacking visibility to other actors in the political arena who do possess such resources, they remain cumulatively unsuccessful in the political arena. Polyarchy may work for the Irish, Italian, or Polish immigrants, but it is less "workable" for nonwhite minorities and the poor whites.

Extending this critique, Kariel, Lowi, and McConnell have written not simply of group poverty but of a poverty of arena pluralism itself. In Kariel's phrase, "the poverty of liberalism" is an intransigence in the system, a frozen system in which low resource groups are not only excluded from the political arena but are excluded indefinitely. *Homo civicus*—and some would-be examples of *homo politicus*—is locked out of the political arena by a prevailing "liberal" ideology and a semipermanent constellation of dominant groups. Lowi has argued that the pluralist system produced a "non-juridical" or "interest group politics" climate in U.S. politics.[166] For Lowi, various actors within the political arena have preempted most of the political resources necessary for pluralist politics. They need not—and do not—include the policy wishes of *homo civicus* in their policy deliberations. Lowi argues that a "juridical" cure is needed. Actors within the political arena must be rigidly constrained by law in what they can and cannot do. The alternative to a Congress accountable for developing explicit law is, for Lowi, a continuation of the semipluralism of interest group politics. In *Private Power and American Democracy*, Grant McConnell presented a detailed longitudinal study of American agricultural, labor, and business policy. Like Lowi, McConnell argued that within their own areas of concern, business and agricultural groups have been able to exclude other interested parties from the political arena—they have "privatized" policy-making within the political arena.[167] Thus, groups such as the National Association of Manufacturers, the Business Council, and the American Farm Bureau exert a disproportionate influence upon the political system. Once again, arena pluralism is criticized as not being pluralistic, but semipluralistic.

The net effect of the permanent minorities critique is twofold. First, critics have attacked the conventional or "arena theory" of polyarchal pluralism and advanced serious criticisms of its alleged "nonjuridical" or "privatized" political process. Second, they have—at least implicitly—presented an alternative explanation of interest group politics. Assuming that such an alternative model can be abstracted from the permanent minorities critique, we have depicted it (see Figure 2.2) as the "privatized" variant of pluralistic politics.

Figure 2.2
The "Privatized" Variant of Pluralist Politics

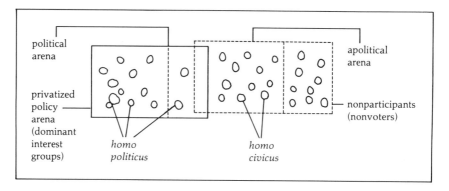

Both bodies of criticism just reviewed discuss Dahl's polyarchy in terms of what has been described as the arena theory variant. Further one set partially agrees with arena theory as a descriptive theory, while a second partially disagrees. There is a third critique which, as before, characterizes Dahl's polyarchy in terms of arena theory but which wholly rejects the arena theory explanation of American politics.

THE POWER ELITE CRITIQUE: ARENA THEORY
VS. ELITE THEORY

"Elite" theorists have challenged Dahl's arena theory at two levels. C. Wright Mills, Suzanne Keller, and G. William Domhoff have suggested that national politics in the United States is hierarchical rather than plural-istic.[168] Domhoff, Floyd Hunter, Peter Bachrach, and Morton Baratz have made similar arguments about American subnational politics. Although there are differences of degree among the elite school members, they share similar attitudes regarding: (1) Dahl and what he means by "polyarchy," (2) the efficacy of arena theory in explaining national or local politics, and (3) what constitutes an accurate description of American national or sub-national politics.

Since the publication of *The Power Elite* in 1956, elite theorists have tended to assume the existence of a common definition of pluralism. As a result, elite theory adherents tend to blur important differences in such writers as Bentley, Truman, Riesman, and Dahl. The pluralist paradigm criticized by the elite writers has come over time to resemble the arena theory of pluralism. For elite theorists, the pluralist paradigm means a bifurcated political system comprised of political actives and inactives with multiple and overlapping groups which shift with some degree of frequency between the political and apolitical arena. It is, in short, a system in which political competition is meaningful, fairly widespread, and serves to check the activities and aspirations of those within the political arena.

In a recent (1978) reexamination of Dahl's New Haven study, Domhoff has restated the elite view of what Dahl means by polyarchy. Domhoff's explanation follows closely the outlines of arena theory assumptions. Dahl, he notes, draws from conclusions about New Haven politics:

(1) The first is that there is inequality in New Haven, but it is not an inequality that favors one specific group or class, as it did in the past. . . . (2) A second major conclusion drawn by Dahl is that movement into the small stratum of individuals who are highly active in politics, a stratum he calls the political stratum, is relatively "easy." . . . (3) The net effects of political competition in New Haven are quite significant, and . . . (4) "Numbers" (the majority of voters) would triumph over "Notability" if the goals of the majority were to become different from those of economic and social notables.[169]

That adherents of elite theory reject arena theory is quite clear. Rejecting the argument that politics is characterized by reciprocal bargaining among many—if not most—of society's citizens, Domhoff argues that "wealthy businessmen are at the center of the upper social class and are the rulers of New Haven—and America."[170] Other members of the power elite critique share a similar perspective. To these analysts, a narrow group of people sharing sufficient amounts of a unique resource (be it social standing, monetary resources, crucial information and skills, or a strategic position in society) and possessing mutually compatible goals and perceptions exercise a preemptive degree of control over the policy outcomes of the American political arena. Discounting arena theory as a descriptive explanation of American politics, elite theory adherents have suggested in a series of studies that a "power elite" or members of the "higher circles" set the agenda of foreign and domestic national policy.[171] Floyd Hunter argued that "community influentials" exert a similar influence upon Atlanta city politics. In summary, then, Domhoff, Hunter, and other adherents of the power elite thesis reject Dahl's polyarchal explanation of American politics (see Figure 2.3).

Figure 2.3
The Elite Theory Description of American Politics

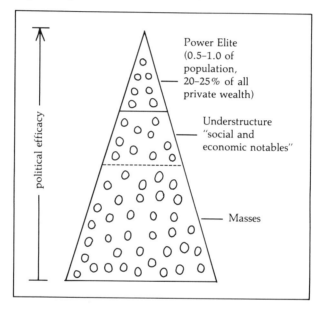

THE THEORETICAL CRITIQUE: CONCLUSION

Four bodies of criticism of Dahl and polyarchy have been identified. Adherents of the apologist, apathy, permanent minority, and power elite critiques have credited Dahl with using an "arena theory" variant of pluralism. Further, several of these critics have taken issue with arena theory, either on normative or descriptive grounds. Two sets of critics, the adherents of "privatized" pluralist or "power elite" explanations, have put forth alternate and competing descriptive paradigms of American politics. We turn now to a final theoretical criticism of polyarchy. This view assumes that Dahl has employed an arena theory variant of pluralism and argues that Dahl's revision of classical democratic theory has both normative and methodological shortcomings. As such this critique serves as a bridge between theoretical criticisms raised earlier and methodological criticisms of Dahl which have yet to be discussed.

THE THEORETICAL CRITIQUE: DAHL AS DEMOCRATIC ELITIST

Several scholars have recognized Dahl's effort to revise "classical" democratic theory but have rejected his reformulation.[172] Citing normative objections, such critics argue that polyarchy shares weaknesses with the earlier democratic-revisionist theory set forth by Joseph Schumpeter in 1942.[173] Dahl, they argue, subverts rather than extends earlier democratic theory. In an argument that parallels earlier critiques, Dahl is charged with abandoning the emphasis upon maximum citizen participation which is at the very core of classical democratic theory. In the strongest expression of their criticism, these critics argue that Dahl's variant of pluralism is so distant from the basic tenets of classical democratic theory as to be "inadequate as a guide" for serious students of democracy and politics.[174]

The neoclassicist argument involves several assumptions: First, that a unified traditional or classical theory of democracy exists; second, that Dahl's theory of polyarchy (as with the earlier critics, understood in terms of arena theory) is a departure from classical precepts; and, finally, that Dahl and Schumpeter are not democratic theorists at all but, rather, "democratic elitists."[175]

Neoclassicists suggest that democratic theory has two "traditions"[176]— one classical, the other modern.[177] Classical democratic theory includes three key assumptions: (1) "the concept of an active, informed citizenry . . . [is] the most distinctive feature of the traditional theory. . . . [T]he principle orienting value of classical democratic theory was its emphasis on individual participation in the development of public policy"; (2) "the classical theorists accepted the basic framework of Lockean democracy, with its emphasis on limited government"; (3) the classicists "were not primarily concerned with the policies which might be produced in a democracy; above all else they were concerned with human development, the opportunities which existed in political activity to realize the untapped potentials of men and to create the foundations of a genuine human community."[178] This third tenet is critical. The emphasis of classicism is not upon the political system as such, but upon the free and active movements of the citizens within the system. Systemic function and maintenance, even policy outcomes of the system, are secondary to the emphasis upon free and active movement within the system. Indeed, for the neoclassicists such an active citizenry is or should be the constitutive element of real or classical democracy.

The neoclassicists grant that the requisite conditions for a classical democracy have not always existed in modern times. Agreeing with social scientists who claim that high levels of citizen participation are infrequently found in modern American society,[179] the neoclassicists argue that current levels of citizen apathy are a malaise indicative of a problem in the modern body politic. Walker, Duncan and Lukes, Pranger, and Kariel[180] warn that current levels of participation need to be raised dramatically to prevent an "eclipse of citizenship." As Kariel notes, the development of a true democracy is hindered by the presence of "oligarchically governed hierarchies . . . [which] now place unjustifiable limits on constitutional democracy."[181] The new threat of polyarchal pluralism is guilty of hindering rather than promoting genuine democracy. "Because the theory of pluralism under conditions of large scale technology conflicts with the principles of constitutional democracy," the American political structure and practice ought to be aligned with a specific segment of the classical tradition—namely, "the still unfashionable one of Rousseau . . . [a movement] from a hierarchical public order toward an equalitarian one."[182]

Neoclassicists have argued that Dahl's arena theory is the latter-day expression of Schumpeter's "democratic-elitist" argument.[183] As does Schumpeter, Dahl puts forward the hypothesis that "a relatively small proportion of individuals in any form of social organization will take up decision-making opportunities."[184]

Carole Pateman has characterized Dahl's arguments:

[T]he lower socioeconomic groups, the majority are "triply barred" from [full equality with participatory elites] . . . by their relatively limited access to resources, participatory elites and—in the United States—by "Madison's nicely contrived system of constitutional checks." In a modern theory of democracy, "political equality" refers to the existence of universal suffrage [one man, one vote] with its sanction through the electoral competition for votes and, more importantly, to the fact of equality of opportunity of access to influence over decision makers through inter-election processes by which different groups in the electorate make their demands heard. "Officials not only listen" to various groups, but "expect to suffer" in some significant way if they do not placate the group, its leaders or its most vociferous members.[185]

A reading of Dahl's early writings tends to support the suggestion that he is a latter-day democratic-elitist. As Ricci notes, Dahl's view of democracy must be judged equivalent to Schumpeter's classic definition: "the democratic method is that institutional arrangement for arriving at political decisions in which individuals acquire the power to decide by means of a competitive struggle for the people's vote."[186] In *Who Governs?* Dahl argues that New Haven is more than less democratic; "New Haven is a republic of unequal citizens, but for all that a republic."[187] In the same year Dahl wrote:

What we call "democracy" . . . does seem to operate with a relatively low level of citizen participation. Hence it is inaccurate to say that one of the necessary conditions for "democracy" is extensive citizen participation. It would be more reasonable simply to insist that some minimal participation is required. . . . For such control as we exert over our political leaders, that is, on their constant and unending rivalry in satisfying the demands of relatively small groups.[188]

Thus, we arrive at a picture of Dahl's polyarchy consistent with the arena theory variant of pluralism discussed earlier. Dahl's polyarchy is, argues one observer, the combination of Schumpeter's assumptions with the concept of the political stratum.[189] Polyarchy is a bifurcation of political society into a political and an apolitical strata coupled with the observation that such a process "roughly and crudely approximates" democracy due to the competition among the ranks of *homo politicus* for the electoral support of *homo civicus*. Again, it is worth noting that the commentators who criticize Dahl's polyarchy as a democratic-elitist paradigm are offering an understanding of Dahl that is consistent with the arena theory explanation of polyarchy.

THE DEMOCRATIC-ELITIST CRITIQUE

In a careful study, Pateman ranks Dahl, along with Bernard Berelson and Giovanni Sartori, as one of the three leading members of the democratic-elitist school. Several critics who share Pateman's assumption criticize the democratic-elitist element in Dahl on either normative or descriptive grounds.[190]

Along normative lines, Dahl's "crude" and "rough" translation of classical democratic theory into contemporary polyarchy is charged with fundamentally altering democratic theory and altering it for the worse. The normative critique extends to two considerations: the proper focus of democratic theory and the proper role of citizen participation. This leads, not to a concern with the individual citizen and his or her well-being and role within the system but, rather, to a discussion of the macro-political system itself. As a result, Walker argues, Dahl has "conservatized" democratic theory. By discussing system stability rather than human potential, by evidencing a belief that low levels of citizen participation are likely to continue as a condition of modern polyarchal politics rather than attempting to increase present participatory levels, Dahl has "fundamentally changed the normative significance of democracy, rendering it a more conservative doctrine in the process."[191]

The conservatizing argument is two-edged. On the one hand, Dahl is criticized for sharing with other pluralists and democratic-elitists an emphasis on system stability.[192] Thus, criticisms that have been made of Berelson, Sartori, Eckstein, Etzioni, Bentley, and Truman were extended to Dahl. System stability is an inherently conservative focus. In this sense, Dahl is charged with rendering democratic theory more conservative. A more powerful conservatizing charge follows the earlier one. Walker, Kariel, Duncan and Lukes, Pateman, Pranger, and Bachrach and Baratz charge Dahl with conservatizing democratic theory by removing its most radical constitutive element. Citizen participation, they argue, is the sine qua non of classical democracy. The "new realism" of Dahl and others has disarmed democratic theory. Classical democratic theory focused not on the system and its stability but upon the individual citizen and his or her human potential. This was the truly radical raison d'être of democratic theory. It alone, of all theories of government, allowed citizens to express themselves and develop to their fullest potential. It did this by providing the opportunity and inducement for expression via participatory government. Even if citizens did not fully participate at any given time, the role of the democratic state and its institutions is to create and promote such activity in the future via arenas of free access and educational activity. Here the dispute between Dahl as elitist and his critics becomes most clear. Reminiscent of John Dewey, the critics argue that if present levels of citizen participation are not suitably high in political society, the state ought to educate the citizens to democracy, ought to create schemes of functional or workplace representation to facilitate maximum levels of citizen participation in political society.[193]

The conservatizing critics charge Dahl with abandoning the commitment to increasing levels of citizen participation and, in Walker's phrase, reducing the noble theme of classical democracy to a "noble lie." "The ideal of democratic participation is thus transformed into a 'noble lie' designed chiefly to insure a sense of responsibility among political leaders."[194] Thus, the average "deme" or citizen no longer legitimizes politics and policy decisions. Political leaders now serve this function for Dahl. As one critic notes:

Dahl concludes in his study of New Haven that the skillful, active political leaders in the system are the true democratic "legitimists." Since democratic procedures regulate their conflicts and protect their privileged positions in the system the leaders can be counted on to defend the democratic creed even if a majority of the voters might prefer some other set of procedures.[195]

In a sentence, the normative critics argue that Dahl replaces a democratic theory of substantive citizen participation with a polyarchal theory of elite political participation—participatory substance has yielded to participatory shadows. Writing on polyarchy's descriptive utility, Jack Walker argues that polyarchy is inadequate as a "guide" for students of democracy. Polyarchy, for Walker, is both theoretically and empirically unsound as a guide for research. It is theoretically unsound because Dahl and the democratic-revisionists "have stripped democracy of much of its radical elan and diluted its utopian vision, thus rendering it inadequate as a guide to the future."[196] Both Walker and Pateman argue that Dahl's democratic-elitism is empirically unsound. Going beyond the argument that the theory is descriptively accurate but normatively unacceptable, Walker and Pateman suggest findings that challenge the semipermanence of citizen inactivity. Walker argues:

The most unsatisfactory element in the theory is its concept of the passive, apolitical common man who pays allegiance to his governors and to the sideshow of politics while remaining primarily concerned with his private life, evenings of television with his family, or the demands of his job. Occasionally, when the average citizen finds his primary goals threatened by the actions or inactions of government, he may strive vigorously to influence the course of public policy, but *"homo civicus"* as Dahl calls him, "is not by nature a political animal."[197]

For Walker, citizen apathy is not the result of psychological predispositions to political inactivity, but more probably the result of "the use of force, or informal, illegitimate coercion in the American political system."[198] Thus, nonwhite ethnic groups have been excluded forcibly rather than voluntarily from all but recent political participation. Pateman presents a careful study of workers' self-management to support her claim that *homo civicus* will actively participate in his or her own governance if the political system is conducive to such participation. Walker, making a similar contention regarding American politics, argues that "a tendency of the prevailing political system to frustrate strong leaders" has, in turn, repeatedly frustrated "the great social movements which have marked American society in the last one hundred years."[199]

In sum, Walker and Pateman charge Dahl with "uncritically accepting the values of the going system in the name of scientific objectivity."[200] Such critics charge that Dahl's bias in favor of the system has precluded the possibility of polyarchy being an accurate scientific account of American politics. A final set of critics has extended this argument, raising questions about Dahl's social science methodology and his "objectivity."

DAHL AS (FAILED) SCIENTIST

Dahl's methodology has been attacked on two fronts: one philosophical, the other methodological. He has been accused of adopting a "value-free" behavioral approach and, alternately, of committing various errors in research design and methodology.

Much of the commentary on the early behavioral movement springs from a distinction first raised by Max Weber. Weber suggested that societal inquiry was characterized by two views of science: *wertfrei* and *wertlos*.[201] *Wertfrei* he defines as a working science that is truly objective—"free from the prevailing passion and prejudice." *Wertlos*, on the other hand, is a false science or a "scientistic" approach. A *wertlos* approach includes the passions of the day but masks them with a false objectivity. "A *wertlos* positivism . . . amounts to nothing more than an unthinking apologia for whatever is."[202] Dahl has been criticized for aspiring to the former but succumbing to the latter approach. That Weber's either/or typology might itself be flawed or that Dahl might be a member of a postbehavioral generation of social scientists attempting to establish a relatively objective set of findings with admittedly value-laden implications has escaped all but a handful of observers.[203]

The *wertfrei/wertlos* typology offers several advantages to would-be critics of social scientists. Since true science (*wertfrei*) is quite probably impossible—it requires scientists to be removed from the historical setting and emotional entanglements of their times[204]—then virtually all attempts at social science can be criticized for being *wertlos*. At the same time, should any attempt at social science approach the status of *wertfrei* inquiry, it can also be criticized precisely because it is *wertfrei*. Because, according to this argument, a set of findings are scientifically objective—removed from the passions and historical setting of the individual social scientist—the scientist is then alleged to be guilty of using his findings in a value-free way, of not caring about, not attempting to inform or assist his own times or cultural milieu. Thus, we arrive at the critic's equivalent of Catch-22. Either a social scientist has not managed to conduct a value-free project and so is condemned as a "scientistic" example of *wertlos*, or the scientist has managed to conduct a value-free project and for this reason is then guilty, by definition, of a lack of concern with pressing social problems of his or her own times. *Wertfrei* or *wertlos*, the social scientist stands condemned.

Given the *wertfrei/wertlos* orientation of the early criticism of behavioral attempts, it seems hardly remarkable that Dahl was criticized in a similar manner. We turn now to an examination of the three leading critics of Dahl as value-free social scientist.[205]

Two recent commentators have charged that Dahl's work has normative difficulties.[206] By referring to the *wertfrei/wertlos* typology, the arguments of the two authors may be characterized as follows: Dahl's studies, particularly in his *Preface to Democratic Theory*, escape the problems associated with merely "scientistic" or *wertlos* studies. But it is in Dahl's attempt to be analytically rigorous, to be scientifically objective and value-free that problems arise. For in so doing, "Dahl either rejects the ethical problem of democratic theory outright . . . or else he subordinates ethical problems to quasi-ethical or ethically neutral considerations."[207] Dahl, in this view, is too rigorous, too objective. He is guilty of "reversing the Aristotleian sense of practicality. . . . [T]he goal of obtaining political knowledge was defined by Aristotle in terms of the larger objective of attaining the good life. Dahl attempts to drive a wedge between ethics and politics, and to confine political theory to the scientific study of political systems."[208] Dahl is not a student of the good life; he is only a neutral student of political life as it is. Because of his attempted objectivity and rigor, Dahl is not simply "scientistic." As one critic noted:

He has carried research into the gray areas between science and evaluation more clearly, more openly, and I believe more fruitfully than others. He has already done enough, but because he has, it is important to point to the problems that he has clarified. The use of data and laws distinguishes his efforts from less rigorous forays into the gray area, and leads to the hope that someday he will present us *Democratic Theory: Beyond Polyarchy.*[209]

Such critics argue that Dahl's studies are superior to simple "scientistic" or *wertlos* projects—they are, in fact, quasi-*wertfrei*. Yet, Dahl's success is also his failure. He is not informing or commenting upon current political life. He is not interested in promoting the "good life." Walker argued earlier that Dahl's polyarchy is an inadequate "guide" for contemporary students of democratic theory. The critics just examined suggest that Dahl is unconcerned with the task of serving as a guide. By this line of reasoning, Dahl is not concerned with the implications of his work; rather, he is value-free. He is not criticizing or measuring political society against a normative standard; instead, he is merely describing it. George Graham's criticism of Dahl is not concerned with Dahl's descriptive theory of polyarchy but with the fact that Dahl should be prescriptive or normative, that Dahl should go beyond polyarchy.

Three critics who have transcended the oftentimes simplistic confines of the *wertfrei/wertlos* typology are Christian Bay, Stephen Rousseaus, and James Farganis. Rousseaus and Farganis have argued that *wertfrei* is, for all practical purposes, impossible in the social sciences. As they note: "A brute empiricist, devoid of any 'passion' is no more capable of describing the world as it is than is an ideologue who views the world around him solely through the lens of his ideological *weltanschauung*. . . . For facts are themselves the products of our viewing 'reality' through our theoretical preconceptions which, in turn, are conditioned by the problems confronting us."[210]

Rousseaus and Farganis continue their argument:

And the theoretical precepts which determine the relevant facts of a particular view of "reality" are not themselves entirely value-free. Social theories, in short, are the result of our concern with specific problems. And social problems, at bottom, are concerned with ethical goals. Social theorists, furthermore, differ in their theoretical constructions of "reality." They differ, that is, in the problems they see, or, what amounts to the same thing, they see a given problem in a different way. Consequently, they differ as to the facts relevant to a given problem. There is, in other words, a selectivity of facts in the analysis of social problems. Some facts included in one approach are excluded in another; and even those held in common may and, usually do, differ in the weight given to them in their theoretical and casual inferences.[211]

Put more succinctly, social scientists, at least for the present, can only aspire to a quasi-*wertfrei* science; "perhaps the best that we can hope for is some form of objective relativism."[212] Thus, Dahl and the behaviorists cannot be faulted for falling short of pure science, for being less than completely objective in or for having passions or values inherent in their studies. What becomes important at this stage is not the absence of values in a study of social science but an honest and accurate clarification of what values are assumed by, or are implicit in, a given study of politics. Christian Bay has attacked behaviorists generally and Dahl specifically on precisely this point. Bay argues that there are two problems with Dahl's use of values. Bay suggests that Dahl shares a problem common to behavioral researchers —a "persistently implied commitment to a certain political bias, which favors democracy" and the accompanying tacit assumption that democracy means "democracy roughly as it now exists in the West, or in this country."[213]

For Bay, this leads to two problems in Dahl's work. Biased in favor of the current "rough" approximation of democracy, it is conservative. It underwrites the status quo. Second, in accepting the status quo and in not clearly stating what constitutes a democracy beyond the rough equivalency of the going concern in the United States with polyarchy, Dahl fails to provide a way to assess the political process he has described. As Bay notes:

In a *Preface* to democratic theory, and one which demonstrates a high order of rigor in analyzing other theories of democracy, the author's reluctance even to begin to develop operating criteria toward making meaningful the present system, or to provide pointers toward its meaningful further development, is as astounding as it is disappointing.

Bay's criticism of Dahl extends to one further point. Not only does Dahl provide insufficient indices with which to measure the efficacy of polyarchal democracy, but "he will not try to determine if it is a desirable system of government." Admitting that Dahl does offer a "vague" defense of democracy's desirability at the conclusion of *Preface*, Bay noted that Dahl does argue that democracy

appears to be a relatively efficient system for reinforcing agreement, encouraging moderation, and maintaining social peace in a restless and immoderate people operating a gigantic, powerful, diversified, and incredibly complex society. This is no negligible contribution, then, that Americans have made to the arts of government—and to that branch, which of all the arts of government is the most difficult, the art of democratic government.[214]

Still, argues Bay, "the author's ambition not to discuss the desirability of the American government would be difficult to understand to someone unacquainted with the currently prevailing fashion among behaviorists."[215] Presumably, then, Dahl in concert with numerous other behaviorists exhibits a bias in favor of the going mode of politics in the West and fails to provide either an adequate rationale for this choice or a rigorous set of indices with which to measure the efficacy of the polyarchal political system. As such, we have returned to a theme raised earlier. Dahl has provided a descriptive model of American politics—he has failed, however, to provide a prescriptive model of politics.

We turn now to a further set of critics, a group that has avoided the pitfalls of the *wertfrei/wertlos* typology by choosing to focus exclusively upon the more technical aspects of Dahl's methodology.

THE "CRITIQUE OF METHOD"

Those who criticize Dahl's methodology focus upon four major concerns.[216] While some of these concerns (and critics) overlap, they will be dealt with separately. Analysts who have suggested that Dahl's methodology is faulty in the area of issue selection, nondecision-making, potential power, and noncumulative resources will be examined. Before turning to this analysis it is important to enter a caveat. While most of the methodological critics speak to a different set of concerns than those raised earlier by the commentators on Dahl as democrat, Dahl as apologist, or Dahl as democratic-elitist, the critics studied in the present section share with the earlier ones a similar understanding of what Dahl means by polyarchy. For the critique of method school, as for the earlier analysts, "polyarchy" refers to the arena theory explanation of polyarchy. Each set of the methodological critics focuses on a separate concern or problem with arena theory. Some offer an alternative explanatory paradigm, but the point of departure or conception of polyarchy is the same for each group.

ISSUE SELECTION

In the New Haven study Dahl focused upon the substantive issues of urban redevelopment, public education, and party nominations. Thomas Anton, Herbert Danzger, and Bachrach and Baratz have criticized Dahl's methodology in choosing these issues.[217] Anton argues that three issues are insufficient for testing a pluralist hypothesis concerning the structure of power in a large American city. Further, even if three issues were a large enough sample, Anton, Ricci, and Delbert Miller question the salience of the issues chosen.[218] As Ricci notes:

In particular, two of the three major issues studied in New Haven, public education and party nominations, were by Dahl's own admission quite unimportant to the Economic and Social Notables of the city. Most of those people lived in suburban towns, send their children to exclusive private schools, and could neither vote nor hold office in New Haven. The apparent disinterest of so many Notables was significant because it raised the analytical problem of salience. If the economic and social elites of New Haven were by and large unconcerned with public education and party nominations—that is to say, if those matters were not salient in their minds and among their affairs—then Dahl's findings of elite impotence in the city were not entirely persuasive. Critics charged that his research failed to establish conclusively that Economic and Social Notables wielded merely ordinary influence; *Who Governs?* only demonstrated that they were not interested in these particular issues, and perhaps this proved no more than that they permitted other men to make decisions on matters of little importance to themselves.[219]

Thus, Dahl may have studied enough issues but not enough of the right issues in New Haven politics. Ricci and Miller suggest that Dahl would have been better advised to select not only hotly contested issues but, more important, to select issues involving a broad spectrum of the community[220] —an issue that "shakes the community from top to bottom."[221] Ricci suggests right-to-work legislation, affirmative action, or school integration as superior choices.

Danzger and Bachrach and Baratz argue that Dahl "stacked the deck" on issue selection. By using visible conflict as an important selection criterion, Dahl commits a tautological error.[222] By selecting hotly contested issues, one will almost invariably conclude that politics in a given city is pluralistic—that is to say, that it is marked by heated and meaningful conflicts in which policy is the result of contests among multiple participants. As Ricci observes:

If we study matters where conflict flares openly, competing interests and competing power holders will probably be present, and we are therefore likely to conclude that power is dispersed. But his choice of subject matter excludes from consideration many matters where conflict is not evident, where there do not seem to be competing interests and power holders, and where one might therefore conclude that power is not dispersed but is instead so concentrated as to be unopposed.[223]

NONDECISION-MAKING

If the earlier set of critics attacked Dahl's selection of issues on the basis of the size or salience of the sample, other critics object to Dahl's "visibility" criterion. Visible issues may be "safe" issues—issues which community influentials care little about. Dahl ignores what Bachrach and Baratz call " 'nondecision-making', i.e., the practice of limiting the scope of actual decision-making to 'safe' issues by manipulating the dominant values, myths, political institutions and procedures. To pass over this is to neglect one whole 'face of power.' "[224] A study of how and which issues do not become visible and hotly contested might reveal more about the power structure of a given community than Dahl's focus upon already visible issues. The authors point to the failure or "invisibility" of black demands for political equality in the South as an example of nondecision-making community power.

David Easton has made a similar if more sympathetic criticism of focusing upon only visible political issues. Political systems, argues Easton, often have "gatekeepers"—that is, systemic restraints on demands or inputs attempting to enter the decisional arena. Thus, community values, private or public coercive measures, economic or social position may act separately or in combination to monitor or restrict the flow of issues into the public decisional arena.[225]

A final criticism of selecting visible issues was suggested by the late C. Wright Mills. Mills argued that the national and subnational policy arenas are biased in favor of community influentials. Mills criticized political scientists for not studying the latent or "potential issues." Mills wrote:

Only one more point of definition: absence of public issues there may well be, but this is not due to any absence of problems. Their absence from many discussions—that is an ideological condition, regulated in the first place by whether or not intellectuals detect and state problems as potential issues for probable publics, and as troubles for a variety of individuals.[226]

POTENTIAL POWER

A related critique is raised by Anton, Howard J. Ehrlich, Andrew Hacker, Jack Walker, Robert Presthus, and Bachrach and Baratz.[227] In this view, Dahl's focus upon overt issues and outcomes prohibits the examination of potential power in the community. Some issues do not achieve public visibility or, once visible, result in a given set of outcomes because actors within the political arena fear the exercise of potential power held by community influentials. "Ostensibly powerful officials in some communities may be no more than functionaries running errands on behalf of other men, as Hunter contended in Atlanta."[228]

While only a few of the critics suggest that a cohesive set of community influentials exercise the degree of power that reduces elected municipal officials to mere functionaries or "leg men,"[229] several commentators note that municipal officials operate within a community context that influences their decisions and places conditions upon their exercise of authority.[230] Mayor Richard Lee of New Haven may have designed his redevelopment plan within his office or that of his appointee, redevelopment director Edward Logue. Still, is it accurate to say that Lee and Logue were free actors in the development of their plan? Is it unreasonable to assume that the elected officials were impacted, that their decisions were in part "conditioned" by the potential power of others in the community? The lending and "redlining" practices of a community's leading banking institutions, the potential approval or disapproval of major downtown businessmen, and the impact such a plan might have upon ward and city hall politics are all considerations that might operate to influence an ostensibly free agent. As Ricci notes:

In more common terms, suppose the Notables enjoy some influence over the mayor and he in turn influences them to some degree. The process of influence is subtle and implicit; it may operate through a great many proverbial winks and nods. It is difficult to grasp empirically; we know only that there is a circular flow of power—a closed loop—from one point to another and back. But who in the chain exercises more power? Who dominates the relationship? No method as yet has been devised, including the pluralist technique of analyzing specific decisions, for precisely ascertaining the measure of power wielded by all elements of a closed-loop system.[231]

NONCUMULATIVE RESOURCES

In *Who Governs?*, Dahl acknowledges that although all citizens may vote other political resources are unequally distributed.[232] As he notes, "Wealth, social position, access to public officials, and other resources are unequally distributed."[233] However, Dahl disagrees with elite anlaysts who hold that the uneven distribution of resources necessarily results in a de facto political elite. For Hunter, Mills, and Domhoff, uneven resource distribution is at once the raison d'être and the means of perpetuating elite political control of a community. Disagreeing, Dahl insists that the tendency of resources to cumulate into an oligarchical fashion is checked by five "limits to the growth of oligarchy."[234] First, "To the extent to which inequalities persist, tendencies toward oligarchy also exist in advanced industrial societies. But to the extent that inequalities are dispersed rather than cumulative—as I am suggesting that they are in the United States—the growth of a unified oligarchy is inhibited." Wealth, for example, is checked by such factors as ethnicity. Inequalities exist but are dispersed throughout the community. Thus, "the pattern of dispersed inequalities means that an individual or group may compensate for this handicap by exploiting his superior access to a different resource." Patrician wealth, for example, has been balanced by such factors as ethnicity and ethnic electoral solidarity.

Second, the growth to oligarchy is checked because no one resource such as wealth or social standing dominates "all the others in the sense that a person or group superior in the one resource would invariably exert superior influence on a conflict with persons who drew on other resources." A third check on oligarchy is that "individuals or groups who are at a disadvantage in their access to resources can sometimes compensate by using their resources at a relatively high level." Dahl points to New Haven's black community, which has overcome "disadvantages imposed by their incomes, status and occupation"[235] by achieving higher levels of mobilization than other identifiable groups in New Haven politics.[236]

Finally, the growth to community oligarchy is checked "because individuals at a disadvantage in resource distribution may develop a high level of political skill" or "may compensate by combining resources so that in the aggregate these are formidable."[237]

The elite theorists and permanent minorities critics reject Dahl's fivefold argument. Instead, they argue that most of the resources listed by Dahl—

"control of jobs, control of information and the mass media, social standing, knowledge and expertise, popularity, esteem and charisma, legal status and rights, constitutionality and officiality, ethnic solidarity, the vote, certain skills, energy, education, and native intelligence"—have all tended to accumulate cumulatively to the collective disadvantage of the lower socioeconomic members of the apolitical stratum.[238]

SUMMARY OF THE FOUR VIEWS

We have examined four views of Robert Dahl. Using the arena theory of polyarchy as a point of departure, four separate perspectives on Dahl and polyarchy have been culled from the literature. Dahl has been characterized as a democrat or an elitist, and, alternately, as a value-laden apologist or a value-free scientist. The critics of the latter perspective, perhaps the most strident of all the critics of Dahl, have made serious and far-reaching claims both about Dahl's "new" theory of polyarchal democracy and about Dahl's alleged "value-free" or behavioral methodology. In the words of two of the leading critics of Dahl's theoretical contribution, "the 'New Democracy' of the behaviorists has no more in common with real democracy than Mao's 'New Democracy.' "[239] As regards Dahl's allegedly value-free or behavioral methodology, Christian Bay has suggested that Dahl and his fellow behaviorists are analogous to physicians who, when called to a patient's bedside, are willing to diagnose the illness but then refuse to prescribe remedies.[240] A final critic has suggested that Dahl's methodology and the methodology of the behaviorists in general amounts to a failure to confront serious sociopolitical problems. It is literally posturing or "fiddling" while "Rome burns."[241]

Whether, in our time, "Rome burns" is open to dispute. So, too, judging from the disparate views of Dahl one finds in the literature, is the question of whether Dahl is "fiddling" and, if so, to what tune.

3

American Pluralism Responds (I)

As has been noted, Dahl has been called "an uncritical apologist for American pluralism,"[242] a "fiddler" while "Rome burns."[243] Scholars as eminent as Jack Walker and Christian Bay have criticized the "apologetical" tone of Dahl's writings on American politics. Walker has charged Dahl with "uncritically accepting the values of the going system in the name of scientific objectivity."[244] Bay has suggested that Dahl is analogous to a physician who when called to a patient's bedside is willing to diagnose the illness but then refuses to prescribe a remedy.[245] Despite the widespread popularity[246] of this interpretation of Dahl's perspective on American politics it is inaccurate. What shall be suggested in this chapter is a revisionist reading of Robert A. Dahl; a revision that would be unnecessary had the earlier scholars read Dahl more judiciously.

The criticism of Dahl as an apologist is considerably wide of the mark; so, too, is the suggestion that Dahl has not prescribed remedies for the American polity. Dahl has frequently advanced suggestions for further democratizing the "American hybrid."[247] Most of the suggestions are implicit in Dahl's writings. Several, more recently, have been explicit, if not outspoken.[248]

A second, although less popular, interpretation of Dahl's perspective holds that Dahl was once an apologist but has now mended his ways.[249] The purpose of this chapter is to review Dahl's discussion of the American polity and in so doing reject both views. We mean to reject the view of Dahl as apologist and, also, to reject a spin-off of this view in which Henry Kariel and William Connolly have argued that early (pre-1967) Dahl is apologetical while the later Dahl is not.

Connolly and Kariel have suggested that Dahl is not an apologist per se. Instead, Dahl is a reformed apologist—a born-again democrat. Rather than one Robert A. Dahl, there are two. In this view, early Dahl was a Schumpeteresque democratic-revisionist overly "tolerant" of such social ills as undue corporate influence, low levels of citizen participation, cumulative political advantages of those with wealth and social status, and the plight of blacks in the American South. For Connolly et al., early Dahl was an apologist and a revisionist—a scholar with a cynical view of citizen participation and potential, and a scholar who (like Schumpeter) was willing to revise democratic theory in order to bring it into alignment with such an understanding of political man.

In a chapter which includes excerpts from Dahl and other alleged democratic-revisionists including Joseph Schumpeter, Robert Michels, Bernard Berelson, Lester Milbrath, and Harold Lasswell, Kariel writes: "Not demanding much of the individual citizen, not expecting him to be generous or fraternal or altruistic, the revisionists redefine democracy in terms of system maintenance."[250] Later in the same book, in a section devoted to finding ways to restore classical democratic theory and to provide "normative, empirical and analytical" alternatives to the revisionist view, Kariel points to a second Robert A. Dahl; this time, in a chapter that includes excerpts form such scholars as Christian Bay, Dennis F. Thompson, and C. Wright Mills, Kariel includes Dahl's 1967 American Political Science Association (APSA) presidential address entitled "The City in the Future of Democracy." For Kariel, the post-1967 Dahl is a changed man—a born-again classical democratic theorist who in company with others in the final chapter seek to "implicitly postulate the individual as free agent, as self-directed, as active political participant. They postulate a political system that fully makes room for such individuals. And they postulate a model for political analysis and research that accommodates free individuals in a free society."[251]

Like Kariel, William E. Connolly also uses 1967 and the APSA presidential address as demarcation points to separate the "two Dahls." Connolly argues that Dahl's position appears to be shifting: "In *Who Governs?* he is critical of the dogma that democracy would not work if citizens were not concerned with public affairs (280). . . . In the 'City in the Future of Democracy,' the need for participation is emphasized."[252]

Thus, from one perspective, scholars have called Dahl an uncritical apologist for American politics. From a second perspective, Dahl is viewed as a former apologist who has rejoined the mainstream of democratic theorists and scholars critical of contemporary American political practices. Despite their widespread popularity, neither view is accurate. Neither view is supported by a careful reading of what George Von Der Muhll has called Dahl's main or "essential works." The present chapter attempts to refute both the view that Dahl is an apologist and the corollary argument that Dahl has fundamentally altered since 1967. A review of Dahl's writings from 1950 to 1980 suggests that Dahl has been both critical and consistent from his earliest writings to the present. The arguments that Dahl has used from 1950 to 1979 can be grouped under the headings of racial discrimination, political participation, corporate influence, and the influence of wealth and social status in the American political process. Additionally, in an effort to prevent misinterpreting passages selected from Dahl's writings, or of missing relevant background material or recent developments in Dahl's analysis of American politics, the author conducted two interviews with Dahl.[253]

RACIAL DISCRIMINATION

If Dahl were an apologist for the American political system, it seems reasonable to assume that he would have been "apologetical" or "overly tolerant" about such concerns as racial discrimination,[254] impediments to political participation, the extent of corporate influence in politics, and the influence of wealth and social status in the American political process. The charge that Dahl has been apologetical, or inconsistent, is easily dismissed. Dahl has long been critical of the status of nonwhites in American society. Two examples, the first written in 1953 and a second written as recently as 1979, should suffice to demonstrate Dahl's long-standing concern about racial discrimination in the United States. Dahl writes, "In the United States, the South as a whole has never been a polyarchy for Negroes or indeed even for poor whites."[255] Again, in 1979, Dahl reiterated this theme: "It is undeniable that in the United States, southern Blacks were excluded from the demos."[256]

Scholars such as Carole Pateman, Jack Walker, Henry Kariel, and David Ricci, who have argued that Dahl is a democratic-elitist, might be well-advised to read (or reread) the 1979 quotation in its entirety. It reads:

The last two examples beautifully illustrate the absurdities to which we may be led by the absence of any criterion for defining the demos. It is undeniable that in the United States, southern Blacks had been a preponderant majority of the population. Would Schumpeter still have said that the Southern states were "democratic"? Is there not some number or proportion of a population below which a "people" is not a demos but rather an aristocracy, oligarchy or despotism? If the rulers numbered 100 in a population of 100 million, would we call the rulers a demos and the system a democracy? On Schumpeter's argument, Britain was already a "democracy" by the eighteenth century—even though only one adult in twenty could vote.[257]

It seems obvious that by 1979 few readers would seriously suggest that Dahl's writings are Schumpeteresque.

In the period spanning the years 1953-79, Dahl consistently criticized status quo ethnic politics in the United States. In *A Preface to Democratic Theory* (1956), Dahl noted that most "active and legitimate" groups have a possibility of effecting a policy outcome somewhere in the political system—providing that system is what Dahl calls "normal." Abnormal (coercive or violent) political activity naturally impedes full participation. So, too, does group inactivity. As Dahl notes:

Hence, if a group is inactive, whether by free choice, violence, intimidation, or law, the normal American system does not necessarily provide it with a checkpoint anywhere in the process. By "legitimate" I mean those whose activity is accepted as right and proper by a preponderant portion of the active. In the South, Negroes were not until recently an active group. As compared with what one would expect from the normal system, Negroes were relatively defenseless in the past, just as Communists are now.[258]

In New Haven, the picture was less clear than in the American South. As Dahl observed in *Who Governs?*, blacks in New Haven had higher rates of participation in campaigns and elections than did whites (see Figures 3.1 and 3.2). Dahl did not see this as a particularly sanguine indicator for race relations in New Haven. Rather than concluding that this indicated the wide acceptance of blacks as active and legitimate forces in the New Haven community, Dahl argued that most black voters were compensating in their voting habits for inactivity and illegitimacy in other aspects of New Haven life. Dahl notes that "although discrimination is declining in the private socioeconomic sphere of life, New Haven Negroes still encounter far greater obstacles than the average white person. In contrast to the situation the Negro faces in the private socioeconomic sphere, in local politics and

Figure 3.1
New Haven Negroes Participate More than
Whites in Campaigns and Elections

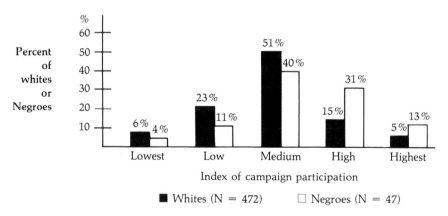

Source: "Figure 26.9. New Haven Negroes Participate More than Whites in Campaigns and Elections," Robert A. Dahl, *Who Governs?* (New Haven: Yale University Press, 1960), p. 295.

Figure 3.2
New Haven Negroes Participate More than
Whites in Local Political Affairs Generally

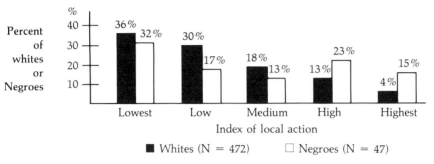

Source: "Figure 26.10. New Haven Negroes Participate More than Whites in Local Political
Affairs Generally," Robert A. Dahl, *Who Governs?* (New Haven: Yale University
Press, 1960), p. 295.

government the barriers are comparatively slight." Thus, black voting
patterns in New Haven and the urban North in general were examples of the
use of "slack resources" by the black community—having few other resources than their vote and their numbers, black community activists urged
northern blacks to compensate for discrimination in other areas by concen-
trating their participation in voting, an area in which their impact was
capable of producing results.[259]

Yet, even factoring in atypically high levels of electoral participation by
northern urban blacks, Dahl has noted that as recently as 1971, blacks as a
group were "still underrepresented in political life."[260] In a set of comments
that emphasize Dahl's assessment of race in American politics, Dahl is
guardedly optimistic about progress. He notes, for example, that although
underrepresented as a group "by 1971 there were 1,860 Black elected officials
in the United States"[261] (see Table 3.1).

Dahl has coupled this guarded optimism with a pessimistic—or realistic—
note. In the second edition of his text *Democracy in the United States:
Promise and Performance* (1972), Dahl argued:

Yet the movement toward political equality—which requires higher levels of resources, skills and incentives—is slower than it would be with a greater commitment
by whites. After the historical breakthrough achieved by the Civil Rights Acts of
1964 and 1965, commitment to further progress, at best never a very strong one,
weakened. Meanwhile, spokesmen for other groups suffering from traditional institutionalized inequalities in political resources, skills and incentives—Puerto Ricans,
Chicanos, American Indians, and (though statistically a majority, not a minority)
women—have demanded that the American polyarchy begin to achieve political
equality and consent much more fully than it ever has up to now. Until performance

Table 3.1
Black Elected Officials in the United States, 1970 and 1979

	Total	U.S. and State Legislatures	Cities and Counties	Law Enforcement	Education
1970	1,472	182	715	213	362
1979	4,584	315	2,647	486	1,136
South	2,768	147	1,828	233	560

Source: "Table 27.1. Black Elected Officials in the United States, 1970 and 1979," Robert A. Dahl, *Democracy in the United States: Promise and Performance*, 4th edition (Boston: Houghton-Mifflin, 1981).

has eradicated these traditional institutionalized inequalities, the American polyarchy will continue to exhibit a large and palpable gap between the standards of performance Americans have long public proclaimed as desirable and the level of performance their polyarchy has actually attained.[262]

Thus, from 1953 to 1979, Robert Dahl has frequently and consistently criticized racial discrimination in American politics. We have drawn several illustrations from Dahl's work to demonstrate that the view of Dahl as apologist, at least as regards racial discrimination, is unsound. From his criticism of black electoral exclusion in the South to his explanation for electoral overparticipation by blacks in the North, Dahl has presented a clear picture of a political system that exhibits "a large and palpable gap between the standards of performance . . . long publicly proclaimed as desirable and the level of performance . . . actually obtained."

POLITICAL PARTICIPATION

As early as *Congress and Foreign Policy* (1950) and *Domestic Control of Atomic Energy* (1951), Dahl wrote disparagingly of the factors that impede full participation.[263] The secrecy and technical expertise involved in atomic energy and weapons programs greatly troubled Dahl. Secrecy and technical expertise, while necessary to the development of atomic energy, strongly militate against popular participation in policymaking. With Edward Tufte in *Size and Democracy* (1973), Dahl reiterated a similar theme: the sheer size of large-scale industrialized Western politics presents massive impediments to full and meaningful political participation.[264] Earlier, in *Congress and Foreign Policy*, Dahl argued that the foreign policy process in Congress is essentially undemocratic. Full or popular participation in foreign policymaking is prevented by the fact that the president and his foreign policy advisors are insulated from both the general public and most of the congressional decision-makers in the foreign policy system. In an argument that anticipates the contemporary "Imperial Presidency" criticisms, Dahl speaks of increasing presidential discretion in the foreign policy arena as possibly leading to a "plebiscitary dictatorship." This is hardly the sort of talk one expects from an apologist for the going political concern.

As George Von Der Muhll has observed:

And those who have become accustomed to think of Dahl as an uncritical apologist for American pluralism might be startled to encounter the following passage: Competent choice on questions [of foreign policy] requires a preliminary process of discussion and inquiry. . . . [But] modern urban life is not conducive to the kind of intermediate organizations implied by, say, the neighborhood discussion group. Individual hostility, anonymity, and moral isolation; the physical layout of the city; the bothersome aspects of transportation; the lack of facilities for group life; the intensified satisfactions of passive participation, exploited by highly organized and influential commercial advertising groups; the centralization of control over techniques of influencing attitudes and the consequent standardization and banality of opinion—all militate against the spontaneous growth of local discussion and inquiry groups.[265]

It is worth noting that Dahl's discussion of participation differs markedly from that of his alleged fellow-travelers, Schumpeter and Berelson. Unlike Schumpeter and Berelson, who argued that barriers to full participation exist and are generally beneficial, Dahl has criticized participatory impediments. And, despite the claims of those who point to the existence of two Dahls (pre- and post-1967), Dahl has been consistently critical over time. Additionally, Dahl's analysis has not stopped at merely recognizing the existence of a problem—despite Bay's admonition, the doctor was already prescribing remedies for the American polity and doing so as early as 1950. Two examples should serve to illustrate this point. Both examples—one early, the other recent—illustrate the extent and longevity of Dahl's dissatisfaction with participatory levels. Further, in contrast to the Bay-Walker view of Dahl as a defender of the status quo, both examples illustrate Dahl's willingness to suggest fairly radical prescriptive measures.

The first of these examples is contained in Dahl's *Congress and Foreign Policy*. In a recent review of Dahl's works, George Von Der Muhll argued:

Indeed, perhaps the most enduringly interesting theme within *Congress and Foreign Policy* is Dahl's concern at this point with improving the quality of democratic participation. Again and again, in tones reminiscent of John Stuart Mill and John Dewey, he deplores the extent to which the outcomes of political activity represent manipulative bargains among self-interested elites rather than the fruit of an informed sense of collective purpose. The process by which agreement is reached appears to him quite as important as its substance. . . . It is this perspective, as much as anything, that leaves one feeling that Dahl's first book is still one of his most satisfying.[266]

In *Congress and Foreign Policy*, Dahl argues that the foreign policy decisionmaking process is exclusionary and undemocratic. Many congressional members and most members of the general public are excluded from the debate that produces policy decisions. Dahl noted that a fully democratic process would include widespread participation in the formulation of such policy. Several impediments prevent a fully democratized policy-making process.[267]

Further, "the current state of discussion and inquiry in American life is inadequate to the task." Some discussion groups do exist—ranging from "the family" to "taverns," "town barbershops," and the "Council on Foreign Relations"—but "the likelihood of a widespread generation of small discussion groups systematically devoted to the critical examination of public policy seems slight."[268] Dahl added that

A growth of this kind would have to take place as a broad movement, not as a specialized attack on the single problem of foreign policy. The assorted foreign policy organizations reach too restricted a clientele to be more than pitifully inadequate. The problem requires nothing less than a revolutionary development in the technique and practice of public discussion and inquiry.[269]

Although the generation of small, local discussion units would be difficult, Dahl believed it possible. The British Army discussion program in World War II is cited as an example. Still, the problems which such a proposal faces are formidable. The problems are of two sorts: the first environmental, the second institutional. As Von Der Muhll observed, Dahl was well aware that "modern urban life" presents an environment that tends frequently to discourage full political participation. A second barrier to the full realization of widespread policy discussion groups is a set of administrative or institutional concerns. Dahl argued that such groups presented a basic paradox. How could the national government provide leadership and adequate information for such groups while, simultaneously, not dominating them or using them to achieve or further government policy aims? How could such groups be supported by government and, at the same time independent of it, be simultaneously dependent and autonomous? Such groups might well be possible, he hoped, but their implementation would be nothing short of revolutionary.[270]

Thus, in *Congress and Foreign Policy*, Dahl suggested a remedy and admitted that the remedy was difficult and its success problematic. Still, he concluded that "a sudden burgeoning of organized citizen discussion about public policy" was preferable to what appeared to Dahl in the 1950s to be a drift toward increasing presidential discretion and a possible foreign policy "plebiscitary dictatorship." Dahl's analysis at this juncture sounds very unlike that of an apologist for the going political concern.

Dahl has reiterated his argument that multiple barriers to full political participation exist in the United States. In "On Removing Certain Impediments to Democracy in the United States" (1977), Dahl argued that the framers of the Constitution greatly inhibited the full participation of "women, nonwhites, and some white males. . . . The majority of adults were provided with as little opportunity to give their active consent to the laws which they were bound to obey as their colonial predecessors had enjoyed under the laws enacted by the English Parliament." Further, in "preserving a set of inalienable rights superior to the majority principle—a goal many of us would surely share—the framers deliberately created a framework of government that was carefully designed to impede and prevent the operation of majority rule." Dahl argued:

Thus, when the country committed itself to their framework of government, two different arguments became confounded to this day. There is the liberal argument that certain rights are so fundamental to the attainment of human goals, needs, interests, and fulfillment that governments must never be allowed to derogate from them. But in addition there is the American constitutional argument that the highly specific, indeed unique, set of political arrangements embodied in our constitutional and political practices is necessary to preserve these rights. While the writer accepts the liberal argument, the American constitutional argument seems seriously defective.[271]

Dahl continued his argument by noting that "the framers' antimajoritarian design . . . is unsatisfactory both as a protection for morally inalienable rights and as a device for procedural democracy."[272] Dahl concluded:

The point is, however, that the elaborate system of checks and balances, separation of powers, constitutional federalism, and other institutional arrangements influenced by these institutional structures and the constitutional views they reflect, are both adverse to the majority principle, and in that sense to democracy, and yet arbitrary and unfair in the protection they give to rights. However laudable their ends, in their means the framers were guilty of overkill.[273]

Dahl suggests several catalysts to increased political participation. These include giving

serious and systematic attention to possibilities that may initially seem unrealistic, such as abolishing the presidental veto; creating a collegial chief executive; institutionalizing adversary processes in policy decisions; establishing an office of advocacy to represent interests not otherwise adequately represented in or before Congress and the administrative agencies, including future generations; creating randomly selected citizen assemblies parallel with the major standing committees of the Congress to analyze policy and make recommendations; creating a unicameral Congress; inaugurating proportional representation and a multiparty system in our congressional elections; and many other possibilities.[274]

More recently, in an interview with the author, Dahl advocated the adoption of automatic voter registration. This measure alone, Dahl argued, "might increase voter participation to 75-80% of the eligible electorate."[275]

Thus, from 1950 to 1979, Robert A. Dahl has criticized American levels of citizen participation and suggested remedies. While our survey of Dahl's writings on participation is not exhaustive, it is suggestive. What it does suggest is that Dahl is not an apologist for the going political concern. In a further effort to undermine the Bay-Walker "apologetical" view, we turn now to a review of Dahl's discussion of corporate influence in the American political process.

CORPORATE INFLUENCE

Dahl's criticism of American corporate power and influence has been long-term and unambiguous. The first and second editions of *Politics, Economics, and Welfare* (1953, 1976) are excellent examples of Dahl's position on this topic. In the first edition, Dahl and Lindblom argue that in their view "the Soviet Union and Spain lack all the characteristics of a poly-archy; so do most large American corporations; and many trade unions and some boss-ridden municipalities lack several important ones."[276] In the second edition the authors charged that the American economy is excessively private:

In the realm of attitudes, ideas and ideology, we Americans have an irrational commitment to private ownership and control of economic enterprises that prevents us from thinking clearly about economic arrangements. This irrational commitment to private ownership and control conflicts with the underlying assumption of this book that a modern economy ought to be thought of and treated as a social or public economy.[277]

Dahl and Lindblom explained that "our notion of a good society is one in which the members seek the ends for social action by means of a public economy that is subject to the final say of a democratic government."[278]

Neither wholly private nor wholly governmental ownership seemed adequate to Dahl and Lindblom. They argued in 1976 that "a great deal of additional experience since we wrote confirms our view that ownership of an enterprise by the government, or more vaguely, by 'society,' does not insure public control over the enterprise."[279] In writing of the privately owned and controlled corporation the authors are exceptionally critical. Concluding their discussion of corporations, Dahl and Lindblom argued for a pragmatic and public-private sector mix that will insure an economy essentially public in character. They concluded:

Nonetheless, we are now more inclined to believe that public control of the American economy cannot in fact be achieved without a substantial increase in government ownership. At the very least, there is a need to search for and to introduce new forms of economic enterprise that will contribute more than the existing privately owned and controlled giant corporation to achieving the ends of social action.[280]

Recently, Dahl has continued this line of reasoning. In *Polyarchy* (1971), Dahl noted that private ownership was neither a necessary or sufficient precondition for a polyarchy. In "What Is Political Equality?: Reply" (1979), Dahl again argued that "the economic order ought to be seen as essentially social or public."[281] Elsewhere, Dahl has written of "despotic" corporations. In "On Removing Certain Impediments to Democracy," Dahl argued that

because the internal government of the corporation was not itself democratic but hierarchical and often despotic, the rapid expansion of this revolutionary form of enterprise meant that an increasing proportion of the demos would live out their working lives, and most of their daily existence not within a democratic system but instead within a hierarchical structure of subordination. To this extent, democracy was necessarily marginal to the actual political system in which the members of the demos lived their daily lives. Thus, the transfer of the Lockean view to the corporation was a double triumph. By making ownership the only, or at least the primary, source of legitimate control over corporate decisions, the new order not only excluded democratic controls in the internal government of the enterprise but placed powerful ideological barriers against the imposition of external controls by a government which, for all its deficiencies, was far more democratic than were the governments of business firms.[282]

Dahl concluded the "Impediments" article with a recapitulation of an argument first introduced in *PEW*. The rationale for a management strategy is its "workability." It is not public or private controls per se that are to be favored. Rather, it is the most effective mix of controls that should be used. In a lengthy concluding passage, Dahl reasoned:

If a privately owned enterprise can be justified at all, it must be on the grounds of comparative social effectiveness; that is, of all the possible alternatives, this form provides the greatest social advantage with the least social disadvantage. The only question we need ask, then, is whether a privately owned corporation is more effective in achieving social purposes than all the possible alternatives to it.

In this perspective, any large economic enterprise is in principle a public enterprise. It exists not by private right but only to meet social goals. Questions about these social goals, and the comparative advantages and disadvantages of different forms, are properly in the public domain, matters for public discussion, choice and decision, to be determined collectively by processes that satisfy the criteria of procedural democracy.

To be sure, none of this implies a direct answer to the question of how a large enterprise should be organized, controlled or owned. To arrive at a correct answer depends as much on technical as philosophical or ideological judgements, perhaps a good deal more. Although this assertion contradicts a nearly universal dogma held on all sides, it is readily demonstrable by even the briefest consideration of the range of alternatives. If we were to take into account only the most obvious possibilities with respect to the internal government of enterprises, external controls, markets, prices, and the locus of ownership together with the rights and obligations of owners, we would quickly arrive at a very large array of theoretically possible combinations.

Few of these can be dismissed as a priori unsuitable. Probably none can be shown to be superior to all the others in all circumstances. Consequently what has already become standard practice in advanced countries in this century will, one hopes, be taken for granted by citizens of advanced societies in the twenty-first century; a complex society cannot protect the rights, needs, and interests of its people with one single, prevailing form of economic organization but requires instead a network of enterprises organized in many different combinations of internal government, external controls, and ownership.[283]

This brief examination of Dahl's discussion of the private corporation and the American polity has provided evidence for two arguments suggested earlier. First, Dahl has been critical of the status quo in American political life. Second, Dahl's critical stance has been consistent and long-lived; it began at least as early as 1953—a date much earlier than the 1967-68 period suggested by Henry Kariel and William Connolly.

POLITICAL IMPACTS OF WEALTH AND SOCIAL STATUS

From his earliest writings, Dahl has recognized that American polyarchal practice was flawed in certain respects. In *A Preface to Democratic Theory* (1956), Dahl spoke of differences between the "American hybrid" of poly-archy and a fully polyarchal or ideally democratic regime—regimes that Dahl labeled "egalitarian polyarchies." The discussion in *Preface* and additional passages in *PEW* and *Polyarchy* (1971) highlight the differences that Dahl believes exist between the "real" and the "ideal"—between the "American hybrid" and "egalitarian democracies."[284] One important difference is that the United States is less than a fully egalitarian polyarchy. "In short," as Dahl noted in *Who Governs?* (1961), "New Haven is a republic of unequal citizens—but for all that a republic."[285]

In *PEW*, Dahl argued that an unequal dispersion of wealth and social status in America gives some citizens "strategic positions" in political life. Dahl noted:

The opportunity to exert control through elections and other forms of political activity is never equally distributed. Voting studies and opinion polls indicate that higher-income people tend to be more politically active than lower-income people, and the better educated more than the poorly educated. Moreover, because campaigns are exceedingly costly, the wealthier a person is, the more strategic his position for bringing to bear on politicians; hence, even if in elections the wealthy few cannot always defeat the many with low incomes, a single wealthy man can make his preferences count for considerably more in making government policy than a single poor man.[286]

And, as Dahl observed, differences in wealth allow some citizens to possess advantages in both the private and public sectors: "Differences in wealth generate differences in control outside government and therefore in it; advantages in wealth buy advantages of education, status, knowledge, information, propaganda, and organization and hence advantages of control."[287] Nor does Dahl stop with a merely descriptive account of the American impacts of unequally held monetary and socioeconomic resources. *PEW* includes some prescriptive passages. Dahl and Lindblom tempered their prescriptions with the admonition that simply equalizing wealth and income would probably not "produce approximately equal political activity and control."

As noted, political activity and control are closely correlated with income, education, and status. They are probably also dependent on other variables—personality and intelligence factors— about which little is known. These little-known variables may in turn affect income, education, and through them status. Certainly there is little reason to suppose that approximate income equality would produce approximately equal political activity and control.[288]

"Nevertheless," noted Dahl, "income is a crucial factor—a factor which can and should be rationally influenced."[289] He noted that

Equal opportunity to act is not, however, a product merely of legal rights. It is a product of a variety of factors that make for differences in understanding the key points in the political process, access to them, methods of exploiting this access, optimism and buoyancy about the prospect of success, and willingness to act. Some of these factors probably cannot be rationally influenced given the present state of knowledge and techniques. Three that to some extent can are income, wealth, and education.[290]

Subsequent to the publication of *PEW*, Dahl's criticism—and prescription—have continued unabated. The criticism of inequalities in wealth and income leading to political inequalities has continued apace. The prescription has been brought more sharply into focus—its tone has grown more inclusive and urgent. This, if indeed there is any "shift" in Dahl's writings after 1967, is the only shift in Dahl's analysis of American politics. A few examples should suffice to demonstrate this point. In *Who Governs?* Dahl wrote of the mixed advantages of the "better-off citizens": "Today, two generations later, it is by no means unrealistic for the Better-Off citizen to be somewhat pessimistic about his chances of success in party politics and at the same time relatively confident about his capacity for influencing city officials in various other ways."[291] As Carole Pateman has observed of *Who*

Governs?: "as Dahl notes, the lower socioeconomic status groups, the majority are 'triply barred' from such (full political) equality by their relatively greater inactivity, their limited access to resources, and—in the United States—by 'Madison's nicely contrived system of constitutional checks.' "²⁹²

Dahl has also argued that political inequalities due to differences in wealth or social status are frequently cumulative. In *Democracy in the United States* (1973), Dahl described these cumulative cycles of winning and losing as "the Cycle of Success" and "the Cycle of Defeat"²⁹³ (see Figures 3.3 and 3.4). In the *Democracy* text, Dahl argued that despite a formal legal or political equality, lower socioeconomic groups are frequently locked into a cycle of defeat due to social, historical, and institutional inequalities. Thus, for Dahl, such variables as low political skills and low political incentive levels interact cumulatively to suppress and defeat low-resource groups. Conversely, higher socioeconomic groups with concomitantly higher levels

Figure 3.3
The Cycle of Success

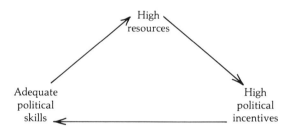

Source: "Figure 27.2. The Cycle of Success," Robert A. Dahl, *Democracy in the United States: Promise and Performance*, 2d ed. (Chicago: Rand McNally, 1973), p. 432.

Figure 3.4
The Cycle of Defeat

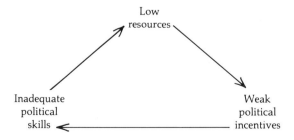

Source: "Figure 27.1. The Cycle of Defeat," Robert A. Dahl, *Democracy in the United States: Promise and Performance*, 2d ed. (Chicago: Rand McNally, 1973), p. 431.

of political skill and resources possess presumably higher political incentives. Thus, the winners and losers in contests for political outcomes are frequently cumulative.

Dahl has suggested that low-resource groups can use their "slack power" to attempt to "break out of the cycle of defeat." Dahl explained:

To break out of the cycle of defeat is particularly difficult if a group is a small minority and lacks even the potential resource of large numbers. . . . With activity and skill, however, a minority may be able to concentrate its numbers so as to maximize their impact; for example, to win local elections and to count heavily enough in nominations and elections for state and local offices so that minority views and leaders gain influence.

[Blacks and other] groups suffering from traditional institutionalized inequalities in political resources, skills and incentives—Puerto Ricans, Chicanos, American Indians, and . . . women—have demanded that the American polyarchy begin to achieve political equality and consent much more fully than it has ever done up to now. Until performance has eradicated these traditional institutionalized inequalities, the American polyarchy will continue to exhibit a large and palpable gap between the standards of performance Americans have long publicly proclaimed as desirable and the level of performance their polyarchy has actually "attained."[294]

Dahl has written elsewhere of the unequal distribution of resources in American society. Perhaps the example that most clearly illustrates Dahl's criticism and his prescriptive remedies is the following: "In American society a number of resources are distributed in extremely unequal fashion. From which it follows—again the conclusion is, as far as I know, unchallenged—that the opportunity to make effective personal choices, and hence the degree of individual freedom and opportunity are markedly unequal in the United States."[295]

Dahl's prescriptive suggestions, especially recently, have been equally unambiguous. Illustrative of this is his argument in a recent colloquy between Dahl and Philip Green in the summer 1979 edition of the journal *Dissent*.[296] The *Dissent* exchange makes perfectly clear that the assessment of Dahl held by Bay and Kariel is simply untenable. Green describes Dahl's position as calling: "for a redistribution of wealth and income ('economic resources') and then adds that 'the form of control should be treated as a problem that is prior to the question of the form of ownership.' " More consistency between the Dahl and Lindblom position in *PEW* (1953) and Dahl's more recent statement would be difficult to show. The 1979 exchange, in fact, is in many ways a verbal overlap of arguments first raised in 1953. Green goes on to disagree that either a redistribution of wealth or Dahl's proposed "industrial democracy" (the placing of labor and general public members on corporate boards) will be significant in his view "as long as the present legal relations of corporate capitalism persist."[297] Indeed, in terms of additional evidence of continuity over time, it should be noted that Dahl's concern over workers' democracy is hardly a product of the 1960s. In fact, one of Dahl's earliest articles was a favorable treatment in 1947 of workers' control tendencies in the British Labor party and on the subject of workers; control of industry more generally.[298] Returning to the Green-Dahl exchange in *Dissent*, it should also be noted that in both his rejoinder and in a subsequent interview[299] with this author, Dahl accepted Green's characterization of his proposed prescriptions. Dahl disagrees with Green about the efficacy of such reforms, but Dahl does not dispute Green's description of his prescriptive recommendations.

SUMMARY AND CONCLUSION

We have examined various assessments of American politics set forth by Robert A. Dahl from 1950 to 1979. While our study has not been exhaustive, it is suggestive. A careful survey of Dahl's work over time reveals it to be both critical and prescriptive. Based on a review of Dahl's work over time, a review that tracks Dahl's arguments across four subject areas central to the development of an "apologetical" perspective, the conclusion that Dahl is an "apologist" is unwarranted. The Bay-Walker-Kariel et al. view is, in a word, incorrect.

4

American Pluralism Responds (II)

There are four views of Robert Dahl in the literature of political science. These views depict Dahl as either a normative democratic theorist, a democratic-elitist, an apologist, or, finally, as a failed scientist or methodologist. The first three of these four views have been covered in earlier parts of this book. Chapter 1 examined Dahl's work, described Dahl as an "institutional pluralist" and accepted and extended Von Der Muhll's characterization of Dahl as a normatively inclined contemporary democratic theorist. In constructing this picture, the view of Dahl as a democratic-elitist has been rejected. Chapter 2 explained the various "views" in more depth, while chapter 3 dispatched the notion that Dahl is an apologist for the status quo in American politics. Hence, the four views have been reduced to two—Dahl as democratic theorist and Dahl as failed methodologist. Of these final two views, only the latter will be examined in depth. The argument for viewing Dahl as a normative democratic theorist has been raised in chapter 1. A comprehensive discussion of Dahl's breadth as a democratic theorist would necessarily include a discussion of his recent (nonpolyarchal) writings on "procedural democracy" and "economic democracy."[300] Such a discussion falls outside the parameters of our current discussion of polyarchy.

What is left is the view of Dahl as a faulty methodologist. This chapter examines this view and chapter 5 raises questions of both method and theory not covered by earlier critics. In so doing, several innovations in both the polyarchal concept and the pluralist methodology of community power research will be suggested.

The purpose of the present chapter is to clarify the status of the critique of method discussed in chapter 2. Although some of the points raised in this chapter are new, many of the criticisms have previously been addressed by various defenders of the pluralist approach to community power research. As such, this chapter draws heavily from such noted defenders of the pluralist perspective as Nelson Polsby, Raymond Wolfinger, and Aaron Wildavsky.[301]

Despite the fact that the methodological critics are among the most thoughtful and careful scholars who have analyzed Dahl and polyarchy, there are difficulties with their perspective. We turn now to a case in point, the methodological critics who focused primarily upon Dahl's issue selection in *Who Governs?*

All of the methodological critics share with the scholars previously discussed a misunderstanding of both Dahl as an individual and polyarchy as a paradigm for American politics. Like earlier critics, the methodological camp misconstrues polyarchy as "arena theory" and Dahl as an apologist. In addition to these more general inaccuracies, the methodologists raise several more specific criticisms of Dahl and polyarchy. These concerns may be grouped under the subject headings of issue selection, nondecision-making, potential power, and noncumulative resources. Each methodological concern will be considered in turn.

ISSUE SELECTION

Thomas Anton, Herbert Danzger, Delbert Miller, David Ricci, and Bachrach and Baratz have criticized Dahl for his selection of issues in the New Haven study.[302] These critics make three basic charges. They argue that (1) the issues were insufficient in number, that studying only three issues (urban redevelopment, public education, and party nominations) is an insufficient number of issues to prove or disprove a pluralist hypothesis; (2) that Dahl selected the *wrong* issues—the critics contend that these issues lacked salience and suggest alternative issues/areas; and (3) that the selection of openly or hotly contested issues amounted to a stacked-deck approach. After all, by selecting hotly contested issues, one will almost invariably conclude that politics in a given city is pluralistic—that is to say, that it is marked by heated and meaningful conflicts in which policy is the result of contests among multiple participants.

While the charge that Dahl et al. selected too few issues to chart in the New Haven study is not without merit, some qualifications should be raised. First, the critics fundamentally misunderstood the "pluralist hypothesis" Dahl was seeking to validate or invalidate. The pluralist hypothesis broadly assumed to be Dahl's focus and described by Connolly as "arena theory" is, rather importantly, not Dahl's focus in *Who Governs?* Instead, polyarchy—the mechanical model of polyarchy as described in chapter 1 and as set forth by Dahl in *Politics, Economics, and Welfare* (1953) and *Preface* (1956)—serves as the hypothesis that Dahl sought to confirm or disprove in his study of New Haven politics. Claims regarding the number, salience, or type of issues notwithstanding, the methodological critics have erroneously assumed that Dahl was testing a hypothesis *different* from the hypothesis actually tested. Although the methodological critics raise several important points later in their analysis, much of their initial criticism is muted by the fact that their criticism is misdirected at "arena theory" rather than polyarchy per se.

Even if the methodological critics misunderstood the basic hypothesis of the New Haven study, their more specific charge that three issues is too few may be correct. It might be argued that an examination of three or even one issue might illustrate much about the politics of an urban area, especially if one of the issues selected was public education and the site selected were Boston, Miami, Cleveland, Indianapolis, or Los Angeles.[303] Still, the appropriateness of these issues and their salience to a thorough examination of urban politics may be locational or idiosyncratic. More issues might have told us more, different issues might have led to different conclusions. In all probability, the New Haven study is weakened by the inclusion of only three main issues.[304] However, the fault for excluding other issues and for (at least as important) focusing upon only one urban area is partially a state of the art of criticism. Few serious studies conducted today would focus upon only one urban area and generalize from a single data base. Yet, at the time it was attempted, the Dahl study paralleled the single-city studies of scholars such as Floyd Hunter and Robert Schulze.[305] To the extent to which the issues selected were too few and the city selected too idiosyncratic, *Who Governs?* is a flawed study. The problem with such criticisms rests on their a posteriori timing and certain problematical aspects of the state of the art of community power research itself. Twenty years after the publication of *Who Governs?* there is still no widespread agreement on such central methodological issues as: How many issues are sufficient in a community power study? What types of issues are central and which are secondary? (Whether, in Polsby's words, we should study "important" decisions, "typical" decisions, "representative" decisions—or all three simultaneously. And, if we did, how we would weight them, if we even should.)[306] What sites and how many are desirable in a serious community power study? Until satisfactory criteria for numbers, types, and locales of issues are charted to the satisfaction of the community power audience, such issues will perennially arise.[307] In the absence of accepted criteria for an adequate number of issues, the adequacy of the New Haven study will probably turn upon an appraisal of the type and salience of issues selected.

Polsby and Wolfinger have argued that the key consideration is not the number but the breadth and range of issue areas measured in a study. Three may seem a small number, but is it if it allows a researcher to test community influence across a broad range of issues? As Polsby notes: "More than a single issue area is always chosen, however, because of the presumption among pluralist researchers that the same pattern of decision-making is highly unlikely to reproduce itself in more than one issue area."[308] And, as

Wolfinger and Polsby have pointed out, pluralist researchers employing this methodology "have seldom been disappointed."[309]

Probably the best measure of the adequacy of issue selection is the fourfold test proposed by Polsby in an appendix to *Community Power and Political Theory*. Polsby argues that important community issues worth studying are determined by using one or a combination of four criteria: (1) "How many people are affected by the outcomes"; (2) "How many different kinds of community resources are distributed by the outcomes"; (3) "How much in amount of resources are distributed by outcomes"; and (4) "How drastically present community resource distributions are altered by outcomes."[310]

Anton, Ricci, and Miller have argued that even if three issues were a large enough sample, the issues chosen were not sufficiently salient—however few in number, they were the *wrong* issues. The Economic and Social Notables of New Haven were not interested in public education, urban redevelopment, or even party nominations. Although public education might have been important to rank-and-file urban dwellers, it was less so to suburbanites.[311] This is also the case with downtown blight, urban redevelopment, and nominations in elections in which several suburban notables could not even vote. Ricci and Miller suggest right-to-work legislation and school integration as superior issue choices.

There are some problems with the methodological critique of salience. First, as Anton et al. admit in their third or "card-stacking" criticism, the issues selected were all hotly contested public concerns. They were selected, in part, because of their voter salience—becaue of public recognition of their centrality. To charge on the one hand that such issues are hotly contested and voter salient but, on the other hand, that such issues are less salient with nonvoting suburban notables is hardly a criticism of Dahl's findings. Quite the reverse. Because an issue is salient only to legal participants in an urban electoral contest is hardly a reason for impugning its salience as a valid concern for an urban political study. In addition, the suggestion that community notables were uninterested in the outcomes of urban redevelopment decisions or party nomination struggles seems on its face to be debatable. Why should suburban notables, presumably connected in some fashion to industrial, financial, and realty concerns of the central city, consider urban realty development and party nominations of little salience. Indeed, the most recent focus of elite scholars is on exactly this set of issues. G. William Domhoff, Thomas Dye, and Harvey Motloch have recently written extensively on the role of local elites in downtown redevelopment—a focus and approach referred to by elite analysts as "the growth machine approach."[312]

Finally, while there is some merit to suggesting alternative issue areas, the Ricci-Miller suggestions are not helpful. School integration and right-to-work legislation are extremely problematic additions to the New Haven issue list. School integration is flawed as an issue both because it duplicates the preexisting public education issue and because it points away from the urban arena to an entirely different political concern. In bringing in the federal court system and, with right-to-work laws, the state legislature, the entire focus of the New Haven study would have been altered to include a discussion of national and state political arenas.

The third charge of the methodological critics is that in selecting the issues Dahl stacked the deck. They charge Dahl with a tautological error. In selecting hotly contested issues with multiple actors, Dahl was inevitably led to support the polyarchal hypothesis. Dahl, conclude the critics, should have included the issues that were not contested, where no conflict existed. In effect, Dahl, Polsby, and Wolfinger are charged here with simply going in and, under the guise of research, accepting the most obvious events in the urban political arena as evidence of the presence of pluralistic politics. As Bachrach and Baratz have phrased it:

Polsby is guilty . . . of the same fault he himself has found with elitist methodology; by supposing that in any community there are significant issues in the political arena, he takes for granted the very question which is in doubt. He accepts as issues what are reputed to be issues. As a result, his findings are foreordained. For even if there is no "truly" significant issue in the community under study, there is every likelihood that Polsby (or any like-minded researcher) will find one or some and, after careful study, reach the appropriate pluralistic conclusions.[313]

There is only one problem with the Bachrach and Baratz critique. It bears little or no resemblance to the criteria actually used by the New Haven researchers in selecting their issues. The "hotly contested" nature of an issue was not the only or even the main criterion used for issue selection. If anything, in selecting urban redevelopment and public education, the New Haven team concentrated not on reputation or open conflict but, rather, on the role of money in New Haven politics. Dahl could, if he had been pressed for an explanation of his choice of redevelopment and schools, have given the same explanation for his choice that Willie Sutton once gave for robbing banks. When asked why he preferred banks, Willie reportedly answered, "Because that's where the money is." The same is true for New Haven politics. Development was chosen for its prominence in Mayor Lee's successful election campaigns and also because New Haven's redevelopment program was the "largest in the country, measured by past and present outlays per capita."[314] Besides being a major financial element of New Haven politics, urban development had the extra advantage of being very simply too visible to ignore. It was, in Polsby's words, "the biggest thing in New Haven. Urban redevelopment had been the focus of several campaigns for re-election by the incumbent mayor, Richard C. Lee. The program had gained nationwide publicity in popular magazines. The federal government had spent, allocated or promised more redevelopment money per capita to New Haven than to any other city in the nation."[315]

Public schools were selected because even though a fifth of the school-age children of New Haven attended private or parochial schools, public schools were the largest single item in the city budget. Schools were also selected because of their prominence as a means of socialization or the indoctrination of ideas and values (a matter, presumably, of no small consequence to any elite that wanted to exercise influence in a community over time).[316] Party nominations were selected both because of the central importance of the electoral process in establishing or disproving a polyarchal hypothesis and because political parties per se were inadequate as a focus. New Haven, unlike many cities, notably Chicago, did not have a dominant political machine at the time of the study. In any given election candidates from either major party could expect to win. "Both major parties in New Haven are well organized and normally have a fighting chance in every election. That is, a popular candidate running on either ticket has a good chance of winning—a circumstance which is not typical of American cities."[317]

Finally, in addition to the *centrality* of the issues (e.g., nominations, schools), the *financial magnitude* of the issues (e.g., schools, redevelopment) and the sheer *scope* or numbers of people affected by the outcome of the issue (e.g., schools, redevelopment, nominations), the issues were selected because as Dahl notes, "they promised to cut across a wide variety of interests and participants."[318] Thus, the New Haven researchers selected their issues to meet a wide set of criteria. Issues selected were not simply "visible" or "hotly contested." They needed, instead, to meet considerations of centrality, financial magnitude, scope, and breadth.

NONDECISION-MAKING

Differing from earlier critics who attacked Dahl's selection of issues on the basis of the number or salience of the issues chosen, Bachrach and Baratz have objected to Dahl's use of "visibility" as a criterion. The Bachrach and Baratz critique is twofold. First, visible issues (presumably redevelopment and public schools) tend to be safe issues. Second, issues that are less visible, decisions that are not made ("nondecisions") ought to be the focus of community studies. Issues which do *not* become highly visible might reveal more about a community power structure. The authors point to the failure or "invisibility" of black demands for political equality in the South as a case in point. To focus only upon issues currently in public debate—"safe issues"—would pass over one whole "face" of power. Such a methodology would tend to obscure repressive elite practices in favor of a narrower focus upon the more open or public policy area.

Thus, for Bachrach and Baratz, nondecision-making is important and serves as an addendum to focusing upon public or hotly contested issues. The process by which issues come into the public arena is itself important. As with blacks in the South, it is possible that dominant community values, mores, and political institutions in a community serve the purpose of limiting the scope of political decisions—in this case, limiting them to racially discriminatory practices.

To the extent to which Bachrach and Baratz have proposed a methodological second check to a focus upon public or contested issues, the nondecisions critique is useful. It seems necessary to reiterate, however, that in addition to visibility and contestation, Dahl used centrality, financial magnitude, scope, and breadth as selection criteria.[319] Nondecisions, as a replacement to Dahl's criteria for selecting issues, and even as a methodological double-checking device, are deficient for reasons both practical and methodological. On the practical side, visible issues precisely because of their visibility often are an advantage. They can be studied, agreed upon, and analyzed. Invisible issues almost by definition present the opposite problem.[320] They lack visibility and present impediments to scholarly agreement and analysis. Additionally, why are issues such as urban redevelopment and public education necessarily "safe" issues simply because they are topics on the public policy agenda? The assumption by Bachrach and Baratz that "public" or "hotly contested" equates with "safe" seems on its face to be a debatable assertion.[321] It may be the case that public discussion of a specific issue in a given locale has been affected by the prior and successful action of a dominant elite, but is this necessarily the case for all issues that eventually emerge as "visible" community issues?

The Bachrach and Baratz nondecisions focus is methodologically deficient for two reasons. It carries an ideological bias[322] about the distribution of power in community politics, and it is faulty as an approach because it is methodologically uneconomical. It duplicates findings of the public issues/policies approach and does so with a less precise methodology. A major problem with the nondecisions approach is that it presupposes the existence of the object of inquiry—namely a community elite that manipulates values and processes to limit the scope of public political decision-making. Additionally, it is frequently unnecessary to use the nondecisions device when explaining community political outcomes. The Bachrach and Baratz example of black repression in the South demonstrates this admirably. Black repression in the South was legally based on concrete and extremely visible policy decisions and actions. *Plessy v. Ferguson*, the black codes, the grandfather clause, literacy tests, sundown laws, poll taxes, property requirements, and the all-white primary were public, visible, and indisputably repressive. Research into possible "nondecisions" that preceded such decisions could provide supportive data, but it is unnecessary to establish the fact of black repression and, in focusing upon "invisible" issues and (non)decisions, is methodologically imprecise and difficult.[323]

Ricci has cited a further methodological criticism of Dahl, a criticism suggested by the late C. Wright Mills. Applying Mills' notion of the importance of less visible or "potential issues,"[324] Ricci extrapolates this to a further criticism of Dahl. He argues that Mills' general criticism of intellectuals in the social sciences might be applied to Dahl specifically. For Mills, intellectuals have a responsibility to identify potential issues and to present these as "troubles" to be brought up for public discussion. Mills noted, "[A]bsence of public issues there may well be, but this is not due to any absence of problems. Their absence from many discussions—that is an ideological condition, regulated in the first place by whether or not intellectuals detect and state problems as potential *issues* for probable publics, and as *troubles* for a variety of individuals."[325]

Again, as chapter 3 indicates, Dahl's work is characterized not by the absence but the presence of problem identification and prescriptive analysis. To twist Bay's analogy slightly, the doctor both diagnosed the illness and prescribed the remedies.[326] One may—as Mills no doubt would—object to both Dahl's descriptive and prescriptive analysis, but that is a separate and debatable charge. Mills' more general admonition that social scientists ought to raise issues for public discussion is clearly inapplicable to Dahl. Dahl has frequently suggested "troubles" and remedies for public discussion. As we mentioned earlier, two of his most novel and controversial proposals involve adequate public discussion of foreign policy matters and industrial policymaking.[327] Dahl has called for a public dialogue involving these issues and suggested the consideration of such measures as governmentally sponsored public discussion groups and "industrial democracy" (the placing of labor and general public members on corporate boards).

POTENTIAL POWER

Thomas Anton, Howard Ehrlich, Andrew Hacker, Jack Walker, Robert Presthus, David Ricci, and Bachrach and Baratz have raised a similar critique.[328] Anton et al. raise three points. First, some issues are not raised publicly because of the retaliatory capabilities ("potential power") of community notables.[329] In this view, elected public officials are more often "legmen" for more powerful community elites. Second, even if the potential power of community notables does not relegate elected officials to the status of "legmen," it *conditions* the decision-making process. Thus, Mayor Lee and his redevelopment chief Logue were not free actors. Rather, they and the redevelopment plan were impacted or conditioned by the potential power of others in the community. Third, Ricci has suggested that even if the potential power argument raised above is invalid, it brings up an important point—who has the most power in a community? Who *dominates* (if any one person or group does) the policymaking process? How are we to weight the various actors and their resources? Ricci argues that

In more common terms, suppose the Notables enjoy some influence over the mayor and he in turn influences them to some degree. The process of influence is subtle and implicit; it may operate through a great many proverbial winks and nods. It is difficult to grasp empirically; we know only that there is a circular flow of power—a closed loop—from one point to another and back. But who in the chain exercises *more* power? Who *dominates* the relationship? No method has yet been devised, including the pluralist technique of anlayzing specific decisions, for precisely ascertaining the measure of power wielded by all elements of a closed-loop power system.[330]

The potential power perspective suggestion that public officials operate as "legmen" for community notables shares a methodological problem with the nondecision approach. Both approaches assume the existence of a group that methodologically *ought* to be open to question. Both approaches implicitly *presume* that a monolithic and powerful community elite exists.[331] If, as Ricci suggests, focusing upon public and contested issues favors a pluralistic finding (an assertion that is debatable at best),[332] it may also be the case that slanting the focus in the other direction poses a similar bias, a bias in favor of the elitist position. Interestingly, just such a problem cropped up in the New Haven study.[333] Originally, as Polsby and Wolfinger have described in published work, the New Haven team attempted to develop a reputational "net" around the three issues of education, redevelopment, and nominations. The problem—and the eventual reason that this attempt failed—was, in Polsby's phrase, the result of a "competence differential" among the reputational respondents. In fact, there was an unacceptably high level of sheer ignorance in the respondent pool vis-à-vis knowledge about the central issues, an ignorance extending to such items as reputationally identified respondents demonstrating that they simply did not know the names of central actors in the process.[334]

In fact, in contrast to the reputational method, the strongest selling point of the pluralist approach may be the less ideologically biased way in which it approaches the study of community power. This nonideological or nonjudgmental starting point is crucial to the pluralist approach. As Polsby notes: 'The first and most basic presupposition of the pluralist approach is that nothing categorical can be assumed about power in any city."[335]

In addition to its ideological bias, the potential power approach carries with it several other assumptions, many of which may prove, at best, problematic when studying political outcomes in a given community. Polsby notes that the potential power view assumes that "none of the following possibilities has empirical reality":

1. That no explicit decision-making took place at all, and that beneficiaries, far from actually governing, are simply reaping windfall benefits (e.g., largely powerless Black Panthers who oppose gun control are beneficiaries of the fact that there are no gun control laws).

2. That beneficiaries are receiving benefits from decisions made outside the com-

munity and over which they have no control (e.g., shopkeepers in a community prosper from a decision made in a far-off corporate headquarters to operate a local plant on overtime).

3. That beneficiaries are the unintended recipients of benefits resulting from decisions made by others within the community (e.g., apolitical, absentee, or deceased owners of adjacent real estate prosper because of decisions made in a bureaucracy to site a public facility).

4. That the powerful are intentionally conferring benefits on the nonpowerful (e.g., in at least some welfare systems).[336]

Potential power critics have criticized Dahl for a related point. Even if potential power exercised by community notables does not control the actions of elected officials, it "conditions" them. Thus, Mayor Lee and others are not free actors. Rather, they are conditioned in their options by the environment and the structure of influence that existed in New Haven. This criticism is both trivial and misguided. It is misguided because it demonstrates how loosely many of Dahl's critics have read his work, particularly *Who Governs?*; it is trivial in that it results from such a misreading. Obviously, Dahl would have been ill-advised to suggest that New Haven politicians were free actors. All such actors operated within a political culture and environment that presented legal, social, and environmental restraints.[337] Dahl never claimed otherwise. In fact, Dahl's depiction of patrician mayors succeeded by entrepreneurs, succeeded in turn by ex-plebes and "new men" illustrated these restraints. Not only did New Haven mayors feel restraints due to party and constituency challenges, but frequently both mayor, party, and milieu were constrained, then replaced by competing political subsets. The picture this presents is hardly that of *homo politicus* as free actor, operating without political constraints.

David Ricci has offered a final potential power criticism, a criticism which in many ways is the most important criticism of Dahl's methodology. In *Community Power and Democratic Theory*, Ricci argues that even if the potential power argument is invalid, it raises important questions.[338] Among these are: How are we to measure political influence by community notables or other groups? How does a researcher determine who in the policy chain exercises more power? Ricci's criticism is accurate—in fact, it should be extended. Ricci's measurement inquiries[339] suggest two sets of concerns, one methodological, the other normative. First, is it possible and, if so, how are weights to be assigned to individual actors and groups in community power studies? What is the best normative democratic role and weight of groups in a democratic polity? Should some groups be stronger than others at the local level and, if so, why? The question, in the narrow legal sense, seems answered at the individual level. In *Baker* (1962) and *Reynolds* (1964), the Supreme Court interpreted equal protection of the law under the Fourteenth Amendment to mean "one man, one vote."[340] What is the parallel normative criterion for groups, both in community politics specifically and in democratic (or more everyday, polyarchal) politics generally?

A final query, which extending Ricci's criticism suggests, is inquiring into not only the normative benchmark for group participation but also the practical benchmark. What is the optimal representation that groups might achieve in a polyarchal regime? What is their most advantageous state? What is the optimal representation for which underprivileged groups may strive, and what—in more precise terms—does one mean by the optimal political participation of groups in community politics? While a full discussion of these and related concerns would lead us astray from addressing criticisms of Dahl and polyarchy which have been raised in the literature, we shall have occasion to return to the question of methodological, normative, and optimal measurements for groups in the final chapter of this book.

NONCUMULATIVE RESOURCES

Dahl argued that there are five checks on the growth of oligarchy in community politics: (1) "inequalities are dispersed rather than cumulative"; (2) no one resource dominates all the others; (3) disadvantaged individuals/groups can mobilize large numbers of members, or (4) develop and exercise "a high degree of political skill," or (5) "compensate by combining resources so that in the aggregate these are formidable."[341]

Ricci and the critique of method scholars reject Dahl's fivefold argument and focus their objections of Dahl's first contention: inequalities, they argue, are dispersed *but* cumulative. Interestingly, Dahl has only disagreed with the "dispersed but cumulative" formula once. He did so in a symposium on pluralism and inequality in the course of a discussion of checks upon oligarchy and using language that Dahl has subsequently described as "loose" and "very unfortunate."[342] Importantly, in each of his writings on polyarchy and community power studies, Dahl has insisted that inequalities in the United States in general and in New Haven in particular are both widespread and cumulative.[343] In only the symposium passage and in a second one in *Preface*, more difficult to misconstrue, could Dahl's intent be misinterpreted.[344] Dahl's answer in the symposium was in response to the more general consideration of whether barriers to elite control existed in community politics. In *Preface* (1956), as demonstrated in chapter 2, Dahl argued that in the normal American process, most "active and legitimate" groups have a possibility of achieving their political aims.[345] Dahl was careful in *Preface* to stipulate what he meant by a normal (nonexclusionary) American political process and by legitimate and active groups. It is clear from his discussion that most underprivileged groups had barriers to activity, were often considered to be "illegitimate" participants, and were subjected to what Dahl would consider an abnormal (in normative terms, an incorrectly functioning) political system. Yet these are the two passages that critics of Dahl have cited as the basis for a claim that Dahl believes unequal resources to be distributed noncumulatively.[346] These two examples do not fit with the review of Dahl's work from 1953 to 1980 presented in chapter 3. The reading of Dahl that suggests to scholars that he believes that unequal resources interact noncumulatively is undoubtedly an honest mistake. It is also a careless one.

SUMMARY AND CONCLUSION

The misreading of Dahl inherent in the critique of method is illustrative of the state of commentary on Dahl in the literature of political science. As the first three chapters of the present study demonstrate, Dahl has not been without his critics. Serious criticism has been leveled at his theory of polyarchy, his description of American politics, and his research methodology. The basic argument of this, as with the preceding chapters, is that Dahl's critics have directed their criticism somewhat wide of the mark. In the present chapter we have analyzed the critique of method and, with the qualified exception of David Ricci, have suggested its inadequacy. We turn now to an extrapolation from Ricci's criticism.

5

Researching the Urban Laboratory

Once again, it would be possible and indeed easy to create a mask in order to put a strong face on a slack-jawed theory. It is tempting, for example, to interpret the theory as a multiple regression equation. But in the absence of satisfactory data from which to construct the predictor variables, the values of the constants would be fictitious.

Robert A. Dahl, *Polyarchy* (1971)

The state of the literature today does not immediately suggest a research agenda fundamentally different from the sorts of problems that could have been tackled fifteen years ago. It still seems to me a good idea to proceed comparatively, first specifying a set of dependent variables that makes more sense than pluralism vs. power elite and *then* seeking causal variables. As students gain experience in analyzing the scopes and styles of community politics, propositions that are promising candidates for general application will no doubt emerge and be subjected to critical scrutiny. One continues to hope that these in turn will tutor our expectations and shape our conclusions about power in local communities.

Nelson Polsby, *Community Power and Political Theory* (1980)

Whenever possible, substitute constructions out of known entities for inference to unknown entities.

Bertrand Russell, *Our Knowledge of the External World* (1924)

David Ricci's criticism,[347] like the bulk of the critical literature reviewed earlier, misaddresses Dahl's polyarchy as "arena theory," misgauges Dahl's assessment of American politics as "apologetical," and mistakes Dahl's methodology as *necessarily* "pluralistic" in its findings. Nevertheless, Ricci has advanced important methodological criticisms—criticisms which, if extended, are profitable as a guide to any future discussion of Dahl and polyarchy. If we assume, as the preceding chapters suggest, that much—if not all—of the critical literature on Dahl is deficient in important respects, then we are striking out on new ground. The purpose of this chapter is to suggest the shape that a new dialogue on Dahl might take, a dialogue which, one hopes, is premised upon a more realistic understanding of both Dahl's polyarchal theory and his methodology.

The present chapter is offered as the opening round in what we hope shall emerge as a new and wider discussion of polyarchy and pluralist urban research methodology. As such, it seeks to raise questions of both theory and method not covered by earlier critics and to suggest several innovations in both the polyarchal concept and the pluralist methodology of community power research. We turn now to the first of these concerns.

TWO ENDURING PROBLEMS: WEIGHTING AND LABELING

In 1971, Robert Dahl and David Ricci advanced criticisms that focused on attempts to weight variables in the polyarchal model and in community power research.[348] Ricci's criticism focused on methodological problems and upon such concerns as: How are we to measure political influence exercised by community notables and other groups? How does a policy researcher determine who in the policy chain exercises *more* power? Dahl's criticism was of the entire polyarchal model. "Polyarchy," he charged in the conclusion of *Polyarchy* (1971), "is a slack-jawed theory."[349] It is slack-jawed because as a social science paradigm it suffers both from an absence of weighting and measurable variables and an absence of genuine predictive capabilities. Both criticisms are accurate. Both may profitably be extended. It is possible to extrapolate from these arguments to consider two problem areas for polyarchal theory: polyarchy and the problem of weighting, and polyarchy and the problem of labeling. As a preview of the discussion that follows, we should note that we are considerably more sanguine about the problems surrounding polyarchy and labeling than we are about the issue of empirically weighting the polyarchal method.

The issue of weighting is a problem in both Dahl's community power methodology and in his theory of polyarchy. Methodologically, the problem, although troublesome, may be solvable.[350] The problem is one, as Ricci notes, of assigning a weight to each (discernible) actor in the policy chain—determining, in fact, which actor has *more* influence than others.[351] While such measures assigned to groups may initially be subjective, it is possible that community power scholars could agree upon a taxonomy of influence and resources along with a corresponding weighting schema. The disadvantages of such a proposal seem obvious. The weighting might appear to be subjective—either its construction or its application in a specific case. Second, as the potential power criticism suggests, all of the actors in the policy chain may not be known or their resources/influences be adequately assessed—or assessable.[352] Third, even if the actors on each policy issue could be charted and assigned a defensible weight which explained a given community politics outcome, such explanations would tend at best to be a posteriori and descriptive. While such weighted descriptions might better explain past outcomes, they would appear to have little predictive value for community power scholars.

There are also theoretical and normative dimensions to the weighting problem. Dahl himself admits that as a model polyarchy can be used atheoretically. Recently, Dahl used Mexico as an example to illustrate this problem.[353] Is Mexico a (working) polyarchy, he asked? Does it have all eight of the processes and institutions required by the model? Does it meet requirement 5, the right of political leaders to compete for support? Does it satisfy requirement 7, the requirement of free and fair elections?[354] Are elections in Mexico really contested and fairly administered? In the end, Dahl concluded by suggesting that recent elections in Mexico probably were contested and fairly conducted. Thus, one could probably be safe in arguing that a genuine political opposition exists and exists legally in Mexico. If so, he concluded, then Mexico *probably* is a polyarchy.

The problem, as the example of Mexico illustrates, is that without weighting, the theory of polyarchy is open to atheoretical uses. Is Mexico a polyarchy, or is it not? Is Chicago? Is Atlanta? If two scholars disagree on such a point, how is it to be resolved? In the absence of quantifying the eight institutional conditions of polyarchy and measuring them against the conditions of actual polities (e.g., Mexico, Chicago, Atlanta), how are we to know *objectively* if and when polity *x* is a polyarchy? The problem could be partially solved by suggesting that polyarchal development is a zero-sum game. A polity either has some (thus, all or enough) of the eight conditions or requisites or it has none. Stated differently, if it has any amount of each of the eight conditions, it has all the amount necessary to satisfy the model.

The zero-sum "solution," however, only removes the weighting to a second level of abstraction. If we assume, as Dahl does in *Polyarchy*, that the United States, Great Britain, France, West Germany and Sweden are all polyarchies,[355] does the model suggest which is *more* polyarchal? Which polity has developmentally the least distance to travel to become an ideal democracy (egalitarian polyarchy)? The fact that as a theory polyarchy is a developmental model suggests that one of these actual polities (polyarchies) may be more polyarchal than the others. But, in the absence of any assigned weights, scholars attempting to use the model are forced to assign developmental weights among the polyarchal countries as they subjectively see fit or, alternately, they may reject such subjective measurements and insist on the basis of the zero-sum assumption that all polyarchies are roughly equally weighted since *all* polyarchies have *all* the qualities of a polyarchy.

A further aspect of the weighting problem exists at the normative or prescriptive level. Assuming for the moment that the methodological problems associated with assigning weights to groups in community power studies might be resolved, what might be the normative implications of such research? What *ought* to be the distribution of group political weight in community politics? What is the best (most polyarchal) array of community groups in a given locale? The question of best weighting arises at two levels: one normative, one tactical. At the normative level, is it possible to develop a research methodology that informs the researcher about the current weight of groups in community politics *and* tells the researcher how distant the present group weighting is from an ideal normative distribution of group weights? And what, in fact, is the normative benchmark for such an ideal? A major theoretical failing of polyarchal theory—as well as group politics theory in general—is the absence of any normative criterion for group participation.[356]

A second and perhaps more tactical or practical concern is the absence of any practical participatory benchmark. What is the optimal representation that groups may achieve in a polyarchy? What is their most advantageous state? What pattern of organization and resources would lead, for example, an underprivileged group to optimize its political efficacy? Further, what is the best normative nexus between optimality and equity in group politics? By what constellation of weighting may a community of groups be most efficient and, simultaneously, most equitably or most polyarchally weighted?

Assuming that the methodological impediments to weighting could be overcome, polyarchy might well be able to address these and similar issues. However, for the present, the impediments to resolving the weighting problem successfully appear formidable. Contemporary attempts at weighting the power and resources of the players in community power studies are arbitrary and incomplete. Attempts to weight the variables in the theory of polyarchy itself have failed.[357] Finally, polyarchy lacks a normative weighting schema that would facilitate such judgments as what ought to be the weight appropriate to each group in a given polity in terms of both group efficiency and political norms—what is the most polyarchal distribution of groups and resources for a given community? And how would one go about making such a determination?

Of these three weighting problems—weighting community influentials, weighting the elements of polyarchy and polyarchies themselves, and normatively weighting groups within a polyarchal polity—we propose in the remainder of this study to address only the second concern; that is, the problem of weighting the various elements within the polyarchal model and of weighting polyarchies themselves. Before discussing a remedy to this aspect of polyarchy's weighting dilemma, it is necessary to discuss a parallel concern, the problem of using the term polyarchy meaningfully in a social science sense. We refer to this below as the "meaningful label problem."

POLYARCHY AND THE MEANINGFUL LABEL PROBLEM

If read closely, the polyarchal model is clear and unambiguous. A (working)[358] polyarchy is an actual polity that has met several specified preconditions and exhibits all eight process variables. Thus, in a social science sense, polyarchy is unquestionably a meaningful and informative descriptive label. It is a useful tool in describing developmental differences in actual polities—whether these polities be cities or nation-states. For example, it stresses and explains certain important similarities that countries such as the United States and West Germany exhibit vis-à-vis more hegemonic actual regimes such as the Soviet Union or East Germany. Nevertheless, there are important policy, process, and institutional differences among polyarchies. Some (nation-state) polyarchies have nationalized major industries and services. England, for example, has nationalized steel production and health care. The United States leaves the production of steel to the private sector. Process differences among the polyarchal polities are also significantly different in Great Britain or West Germany than in the United States; so, too, are election processes and laws on the U.S. East Coast or in the Northeast corridor different from the nonpartisan elections of the West Coast and northwestern U.S. cities. Institutional differences also abound. The United Kingdom is a parliamentary regime and a unitary state. The United States, on the other hand, has a Congress and a separately elected chief executive. Additionally, far from being a unitary state, the United States has a governmental structure premised upon the principle of federalism. At the urban level, some polyarchies have at-large elections, others have council, district, or ward elections. Some have consolidated city and county electoral structures while, to mention the extreme case of Washington, D.C., one major U.S. city exists as a semiautonomous ward of the federal government.

Despite all of the differences noted above, Dahl and the polyarchal model assume these countries to be similar—to be, in fact, polyarchies. A problem arises, though its magnitude is far from clear at this point. As a model, polyarchy yields to the researcher a matrix with which to determine if a polity is, in fact, polyarchal. This is accomplished by determining if polity x exhibits eight similarities with other known polities. Assuming an affirmative finding is obtained, the model then gives little guidance in explaining the empirical differences which then may be found to exist between actual polities; differences between, for example, the United States and Great Britain, or between New Haven and San Francisco. In fact, given little guidance in explaining such differences, is the researcher to assume that any observed differences are, at least theoretically, unimportant? Possibly so. Yet, if so, does this contradict the implied logic of a developmental model? As chapter 1 demonstrated, three of the four main subparts (B, C, and D) of the polyarchal model are developmentally related to each other. D is prior to (less developed than) C, which in turn is prior to B. If the subsections of the model are developmentally related to each other, why would the same relationship not be true *within the subsections*? Are there no normative or theoretical distinctions to be made based not only upon the similarities of polyarchies but also upon their differences? At best, the polyarchal model is ambiguous on such questions. Polyarchy succeeds because it describes certain macrolevel institutions and process similarities which actual polities may hold in common. In so doing, polyarchy as a model yields a taxonomy of polyarchal and nonpolyarchal or nonhegemonic and hegemonic states. Because it focuses upon a macrodescription of competitive electoral institutions and processes—though the format, timing, and administrative laws of each polyarchy's electoral system may differ greatly—polyarchy is useful as a descriptive and prescriptive theory of democratic politics. It is not, however, a predictive theory. It cannot, for example, demonstrate that certain nonpolyarchal states are likely to become polyarchies over time.[359] It can only describe the fact that some have changed and others have not. Perhaps polyarchy, without weighting and without further refinement is, as Dahl says, necessarily "slack-jawed." On the other hand, it may be that it is possible to supplement polyarchy's descriptive and prescriptive capabilities by constructing a subprocess theoretical addendum. If so, such an addendum might provide limited predictive capabilities for the polyarchal model.

What shape would a subprocess addendum take? Like its promise, its exact theoretical parameters are difficult to chart. Tentatively, we might suggest that a subprocess addendum that collated and attempted to explain differences among the polities grouped in each subset might prove of some benefit. Perhaps focusing upon cities or countries labeled as near-polyarchies and, alternatively, those labeled as polyarchies and describing their differences would be useful.

As a model, polyarchy focuses on similarities. Unquestionably, it is meaningful and informative to label both Britain and the United States or New Haven and San Francisco as polyarchies. But perhaps the meaning of such labels can be increased in proportion to the number of significant qualifiers researchers attach to them.[360] Given enough significant differences observed among the members of the subset of near-polyarchies, would it not be reasonable to assume that those actual states at the upper end of the spectrum are more likely than the other states in the subset to become polyarchies? Obviously, the construction of such microlevel distinctions—like the weighting problem presented earlier—may prove difficult, if not impossible. Nevertheless, the current state of polyarchal theory would seem to suggest such efforts. The polyarchal developmental theory is itself still developing. Although polyarchal theory has remained essentially the same since first presented in 1953, there is much that might be accomplished by serious attempts at both criticism and revision. The section that follows presents an empirical polyarchal model designed to respond to some of the weighting and labeling criticisms noted above.

A TENTATIVE EMPIRICAL MODEL

Polyarchy has eight processes or conditions. These are: (1) free association, (2) free speech, (3) the right to vote, (4) office eligibility, (5) leadership competition, (6) alternative sources of information, (7) free and fair elections, and (8) other public preference/policy outcome-linking institutions. The questions facing comparative researchers are, when studying one or more polities: (1) is polity x (and/or polity y) a polyarchy? (2) how strong or weak a polyarchy is polity x? Is it not a polyarchy at all, but a more hegemonic political regime (a near-polyarchy, a mixed-regime, or an oligarchy)? If x and y are both polyarchal urban political regimes, which city (if either) is more polyarchal and why? Assuming that the polyarchal strength of one city exceeds that of a second, are these traits, institutions, or practices practiced in the more polyarchal city transferable to the second city—or are the factors that yield a stronger polyarchal regime in one city nontransferable aspects having to do with that city's electoral history, region, ethnicity, or political culture generally? Can, in short, cities be typed in categories or ranged along a continuum due to the presence (or absence) and strength (or weakness) of polyarchal conditions in that city? This is, at any rate, the goal of the empirical model of polyarchy presented in Table 5.1.

The empirical model was designed to test for both the presence and strength of polyarchy in a given political unit—in this case, cities in the United States. To do this, and to perform the task with some measure of economy while still ensuring representativeness, a two-tiered test was designed. In the model, each city is tested for both the presence and strength of the eight conditions of polyarchy. Thus, each city is subjected to sixteen queries—one each to test for the presence of each polyarchal variable and one each to test for the strength of the process variable (polyarchal condition) in the given city. This yielded a set of sixteen questions.

Thus, in the first sixteen questions, cities are checked to see if the legal right to polyarchal conditions one through seven is legally guaranteed in the city. Hardly surprising, all U.S. cities possess legal guarantees (via the U.S. Constitution) for the conditions and practices listed on polyarchy's first seven conditions.[361] Second, each of the first seven conditions is tested not simply for its legal presence in a given city but for some estimate of its strength or vigor. Hence, the first fourteen questions attempt to gauge if seven of the polyarchal process conditions exist in a given city and how strong or weak these polyarchal processes or conditions are in a given city. The final polyarchal variable—the presence of institutions linking public preferences and policy outcomes—was tested by checking, as in the earlier cases, for its legal presence and strength. The existence of any one of the following: initiative, referendum, recall, town meetings, or political parties, was taken as an indication of the legal presence of linkage institutions. The presence of two or more such institutions was counted as a measure of strength of the linkage institutions in a given city. (See appendix A for a more detailed explanation of the criteria and methodology used to measure the strength and presence of polyarchy in the two cities tested.)

Table 5.1
Empirical Polyarchy Model: Objective Axis

Condition	Objective Measures	
1. Free Association	1. Legal Right? Yes/No 1, 0	2. Membership Barred? Yes/No 0, 1
2. Free Speech	3. Legal Right? Yes/No 1, 0	4. Restrictive Laws? Yes/No 0, 1
3. Right to Vote	5. Legal Right? Yes/No 1, 0	6. % of Population Registered 0-100% 0-1
4. Office Eligibility	7. All Adults? Yes/No 1, 0	8. % Adult Pop. Candidates in Last Election 0-100% 0-1
5. Leader Competition	9. Legal Right? Yes/No 1, 0	10. Electoral Competition Index 0-100% 0-1
6. Information Sources	11. Legal Access? Yes/No 1, 0	12. Press Pluralism Index 0-100% 0-1
7. Free/Fair Elections	13. Legal Access? Yes/No 1, 0	14. Vote Challenged or Electon Law Changes Yes/No 0, 1
8. Other Preference- Policy Linkage Institutions	15. Any 1 of: Initiative, Referendum, Recall, Town Meetings, or Political Party? Yes/No 1, 0	16. Any Additional 1 of: Initiative, Referendum, Recall, Town Meetings, or Political Party? Yes/No 1, 0

While polyarchy tends to focus on legal institutions and political processes, other linkage institutions are important to the health of a representative urban polity. Two points should be raised at this point. First, as Michael Lipsky has noted, legal institutional linkages extend further and are more decentralized than might seem the case. In *Street Level Bureaucracy*, Lipsky shows that for many city residents, the cop on the beat not only represents city hall—he or she *is* the city bureaucracy. In effect, street patrols become street-level bureaucracies linking the public with its government. Thus, a fully polyarchal model would attempt to measure the strengths of these decentralized institutionalized linkages between citizen and government.[362] In this respect, the model as presented in this chapter falls short of the ideal. The model is also deficient in that it describes some long-term linkage institutions (e.g., political parties) but incompletely describes others. These include the friends and neighbors political networks described in the Providence and Foster case studies below, and the role and strength of ad hoc intermediary linkage community groups such as the Woodlawn Organization (TWO) in Chicago or the Mission Coalition in San Francisco.[363]

The test described above, in which cities are tested for the presence and strength of the eight conditions of polyarchy, has two obvious flaws. It tests only one dimension of urban polyarchal life. It concentrates on "objective" or de jure measures of polyarchy. Second, it bodes poorly for comparative urbanology, as most U.S. cities would have similar—if not identical— scores on at least the first seven questions. All U.S. cities will show a positive finding for the legal presence of polyarchy's first seven conditions, and most cities will show the legal presence of all eight polyarchal conditions. Thus, at least along the legal presence dimension, U.S. cities will show few differences. This is as it should be. U.S. cities are, in many respects, similar, and a model that did not indicate this would be faulty in the extreme. The question remaining, then, is whether the remainder of the model can clarify and highlight unique features of American local polyarchies, or whether the model fails to capture such nuances and distinctions. In order to facilitate such measurement and to respond to the earlier charge that the sixteen measures discussed thus far concentrate on only one aspect of urban polyarchal life, a second axis or focus was added to the empirical model.

The first sixteen questions are designed so that a researcher or team of researchers may, by examining the voting records, laws and ordinances, and newspaper circulation in a given city, make an "objective" determination of whether or not the city in question is a polyarchy. However, this focus on legal or de jure aspects has serious deficiencies. As the potential power critics suggested, a city might have the legal *forms* of a polyarchy (be a de jure polyarchy) but lack the *substance* or practical reality of a polyarchy. The difference here is the same as that between a school district or city that does not have legal or de jure segregation in its schools but does have practical or actual—de facto—segregation because of private school policies, ethnic neighborhood patterns, or school board practices. The danger, it seems, would be in not distinguishing between a de jure polyarchy (a city with the legal forms of a polyarchy) and a de facto polyarchy (a city with a strong and vigorous level of polyarchal activity).

As Jack Walker once observed of democracy, a polyarchy with only the forms intact is hardly a polyarchy at all—it would be a polyarchy stripped of its "radical élan."[364] As Dahl has insisted repeatedly, polyarchy is a theory of near-democracy. To find out how nearly democratic U.S. cities are, we need inquire beyond the legal forms into the substance of the nearly democratic (polyarchal) practices and way of life in each city. To facilitiate such an inquiry, a second set of sixteen questions (see Table 5.2) was added to the original sixteen "objective" test questions. The two sets will be distinguished by referring to the original sixteen as the objective questions or the "legal-institutional axis" and referring to the second set of sixteen questions as the "subjective" questions or the "social-psychological axis." The subjective questions are designed to ask a representative sample of citizens in each city to describe feelings, perceptions, and activity vis-à-vis local government policies and practices in the city (see appendices B and D for a more extensive description of the questions and interview schedule used for the subjective aspect of the municipal polyarchy test).

To capture this subjective dimension of local polyarchy, a telephone survey was conducted in two cities and respondents were asked a series of questions.[365] The interview was designed to provide a subjective judgment by each citizen on the strength and presence of each of the eight conditions of polyarchy in the city. The respondents were screened for residency and age. If they did not live within the city limits or if they were younger than eighteen, they were excluded from the survey. Additionally, the samples were adjusted to reflect the male-female breakdown of the interview cities. A final score was obtained by scoring each of the 32 questions (16 on the objective axis, 16 on the subjective) on a scale of 0 to 1 for each respondent and then dividing each city's score by the number of respondents. In theory, then, either city could have emerged from the study with an empirical polyarchy score ranging from 0 to 32.

A TALE OF TWO CITIES: PROVIDENCE AND FOSTER

Founded by Roger Williams in 1636 and incorporated in 1832, Providence is a city divided by a river and built on seven hills. The topographical, if not political, similarity to both San Francisco and Rome is the source of a great deal of justifiable civic pride. Providence is the capital of Rhode Island and a moderate-sized (1980 pop.: 156,804) New England city with many of the problems that plague other urban areas on the Northeast Atlantic seaboard. These problems include outmigration, a not-

Table 5.2
Empirical Polyarchy Model: Subjective Axis

Condition	Subjective Measures	
1. Free Association	17. Membership? Yes/No 1, 0	18. How Many? 1-3 0, .25, 1
2. Free Speech	19. Free Speech Index 1-4 1, .66, .33, 0	20. KKK/Nazi Rallies? Yes/No 1, 0
3. Right to Vote	21. Vote Last Election? Yes/No 1, 0	22. Voter Satisfaction Index? 1-4 1, .66, .33, 0
4. Office Eligibility	23. Citizen Role? Yes/No 1, 0	24. Able to Run? Yes/No 1, 0
5. Leader Competition	25. Follow Politics? 1-3 1, .25, 0	26. Follow Campaigns? 1-3 1, .25, 0
6. Information Sources	27. Newspaper Attentiveness 1-4 1, .14, .10, 0	28. TV and Radio 1-4 1, .14, .10, 0
7. Free/Fair Elections	29. Election Legitimacy Index 1-5 1, .75, .50, .25, 0	30. Reason Able to Run? Yes/No 1, 0
8. Other Preference- Policy Linkage Institutions	31. Support Political Party Yes/No 1, 0	32. Participate in: Initiative, Referendum, Recall, or Town Meeting? Yes/No 1, 0

too-distant history of political machines, the high cost of energy and heating oil, labor unrest, and the decline of the once mighty textile and jewelry industries.

The city has declined from its peak period of population in-migration in 1940 and since that time has, like many of its urban compatriots nationally, been steadily losing residents. In the last ten years, the population of Providence has declined 12.4 percent from 179,116 to 156,804 residents. Politically, Providence has shared a history of ethnic politics much like that described by Dahl in *Who Governs?*[366] Patrician elites, whose names still adhere to the leading streets and private schools, have long since been electorally submerged by succeeding waves of immigrant workers. Today, Italian and Irish voters and politicians and—to a lesser extent—Portuguese and black voters tend to prevail in mayoral and council elections. This was not always the case. As late as the 1920s, Providence had property requirements for city voters, although the state of Rhode Island eliminated such requirements for state voters after the Dorr Rebellion of the 1840s, during which for a time Rhode Island "had two separate governments, each claiming sovereignty."[367] The property requirement for voting in local elections allowed the financial and business or patrician class residing on the east side of the Providence River to prevail in election contests from the early days of Providence up until the early part of the twentieth century. The balance of electoral power shifted with the participation of "thousands of immigrants, especially women who had never voted before."[368] These immigrant groups changed the complexion of city politics dramatically. The "East Side" voters of College and Lippit Hills saw "their" city hall physically relocated across the river, and elections of the late 1920s marked the emergence of Italian politicians from Smith and Federal Hill, Portuguese politicians from Fox Point, and the emergence of black electoral strength from Providence's South End or Edgewood neighborhood.[369]

It is generally agreed that the shift from patrician politics to the politics of the immigrant "new men" in the early 1900s did not end the role of political machines in Providence. Rather, as Richard Gabriel has argued, the older Republican machines were replaced with Democratic machines in Providence, as well as in the state's other large urban areas, Warren and Pawtucket.[370] Whether the political machine as such is moribund is still a highly relevant topic—and a frequently asked question—in Providence political circles. As such, Providence seemed an excellent prospect for a study of polyarchy. To wit, how nearly democratic (polyarchal) is the city of Providence? How polyarchal do its institutions and practices appear? And how polyarchal does Providence seem to the average Providence resident? How polyarchal are the attitudes and practices of Providence residents? Finally, how does the picture of Providence which emerges from this study compare with Foster, a small New England village located near Rhode Island's western border with Connecticut?

Foster, a New England town of 3,370 residents, is in many respects the polar opposite of Providence.[371] It is extremely small in population, although unlike Providence it is gaining population. The decade from 1970 to 1980 saw a 28 percent increase in population, as Foster grew from 2,626 to 3,370 residents. Unlike Providence, the town topography is flat, allowing many of the residents to tend farms and apple orchards which antedate the Revolutionary War. Unlike Providence, Foster is predominantly Republican in its town electoral politics,[372] and—again, unlike Providence—still retains the New England practice of conducting important town business and the annual budget via the process of town meetings. Indeed, during a recent two-year span (1981-82), Foster called town meetings on topics as diverse as gypsy moths, an interstate freeway construction project, and the proposed relocation of the Town Hall.[373] Furthermore, Foster is so small, and most of its residents are long-term and well known to each other, that much of the town's politics would appear to be conducted over backyard fences or, as is more typically the case, low stone walls. Many Foster residents (25 percent of the sample) either currently served in public office, were related to someone that was a politician, or had a politician as "a close family friend."[374]

Thus, Foster seemed, at least intuitively, an ideal polyarchal contrast to Providence. On almost every intuitive measure scholars and residents would probably agree that Foster is more nearly democratic (polyarchal) than Providence. The trick, however, is to prove it. Foster's smallness, its social and geographic compactness, its apparent ideological homogeneity, its high percentage of long-term and familiar residents, its long tradition of town meetings, its enhanced avenues for addressing the political system—either directly via the town meeting or indirectly via the social network[375] of neighbors, friends, and relatives—all suggest that Foster is, or should be, much more polyarchal a town than Providence. But is it? And if so, by how much, and why? If not, why and by what degree and with what precision of measurement?

Although the empirical model that follows is in many respects a less than perfect measure, it allows community power scholars to provide an empirical answer to the question of which community(ies) is (are) polyarchal and to what degree. Absent such a model, the discussion must necessarily proceed at the level of tastes, preferences, and intuitive judgments. Worse, even cases that seem on their face to be clear—the Providence/Foster contrast for example—are not demonstrably clear. It is this ambiguity that the empirical model of polyarchy was designed to remedy.

OPERATIONALIZING THE MODEL AND
ANALYZING THE FINDINGS

The intuitive case is clear. Foster seems intuitively more nearly democratic than Providence. Foster's small size, town meetings, friends and neighbor politics, its well-informed population (over 900 of the 3,000 adult residents subscribe to the morning or evening newspaper), its political and ideological homogeneity all combine to present an image of a strongly polyarchal New England village—a town quite unlike its more urban neighbor.

The empirical model presents a somewhat different picture. The empirical scores are: Providence 19 and Foster 23 (see Table 5.3). While the empirical scores are consistent with the intuitive view of Foster as more polyarchal, there are important and nonobvious differences between the intuitive and empirical views of the two municipalities. First, the distance between the two towns on a polyarchal scale is much less than assumed in the intuitive model. The view of Providence as less polyarchal than its country cousin is accurate but requires some qualification to be meaningful. The differences between the two polyarchies are best explained by reference to an explanatory typology of polyarchies. Put simply, the two polyarchies are not only different, they are different *types* of polyarchies. Second, Providence is much stronger in some polyarchal respects than the intuitive or conventional view might suggest. Third, there are important nonobvious differences and similarities which the empirical polyarchy model helps to identify and explain. We turn now to a brief analysis of these findings.

The closeness of the Providence and Foster scores can be explained by several factors. First, since both cities are polyarchies, both have all eight of the legal rights or conditions of a polyarchy. Thus both will have a total score of 8 on objective measures 1, 3, 5, 7, 9, 11, 13, and 15 (see Table 5.3). All polyarchies, by definition, share this score in common. A city lacking even one of these measures would necessarily be, at best, a near-polyarchy. Since cities can theoretically receive a score ranging from 0 to 32—with polyarchies constituting the 8-32 point end of that range—it is theoretically possible that cities might fall anywhere along this 32-point continuum. While it is probable that most U.S. cities would be polyarchies, it is not necessarily so. The description of Plaquemines parish in appendix D is included as an example of a governmental unit that until recently would have failed to meet the legal rights (especially conditions 2 and 3—the right to vote and the right of leaders to compete for electoral support) that are a basic element of polyarchies.

Second, the intuitive picture was an injustice to the political realities of Providence political life. As the empirical model makes clear, Providence's score is relatively close to that of Foster because both have institutional similarities found in all polyarchies and because, in some respects, Providence is (in five areas) *more polyarchal* than suburban Foster. Providence's score on measures 10, 25, 28, 31, and 32 all exceed that of Foster. More people, in both absolute numbers and in percent of the overall population, in Providence follow politics on a day-to-day basis, follow politics on television or the radio, support a political party, or are likely to participate in public preference-policy linkage activities or institutions than is the case for Foster. The electoral competition index complements these findings by suggesting a higher level of alteration and smaller pluralities in Providence than in Foster. These findings necessitate amending the intuitive view of political activity in   Providence[376] and the ubiquity and control of the Democratic party "machine" in Providence.

As one observer has noted, there is some question whether Providence ever had an urban machine in the sense of Chicago or Tammany Hall.[377] When the property requirements were dropped and immigrant groups entered the Providence electoral arena in 1928, the change was so overwhelming and has remained so permanent that no machine was needed to deal with external threats to Democratic party control.[378] True, the organization of ward politics did and does exist in Providence, but machines as such were more coalitions to secure intramural advantages for various Democrats than to insure city or even statewide advantage to the Democratic party.[379]

The more competitive, more participatory, less ominous view of Providence politics that emerges from the empirical study is consistent with some of the remarks of Providence respondents. Far from big-city anomie or machine politics-related alienation, respondents warmly described politics in Providence as a "participant sport"; one in which whole families can and do participate actively.[380]

On the other hand, the intuitive picture of Foster as more polyarchal than Providence is accurate and the empirical model helps to pinpoint several areas in which Providence lags behind Foster. Providence has a lower score than Foster on two important measures on the subjective axis. The legal-institutional aspects of polyarchy are weaker in Providence in two respects. On one measure (objective axis measure 4), Providence received a score of zero because of restrictive laws prohibiting pamphleteering in public parks and because of the lack of procedural due process in the city's ad hoc and irregular manner of deciding whether or not to grant parade permits.[381]

A second problem indicated by the objective axis measures is Providence's election laws and their enforcement. While Providence has no problem qualifying on polyarchy's measure of legal access for adult voters (measure 13), it suffers, rather, from an excess of such access. The 1982 city elections were plagued with election scandal resulting from the dubious handling of mail ballots—primarily from senior citizens and shut-ins—and the curious state of Providence's residency laws. Under the law—changed in 1983 as a result of election publicity and scandal—voters can declare their voting residency in Providence despite the fact that they may actually reside elsewhere in the state. Thus, Providence saw large numbers of citizens from surrounding towns registering to vote and voting in the very close mayoral election of 1982.

On the subjective side, Foster is more polyarchal than Providence on measures 17-19, 21-24, 26-27, and 29-30. Fleshing this out, Fosterites emerge as more likely than Providence residents to belong to organizations and clubs and to belong to several clubs simultaneously. Thus, the stereotype of

Table 5.3
Empirical Polyarchy Score

	Objective Axis (Legal-Institutional Dimension)	Subjective Axis (Social-Psychological Dimension)
Condition		
(1) Freedom of Association		
1. Legal Right? P-1, F-1	2. Membership Barred? P-1, F-1	17. Membership? P-.58, F-.68	18. How Many? P-.32, F-.33
(2) Free Speech		
3. Legal Right? P-1, F-1	4. Restrictive Laws? P-0, F-1	19. Free Speech Index P-.60, F-.67	20. KKK/Nazi Rallies? P-.33, F-32
(3) Right to Vote		
5. Legal Right? P-1, F-1	6. % Adults Registered? P-.80, F-.90	21. Vote last 3 Elections? P-.68, F-.87	22. Voter Satisfaction Index P-.76, F-.79
(4) Office Eligibility		
7. All Adults? P-1, F-1	8. % Adult Pop. Candidates in last Election? P-.06, F-.39	23. Citizen Role P-0, F-.02	24. Able to Run? P-.33, F-.49
(5) Leader Competition		
9. Legal Right? P-1, F-1	10. Elec. Competition Index P-.43, F-.28	25. Follow Politics? P-.49, F-.45	26. Town Council or Mayoral Vote? P-.64, F-.76

(6) Information Sources
11. Legal Access?

P-1, F-1

12. Press Pluralism Index

P-.10, F-.59

(7) Free and Fair Elections
13. Legal Access

P-1, F-1

14. Vote Challenged or Reforms Enacted

P-0, F-1

(8) Other Preference-Policy Institutions
15. Any 1 of:
Initiative,
Referendum,
Recall, Town
Meetings, or
Political Party?
P-1, F-1

16. Any Additional 1 of:
Initiative,
Referendum,
Recall, Town
Meetings, or
Political Party?
P-1, F-1

27. Newspaper Attentiveness?
P-.44, F-.46

28. TV and Radio

P-.57, F-.56

29. Election Legitimacy Index

P-.71, F-.92

30. Reason Able to Run?

P-.28, F-.55

31. Support Political Party?

32. Participate in:
Initiative,
Referendum,
Recall, or Town
Meeting?

P-.46, F-.35

P-.40, F-.36

Objective Axis Score =
Providence   11.39
Foster   14.17

Subjective Axis Score =
Providence   7.59
Foster   8.58

Empirical Polyarchy Score (total) =
Providence   18.98 = 19
Foster   22.75 = 23

the cloistered rural nonjoiner suburbanite probably included in the intuitive view of Foster is disconfirmed by the empirical model. Rather, we get a view of an active citizenry, not only in organization and club membership but also in local elections (measure 21). A further line of argument suggested by the objective axis measures probably has as much, or more, to do with an undertow of antiparty or antiboss politics in Providence as it does with the vigor of democratic yeomanry in Foster town politics. Collectively, Providence's low scores on objective measures 23, 24, 29, and 30 present a picture of Providence citizens with a low feeling of efficacy about their urban polyarchal regime. None of the Providence respondents mentioned the possibility of themselves running for office as part of "the role of the ordinary citizen." Asked if they would be able to run if they wanted to, only 33 percent of the Providence sample saw this as a viable possibility. While considerations of time, experience, and personal inclination were mentioned as factors accounting for this answer, many of the respondents suggested that the process was not open to them—that one had to "know someone," to have the party endorsement, to "be close to a politician," or, more cynically, that the process was closed to outsiders, "fixed," or closed to someone of their gender, income, or ethnic background. In sum, only 33 percent of the Providence residents felt that, if they wanted to, they would be able to run for elective office in their municipality. These attitudes and the electoral practices discussed earlier may explain why, compared to 92 percent of the Foster respondents, only 71 percent of the Providence respondents were willing to describe local elections as "always legal and fair."

Thus, as the empirical model of polyarchy helps to clarify, the intuitive view of Providence and Foster is accurate—but only partially so. The use of the empirical model has allowed us to highlight the degree of difference between the two municipalities, to focus on the significant differences and similarities between the two polyarchies, and to bring to light important and nonobvious components of their respective polyarchal regimes.

A CAVEAT ON METHODOLOGY

Obviously, two cities do not constitute a full-blown comparative study of urban polyarchal regimes. The use of Providence and Foster in the present study is meant as an illustrative example of the possibilities of the empirical polyarchal method. No two cities, however judiciously selected, could possibly be representative of the full panoply of municipal political regimes in the United States. The present study incorporates the two-city study in order to show how the empirical model of polyarchy can be operationalized and to facilitate the discussion of a polyarchal typology which follows.

The empirical model of polyarchy, despite its manner of presentation in the current study, is not a "stand-alone" method for studying community power. While empirical model studies of diverse communities would be intrinsically useful, the method is meant as a methodological double-check to the present pluralist methodology of studying issues in community politics. Thus, a full application of the methodology recommended in the present work would be the empirical model described herein combined—for example, in Providence or Foster—with a study of such issues as party nominations, charter reform, urban or town renewal, and school finances and policies. While the proper issues to study may vary from community to community,[382] the study of such issues[383] coupled with the measures incorporated in the empirical polyarchy model should yield to community power scholars the best available means for describing the politics of a given city, or comparing a given city with other U.S. polyarchal and nonpolyarchal regimes, and finally facilitating prescriptive analysis via the use of polyarchal measaures and norms.

A TENTATIVE TYPOLOGY OF POLYARCHIES

Descriptive Uses of Polyarchies

As Figure 5.1 indicates, municipal polyarchies have been divided into four groups: polyarchy Types I, II, III, and IV. Cities which do not have all eight of the basic legal-institutional conditions or processes of polyarchy are (by definition) nonpolyarchies (see the lower two cells of Figure 5.1). Thus,

Figure 5.1
A Typology of Polyarchies

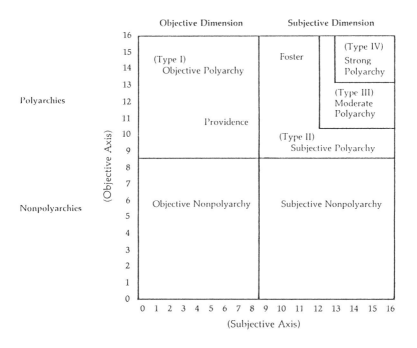

on the objective axis, the first eight points correspond to a city's score on objective axis measures 1, 3, 5, 7, 9, 11, 13, and 15 (see Table 5.3). The remainder of the objective axis corresponds to a city's score on objective measures 2, 4, 6, 8, 10, 12, 14, and 16. The subjective axis represents a city's score on all 16 of the subjective axis measures. Thus, Providence's placement would be the intersection of its objective axis score of 11.39 and its subjective axis score of 7.59. As Figure 5.2 indicates, Providence—a Type I polyarchy—is located in the upper left-hand cell. Foster, with an objective axis score of 14.17 and a subjective axis score of 8.58, is a Type II polyarchy and is located in the larger of the upper right-hand cells. Polyarchies range along a continuum as indicated in Figure 5.2.

Figure 5.2
A Continuum of Municipal Polyarchies

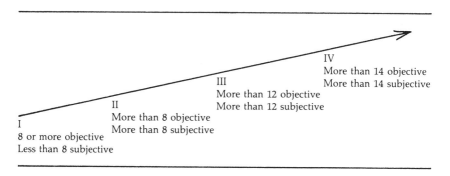

Thus, as the two sample cities illustrate, municipal polyarchies vary not only by degree but also by type. Providence, a Type I or "objective polyarchy," has the legal institutions of polyarchy but some of these institutions are not yet firmly entrenched, or their present configuration allows for weak delivery or can lead to a lack of public confidence. Part of this is subject to change—with the recent reforms enacted by Providence to close election residency and mail balloting loopholes—and part is unlikely to change rapidly, for example, Providence's strong Democratic party, the role that party endorsements, patronage, and party bossism plays in city politics may continue to produce low election legitimacy scores, low able to run, and reason able to run scores (measures 24, 26, and 30) in future subjective axis measurements of Providence politics.

Foster, on the other hand, is a Type II or "subjective polyarchy." In Foster's case, the institutions of polyarchy seem firmly in place and efficacious in their effect. Further, the opinions of residents as to the "polyarchalness" of town government is slightly stronger than is the case for Providence residents. Nevertheless, Foster's low subjective score, while stronger than Providence, indicates that it is quite a distance away from achieving a "strong polyarchy" (Type IV) score. The problems associated with the low polyarchy score for Providence were fairly blunt and obvious—a strong party mechanism, restrictive laws, and election irregu-larities.[384] They are also more easy to repair. Foster's case is more subtle. Foster's problem is the need to remedy defects in the social-psychological dimension of polyarchal life. While a stronger polyarchy than Providence, Foster is not yet a "strong polyarchy" in either a descriptive or normative sense. Even with solid polyarchal forms (e.g., frequent town meetings and a strong political party), few people seem to support either activity. The local dominance by the Republican party (including at the time of this writing an unbroken twelve-year stretch of Republican town administrators), a low resulting election competition index score, the low level of tolerance for socially different ideas and the right to express them, and the lower level of attention to political affairs all suggest subjective axis areas in which Foster could increase its polyarchal performance.

Type III ("moderate polyarchies") and Type IV ("strong polyarchies") represent possible classifications in which municipalities might register increasing levels of both the presence and strength of polyarchal institu-tions. While not a democracy, Type IV polyarchies would represent the subset of U.S. cities that are most nearly democratic in their municipal political performance.

SOME METHODOLOGICAL CONCERNS

There are several methodological concerns that this analysis has not fully resolved. Four such concerns appear uppermost. First, not all 32 variables seem to be equal, in terms of their importance or in terms of testing polyarchy equally well. True, all eight of Dahl's polyarchal conditions are equal. The set does not "work" with only six or seven conditions. Condition 8 (the policy-preference linkage institution), for example, is not a summary variable summarizing conditions 1 through 7. It is a necessary safeguard of the other conditions, and polyarchy is not fully operative without it. There is some question whether the measures incorporated in the empirical model are of the same order or level of analysis. Not all measure their targets equally well. Surely, some could be improved. The "press pluralism index," for example, would be more realistic if it included the television and radio news audience figures for the towns under study. Unfortunately, these figures are simply unavailable.[385] Admittedly, then, some of the measures in the empirical polyarchy model "satisfice" rather than satisfy our research aims.

Second, and partially echoing the first concern, there is the question of parity between the objective and subjective halves of the model. Do subjec-tive variables as a set weigh as much as the objective variables? Do they matter as much? Ought they? In the absence of a definitive answer to such queries, we have arbitrarily assumed that the subjective dimension is as important a dimension to measure as the de jure or objective side and ought to weigh as much. The Providence and Foster findings would seem to bear this out. Type I and Type II polyarchies are rendered meaningful, both descriptively and prescriptively, precisely because they can be compared and, in the normative case, held accountable to polyarchy Type III and Type IV. This dimension of the model seems worth retaining.

Third, the distances and differences between the scores and the subsets (Types I-IV) are ordinally meaningful (e.g., Type III polyarchies are more nearly democratic than Type I polyarchies) and, to some extent, the distance between these two polyarchal types is intervally meaningful in the same way that a centigrade thermometer is meaningful in its distance between 0 and 100 degrees. Still, the units of measurement do not equate to true ratio level measurement. It is not clear, for example, that a city with a score of 30 would be twice as strong a polyarchy as a city with a score of 15. Rather, what the model suggests is that a city with a score of 30 is much stronger than a city with a score of 15.

A final set of problems has to do with definitions. When, for example, is a polity a near-polyarchy? Is a city a near-polyarchy when it has 4, 5, 6, or 7 of the polyarchal conditions? What if it only has voting but the voting objective and subjective axis variables are very strong (e.g., one point each)? Such definitions will always retain a grain of arbitrariness. Nevertheless, we have arbitrarily determined that to be "near" to a polyarchy, a city must have most or a majority of the polyarchal conditions present. Thus, in order to be a near-polyarchy, a city must score at least a total of 5 on the objective axis (measures 1, 3, 5, 7, 9, 11, 13, and 15). Our defense for this five-point cutoff point is that requiring a majority showing on the crucial variables seems the least arbitrary way to proceed.

FURTHER EMPIRICAL EXPERIMENTS

The model and the tentative typology presented in the current study are sufficient for our present purposes. Both the model and the typology[386] would benefit from further efforts in the comparative research of U.S. municipal and urban areas. While such wide-scale comparative urban research has not been in vogue of late,[387] it is hoped that the pluralist study of issues and community power, enriched with the application of the empirical polyarchy model, would reap several descriptive and prescriptive benefits for community power and urban scholars. The descriptive promise of a typology of urban regimes and institutions, as well as the opportunity to create a taxonomy of municipal polities, would seem to lobby strongly in favor of such future research. Our own research agenda calls for an effort to rank several of the largest and smallest U.S. cities via the use of the empirical polyarchy method.

CONCLUSION: PRESCRIPTIVE USES OF THE EMPIRICAL MODEL

Perhaps the strongest argument for the use of the empirical polyarchy model is the prescriptive use which such a model entails. While not belittling the taxonomical or descriptive gains that arise from an application of the empirical model, these are far outweighed by the prescriptive promise of the empirical method. To wit, let us assume for the moment that several cities were studied vis-à-vis the empirical polyarchy method. Assuming a study of, say, thirty cities we might be entitled to suppose that a multiplicity of Type I to Type IV cities would emerge. After categorizing these cities by type, we could begin to draw up a list of possible explanatory variables—one descriptive, the other prescriptive. The descriptive explanatory variables might include such nontransferable variables as region, political culture (e.g., a history of reform, involvement, or activism), ethnicity, and heated electoral contests. Transferable explanatory variables might include such elements as election laws or election administration techniques,[388] campaign spending laws or practices, campaign tactics or strategy, information dissemination by the municipal government or private providers, city council norms or practices, and so on. If—and this is an empirical question yet to be resolved—Type III and Type IV polyarchies are characterized by the presence of transferable features not found in Type I and Type II polyarchies, then the prescriptive requirements of the polyarchal method would seem clear. That is, in addition to classifying and explaining the strength of a polyarchy in a given locale, the implicit prescriptive requirement of the empirical polyarchy method is the recommendation that the transferable polyarchal practices of Type III and Type IV polyarchies not present in Type I and Type II locales ought to be, at the least, attempted for the sake of municipal polyarchal reform. While the political science discipline may be without a universally acceptable prescriptive theory of urban or municipal democracy, it is not without a fully developed and applicable descriptive and prescriptive theory of near-democracy (polyarchy).

Admittedly, the model outlined in the present study is, in many respects, less than ideal. Ideally, a perfect measurement schema would have been designed—one that measured not simply near-democracy but democracy itself. But the study of empirical democratic theory, and particularly the application of that study to local government, has yet to yield an adequate model with which to work. This book is a step in that direction.

APPENDIX A _____
The Empirical Polyarchy Model

THE EMPIRICAL TEST

The model used in the present study is designed to test a given polity for its "polyarchalness"—to measure how nearly democratic a given political unit is. A second purpose of the model is to facilitate comparisons among polyarchies, to answer such questions as how polyarchal (nearly democratic) city x is, and how x compares, for example, with Chicago or New Haven. A third intent of the model is to address concerns of normative democratic theory. To wit: How democratic is city x? Is city x more democratic (or, at the least, more nearly democratic) than y? And, if so, why? What, if anything, can be done in the less democratic city to raise its level of democratization?

Polyarchy has eight conditions or institutional guarantees. These are (1) freedom of association, (2) free speech, (3) the right to vote, (4) eligibility of the general public for elective office, (5) competition for elective leadership, (6) diversity of information sources, (7) free and fair elections, and (8) other institutional processes that link public preferences to public policy. The empirical test used in this study is designed to probe a given community for the presence and strength of these eight polyarchal conditions. Thus, the test measures each condition twice along an "objective axis" and twice more along a "subjective axis." Hence, the model contains 8×4, or 32 variables. Since each variable is scaled to yield an answer in the 0 to 1 range, the highest possible score for any municipal polyarchy would be 32.

THE OBJECTIVE AXIS

The objective axis contains two measures for each of the eight polyarchal conditions. Most of these measures are self-evident and require little explanation (see Table A.1). Cities are studied to determine if, for example, the legal right to association, speech, and voting are present. It is difficult to imagine an American community in which such legal rights do not exist. Similarly, each community is checked for the legal presence of the right of sane and nonfelonious voting age residents to run for public office, to compete for leadership posts, to have legal access to information sources such as the printed news, and to engage in free and fair elections. As with the earlier measures, it is difficult—though not impossible—to imagine an American community not meeting such litmus tests of the presence of polyarchal institutions.[389] For measures of policy/preference linking institutions, we accepted the presence of any two of the following as bona fide examples of such institutions at the municipal level: initiative, referendum, recall, town meetings, or political parties (see measures 15 and 16 in Table A.1).

Eight additional measures attempt to get beyond the legal or de jure focus of the measures previously discussed. Thus, measures 2 and 4 attempt to detrmine if the legal rights to membership in political associations or free speech have been effectively denied by the actions of the city government. To help in this determination, a civil liberties panel was selected for each community. In each locale, a panel was formed using an ACLU board member, a college professor of political science, a political reporter for a local newspaper, and a lawyer/elected politician. Additionally, public records such as city or town council minutes and a newspaper clipping file covering a twelve-month period were used in an effort to corroborate the judgment of the civil liberties panel members.

Measure 6 calculates the percentage of residents eighteen years and older who are registered to vote. The source used was the 1980 *Census of Population*, vol. 1, produced by the Bureau of the Census (U.S. Department of Commerce, March 1982). Comparable small-city figures are available in the "1980 Census of the Population and Housing, Summary Tape File 1-A," microfiche edition.

In a 1967 article which combined elements of Anthony Downs' *Economic Theory of Democracy* with Dahl's theory of polyarchy, Deane Neubauer suggested an "index of democratic performance."[390] Neubauer's democratic performance index contains three measures of polyarchy that are applicable to the present study. To determine if conditions 3 (right to vote), 5 (right of political leaders to compete for support and votes), and 6 (alternative sources of information available) were present, Neubauer relied upon a calculation of the percent of the adult population eligible to vote, an "information equality" index, and a related measure of electoral competition.

Percent of the adult population eligible to vote is a measure of the extent to which voting-age members "excluded from suffrage for whatever reasons (sex, race, residence, literacy, etc.)." Adopting Neubauer's comparative measure for use in the present urban politics study, cities "which score the highest are those which most closely approximate the norm of permitting all adults to participate in the choice of a preferred set of leaders."[391]

As a measure of "the degree to which multiple sources of information are available to citizens of a given country," Neubauer used the following formula:

$$\text{number of separately owned papers} \times \frac{\text{average circulation}}{\text{size of capital}}$$

This formula attempted to measure the degree of pluralism of press ownership and "since adequate data of this form exist only for large cities, the indicator is explicitly concerned with the pattern of newspaper ownership in capital cities."[392] For the current study, which focuses exclusively on municipal polyarchies in the United States, Neubauer's formula has been changed to:

Table A.1
Empirical Polyarchy Model: Objective Axis

Condition	Objective Measures	
1. Free Association	1. Legal Right? Yes/No 1, 0	2. Membership Barred? Yes/No 0, 1
2. Free Speech	3. Legal Right? Yes/No 1, 0	4. Restrictive Laws? Yes/No 0, 1
3. Right to Vote	5. Legal Right? Yes/No 1, 0	6. % of Population Registered 0-100% 0-1
4. Office Eligibility	7. All Adults? Yes/No 1, 0	8. % Adult Pop. Candidates in Last Election 0-100% 0-1
5. Leader Competition	9. Legal Right? Yes/No 1, 0	10. Electoral Competition Index 0-100% 0-1
6. Information Sources	11. Legal Access? Yes/No 1, 0	12. Press Pluralism Index 0-100% 0-1
7. Free/Fair Elections	13. Legal Access? Yes/No 1, 0	14. Vote Challenged or Election Law Changes Yes/No 0, 1
8. Other Preference- Policy Linkage Institutions	15. Any 1 of: Initiative, Referendum, Recall, Town Meetings, or Political Party? Yes/No 1, 0	16. Any addition 1 of: Initiative, Referendum, Recall, Town Meetings, or Political Party? Yes/No 1, 0

$$\frac{c}{p} (.6n)$$

Where c is the combined average news circulation figure, p is the city or SMSA (Standard Metropolitan Statistical Area) adult population, and n is the number of separately owned newspapers in the community. The formula yields a score of 1 or more if 100 percent of the adult population regularly uses 60 percent or more of the available separately owned news sources. Modified in this fashion, Neubauer's formula becomes a "press pluralism index," an empirical measure of polyarchy's condition 6.

We use Neubauer's index of electoral competition as an index of leader competition (condition 5). Arguing that "electoral competition is meaningful only if the nature of the competition is such that the alteration in office of competing sets of leaders is probable as well as possible . . . the measure rewards those countries [cities] which come most close to providing the electorate with this alternative."[393] To do this Neubauer utilizes two measures:

(1) Percent of the time period in which the dominant party held office. Competition may be close, but if no alteration occurs over a long period of time, the nature of the alternative perceived by the electorate is substantially different than that in which alteration actually takes place.

(2) Mean percentage of the vote actually received by the winning party (parties). This indicator actually measures the closeness of the competition. It distinguishes particularly among those situations in which alteration does not occur. Non-alteration with a margin of 51-49 is thus distinguished from non-alteration with a margin of, say, 90-10.

These two measures eliminate the need for a third, obvious measure—the number of parties competing in the election. Single party states [cities] are distinguished from multiple party states by showing no alteration in office, and by the percentage of the vote gained by the winning party.[394]

The model presented in the current study incorporates all three measures of polyarchy developed by Neubauer. The adoption of these measures for the present study requires some qualification—especially in light of the fact that we are using them to measure municipal polyarchies as opposed to national polyarchies. Nevertheless, even with a necessary caveat and (in two cases) substantial modifications, they would appear extremely helpful measures of municipal polyarchy.

The press pluralism index (measure 12) will yield a number ranging from 0 to 1, depending on the availability of alternative sources of printed information. For purposes of illustration, assume that a medium-sized city (SMSA adult population of 1 million) has 3 separately owned newspapers with a combined circulation of 1.3 million. These figures would result in a score of 1.3 million divided by 1 million times 60 percent of 3, for a final score of .72.

While most such scores will probably be quite low, they seem justified in that all the formula requires for a polity to meet condition 6 (measure 12) is for all polity members to have access to most (60 percent) of the sources of printed news in a community. To require citizens to have access to *all* information sources seems much more problematical as a standard. Sixty percent of the separately owned newspapers may seem high as a criterion, but it seems inherently more fair than requiring that citizens obtain and read *all* the various morning, evening, daily, weekly, and specialty newspapers in a given community.

Measure 10—Neubauer's measure of electoral competition—although it requires a caveat, operates in a way similar to that described above (see appendix B). The model assumes that political party competition can be measured in most, if not all, American cities. Thus, in the case of California, Tom Bradley, the mayor of Los Angeles, is a well-known Democrat, while San Diego's former nonpartisan mayor (now U.S. senator) is active in Republican party circles. Presumably, such identification of nominally "nonpartisan" mayors should present the investigators with few difficulties. Neubauer's measure of electoral competition yields a range of scores from a theoretical low of 0 to a high of 200. We have modified Neubauer's calculation slightly. For the purpose of measure 10, a score is arrived at by dividing the electoral competition score by 2, subtracting this halved percentage from a base of 100 percent, and then recording the decimal equivalent. Thus, for example, a city with a Neubauer electoral performance score of 160 percent would result in a measure 10 revised score of 80 percent, which would in turn be subtracted from a base of 100 percent, and the resulting 20 percent would be recorded as a measure 10 score of .20. We shall refer to this final score as an electoral competition index score. For a more detailed explanation of this measure as it was used in Providence and Foster, see appendix B.

THE SUBJECTIVE AXIS

While largely self-explanatory, it should be noted that the subjective axis scores resulted from interviewing respondents in each city, scaling these answers on questions designed to measure their perceptions of the strength and presence of each of polyarchy's eight conditions, totaling the points assigned for the scaled responses for each question, and dividing by the number of responses for each question. Thus, for measure 21, for example, the respondents were asked if they voted in any of the last three municipal elections (scored as 1) or if they had not (scored as 0). These individual scores for all respondents answering the question for a given city were added together and then divided by the number of respondents answering the question (see appendix C). A hypothetical score for measure 21 might include 322 respondents, half of whom answered yes—which, in such a case, would yield a measure 21 score of 161 divided by 322, or a final score of .50.

The questions that served as the basis of the subjective axis scores (see Table A.2) were as follows: measure 17 (interview schedule questions [q.] 16-24 and 26-29), measure 18 (q. 25 and 30), measure 19 (q. 13), measure 20 (q. 33), measure 21 (q. 31), measure 22 (q. 32), measure 23 (q. 9). measure 24 (q. 11), measure 25 (q. 15), measure 26 (q. 34), measure 27 (q. 6), measure 28 (q. 7-8), measure 29 (q. 14), measure 30 (q. 12), measure 31 (q. 44 and 44-probe), measure 32 (q. 36, if Providence; or q. 38-41, if Foster). In cases such as measure 18 where two or more questions were used to construct a measure, the scaled responses of all respondents answering the question in a given community are calculated and that figure is divided by the number of respondents answering the various questions which collectively comprise the measure. Invalid answers such as "don't know," "refuse to answer," and "missing data" are excluded from the calculation.

Table A.2
Empirical Polyarchy Model: Subjective Axis

Condition	Subjective Measures	
1. Free Association	17. Membership? Yes/No 1, 0	18. How Many? 1-3 0, .25, 1
2. Free Speech	19. Free Speech Index 1-4 1, .66, .33, 0	20. KKK/Nazi Rallies? Yes/No 1, 0
3. Right to Vote	21. Vote Last Election? Yes/No 1, 0	22. Voter Satisfaction Index? 1-4 1, .66, .33, 0
4. Office Eligibility	23. Citizen Role? Yes/No 1, 0	24. Able to Run? Yes/No 1, 0
5. Leader Competition	25. Follow Politics? 1-3 1, .25, 0	26. Follow Campaigns? 1-3 1, .25, 0
6. Information Sources	27. Newspaper Attentiveness 1-4 1, .14, .10, 0	28. TV and Radio 1-4 1, .14, .10, 0
7. Free/Fair Elections	29. Election Legitimacy Index 1-5 1, .75, .50, .25, 0	30. Reason Able to Run? Yes/No 1, 0
8. Other Preference- Policy Linkage Institutions	31. Support Political Party Yes/No 1, 0	32. Participate in: Initiative, Referendum, Recall, or Town Meeting? Yes/No 1, 0

THE SAMPLE AND THE SAMPLING ERROR

The two surveys analyzed in chapter 5 were conducted by Alpha Research Associates of Providence, Rhode Island, in October 1982. Supervising the poll was Dr. Victor Profughi, of the Department of Political Science, Rhode Island College. The poll (see appendix C), was based on telephone interviews with 322 adults in Providence and 295 adults in Foster. The sample of telephone numbers actually dialed was selected via the use of random numbers tables and cross-referenced telephone directories containing a complete list of exchanges for the area. For each exchange, 10 percent of the numbers were formed by randomly selecting the last four digits, thus permitting access to listed and unlisted residential numbers. Additionally, the sample was constructed to reflect the male/female ratio of residents eighteen years of age and older in the two cities surveyed.

In theory, it can be said that in 95 cases out of 100, the results based on the entire sample are no more than 5 percentage points above or below what would have been obtained by interviewing all adult Providence and Foster residents. The error for subgroups is larger, depending on the number of cases in the subgroup.[395] The theoretical errors do not take into account a margin of additional error resulting from the various practical difficulties in taking any survey of public opinion.

On a final note, there is an obvious difficulty generalizing from Providence and Foster to other cities, or to the nation as a whole. In fact, it is exactly this problem that the empirical model was designed to avoid—by facilitating measurement and comparison of as many municipal units as possible. Nevertheless, Theodore Caplow has recently argued that generalization from such isolated units to the national picture may be more valid than heretofore assumed. See Caplow's recent article, "Decades of Public Opinion: Comparing NORC and Middletown Data," in which Caplow suggests several continuities between the presumably isolated municipal unit and the nation.[396]

APPENDIX B
Electoral Competition and Press Pluralism Indices

The electoral competition index was computed in the following manner:

1. The mean percentage of the time in which the dominant party or coalition held office. This figure is intended to measure the existence of electoral competition over a twelve-year period. The calculation includes the office of the mayor or town administrator and city council seats. The percentage of time that the mayor's office or a majority of council seats were won by the dominant party/coalition is summed and divided by 2 to produce a mean percentage of mayor/council control.

2. Mean percentage of the vote received by the winning party/coalition. This indicator measures the closeness of competition over a twelve-year period.

3. The combined percentages from items 1 and 2 above are divided by 2. The resulting figure is then subtracted from a base of 100 percent and, then, recorded as its decimal equivalent. Thus, a final score of 32 percent would be recorded as .32.

The Press Pluralism Index was computed in the following manner:

$$\frac{c}{p} (.6n)$$

Where c is the combined daily newspaper circulation figure for the city in question, n equals the number of separately owned print news sources (daily, weekly, biweekly, and monthly) in the city, and p equals the adult (eighteen and older) population of the city. Weekly papers are converted to daily circulation figures by dividing their circulation by 7 and entering only $\frac{1}{7}$ of their circulation in c; similarly, monthlies are entered only for $\frac{1}{30}$ of their overall monthly circulation figure, and so on. Table B.3 gives the numbers and sources for Providence and Foster.

Table B.1
Electoral Competition Index: Providence

Year	Mayoral Winner	Mayoral Vote	Total Vote	Dominant Party %	Dominant Party Mean	Council Majority	% Time Dominant Party Held Mayorship	% Time Dominant Party Majority of Council	Mean Time Dominant Party Held Mayor/ Council Maj.	Means Combined	Divided by 2 and Sub- tracted from base of 100%	Final Score
1970	D	34,524-D 16,641-R	51,165	68%	51%	D	25%	100%	63%	114%	43%	.43
1974	R	26,165-D 26,874-R	53,039	49%		D						
1978	R	23,627-D 29,996-R	53,623	44%		D						
1982	R	22,837-D 32,490-R	55,327	41%		D						

Table B.2
Electoral Competition Index: Foster

Year	Mayoral Winner	Mayoral Vote	Total Vote	Dominant Party %	Dominant Party Mean	Council Majority	% Time Dominant Party Held Mayorship	% Time Dominant Party Majority of Council	Mean Time Dominant Party Held Mayor/ Council Maj.	Means Combined	Divided by 2 and Sub-tracted from base of 100%	Final Score
1970	R	634	1070	59%	59%	R	100%	67%	84%	143%	28%	.28
1972	R	735	1239	59%		R						
1974	R	566	1112	51%		D						
1976	R	712	1313	54%		D						
1978	R	662	1236	54%		R						
1980	R	881	1508	58%		R						
1982	R	885	885	100%		R						

Table B.3
The Press Pluralism Index: Summary Information

City	Newspapers*	.6n	Combined Circulation	Population
Providence	7	4.2	46,083	110,667
Foster	1	0.6	822**	2,309

*Source: *1982 Ayer Directory of Publicatons* (Bala Cynwyd, Pa.: IMS Press, 1982), pp. 809-10.

**Source: *Providence Journal-Bulletin Almanac, 1982* (Providence, R.I.: Journal-Bulletin Co., 1982), p. 211.

APPENDIX C
Interview Schedule

Code Number_____
                              (1-3)

Interviewer Name:_____

1. Municipality   (4) Providence   1
                                       Foster   2

2. Gender   (5) Male   1
                                       Female   2

Screening Questions: Do Not Code
    Are you a resident of (name of municipality)?
    And are you 18 or older?

3. About how long have you lived in (municipality)? (6)_____

4. And were you born in (municipality)?

                        (7) Yes   1
                             No   2
                             Dk/Ra   6

5. Would you say that you follow town (or city) politics and government regularly, from time to time, or almost never?

                        (8) Regularly   1
                             Time to time   2
                             Almost never   3
                             Dk/Ra   6

6. What about newspapers? Do you follow local politics and government in the newspapers every day, once a week, from time to time, or almost never?

	(9)	Every day	1
		Once a week	2
		Time to time	3
		Almost never	4
		Dk/Ra	6

7. And what about radio? Do you listen to news of local politics and government every day, once a week, from time to time, or almost never?

	(10)	Every day	1
		Once a week	2
		Time to time	3
		Almost never	4
		Dk/Ra	6

8. How about television? Do you watch it for news about local politics and government every day, once a week, from time to time, or almost never?

	(11)	Every day	1
		Once a week	2
		Time to time	3
		Almost never	4
		Dk/Ra	6

9. Most people have personal interests or problems that take up much of their time. In view of this, what part should the ordinary person play in (Providence or Foster's) politics and government? (PROBE, if needed) What specifically should the ordinary citizen do?

_____ (12)
_____ (13)
_____ (14)

10. Where do you think a person's vote counts the most—in a local election, in a statewide election, or in a national election?

	(15)	Local	1
		Statewide	2
		National	3
(Volunteered)		All the Same	4
(Volunteered)		Doesn't Count	5
(Volunteered)		Dk/Ra	6

11. Suppose you were interested in running for office in (municipality), do you think you would be able to run for office, or don't you think you would be able to run?

	(16)	Yes	1
		No	2
		Dk/Ra	6

12. Why? _____

_____

(17)

13. I am going to read you four brief statements. Tell me which one comes closest to the truth in (Foster or Providence). When talking about politics . . .

(18)	People can say anything they please	1
	People can say almost anything they please	2
	People can say some things but they have to be careful what they say out loud	3
	People who don't talk the party line have a hard time	4
	(Dk/Ra)	6

14. How legal and fair would you say elections are in (name of municipality), are they almost always legal and fair, usually legal and fair, seldom legal and fair, or almost never legal and fair?

(19)	Almost always	1
	Usually legal and fair	2
	Seldom legal and fair	3
	Almost never legal and fair	4
	(Dk/Ra)	6

15. How much attention do you pay to the campaigning that goes on at the time of a local election—a lot of attention, a little attention, not much attention, or no attention at all?

(20)	A lot of attention	1
	A little attention	2
	Not much attention	3
	No attention at all	4
	(Dk/Ra)	6

I'm going to read you a short list of a few types of organizations, groups, and clubs. Tell me if you are a member of each type (if "yes," ASK "How many?") Are you a member of a . . .

16.	Labor union	(21)	_____
17.	Business group	(22)	_____
18.	Social club	(23)	_____
19.	Professional association	(24)	_____
20.	Neighborhood group	(25)	_____
21.	Farm organization	(26)	_____
22.	Fraternal group	(27)	_____
23.	Veterans group	(28)	_____
24.	Sports club	(29)	_____
25.	Political club	(30)	_____
26.	Service club	(31)	_____
27.	Hobby or garden club	(32)	_____
28.	Religious organization	(33)	_____

29. Any other organization or club _____

_____

                                                   (34)   (35)

30. (If a member of some organization or club) Of the organizations to which you belong, which ones are concerned with governmental or political affairs?

_____ (36-39)

31. Have you voted in any of the last three local elections in (name of municipality)?
        (40)   Yes   1
               No   2
               Dk/Ra   6

32. I'm going to read you four brief statements. Which one comes closest to describing your feelings when you go to vote. (Read Answers)
        (41)   I get a feeling of satisfaction out of it   1
               I do it only because it is my duty   2
               I feel annoyed, it's a waste of time   3
               I don't feel anything in particular   4
                                 (Dk/Ra)   6

33. In your opinion, do you think that groups like the Ku Klux Klan, the American Nazi Party, or the Socialist Worker's Party should be allowed to hold rallies in (name of city) city parks?

_____

                                                   (42)

Foster interviews skip to Question 37

34. Providence interviews ask: Thinking back to the last election for mayor in 1978, did you vote in that election between Buddy Cianci and Frank Darigan?
            (43) Yes   1
                 No   2
                 Dk/Ra   6

35. (If no, skip to Question 36). If "yes," ask: And what person did you vote for—Frank Darigan, the Democrat, or Buddy Cianci, the Republican?
            (44) Darigan   1
                 Cianci   2
                 Dk/Ra   6
36. And in 1980 did you vote in the city home rule charter referendum?
            (45) Yes   1
                 No   2
                 Dk/Ra   6

Providence interviews skip to Question 42

37. In Foster, did you vote in the last election for Town Council in 1980?

	(46)	Yes	1
		No	2
		Dk/Ra	6

38. Have you attended any of the town meetings that dealt with the gypsy moth problem in Foster?

	(47)	Yes	1
		No	2
		Dk/Ra	6

39. Have you attended any of the town meetings that discussed the relocation and renovation of the City Hall in Foster?

	(48)	Yes	1
		No	2
		Dk/Ra	6

40. Did you attend any of the town meetings that were held to discuss the Stop I-84 problem?

	(49)	Yes	1
		No	2
		Dk/Ra	6

41. Have you attended any of the annual town meetings to discuss the town budget over the last three years?

	(50)	Yes	1
		No	2
		Dk/Ra	6

42. In the future, do you plan to continue to live in (name of municipality) or do you expect to move out?

	(51)	Continue to live in	1
		Expect to move	2
		Dk/Ra	6

43. Is there any political leader in (name of municipality) who is a close friend or relative of your family?

_____

_____

(52)

Finally, just a few quick questions for statistical purposes only.

44. As far as local elections are concerned, do you consider yourself a Democrat, a Republican, an Independent, or what?

	(53)	Democrat	1
		Republican	2
		Independent	3
		Dk/Ra	6

If "Independent," "Don't Know," or "Refused," ask, "Would you say you lean toward the Republican side or toward the Democratic side?"

(54)	Democrat	1
	Republican	2
	Independent	3
	Dk/Ra	6

45. What is your religious preference?

(55)	Catholic	1
	Protestant	2
	Jewish	3
	Atheist	4
	Other	5
	Dk/Ra	6

46. (If religious preference) Would you say you go to (church/synagogue) more than once a week, weekly, almost every week, once or twice a month, a few times a year, or almost never?

(56)	more than once a week	1
	weekly	2
	almost every week	3
	once/twice a month	4
	a few times a year	5
	almost never	7
	Dk/Ra	6

47. And is your race white, black, Hispanic, Chicano, Asian, American Indian, or what?

(57)	White	1
	Black	2
	Hispanic	3
	Chicano	4
	Asian	5
	American Indian	7
	Dk/Ra	6

48. And which of these age groups are you in? (READ ANSWERS)

(58)	18-24	1
	25-34	2
	35-49	3
	50-64	4
	Over 64	5
	Dk/Ra	6

49. Is your total family income (READ ANSWERS)

(59)	Under 6,000	1
	Between 6,000 and 12,000	2
	Between 12,000 and 18,000	3

Between 18,000 and 25,000	4
Between 25,000 and 35,000	5
Over 35,000	7
Dk/Ra	6

50. Are you single, married, divorced, widowed, or separated?

(60) Single	1
Married	2
Divorced	3
Widowed	4
Separated	5
Dk/Ra	6

51. How many children do you have?

_____ (61 & 62)

— THANK YOU —

APPENDIX D

Are All U.S. Cities Necessarily Polyarchies?

ON NONPOLYARCHAL U.S. MUNICIPALITIES

In response to the possible assertion that all U.S. municipalities must *necessarily* be polyarchies, I would submit the following article describing Plaquemines parish in Louisiana. The story below, if accurate, leaves considerable room for doubt whether Plaquemines parish meets several of the eight conditions of polyarchy.

Election Signals End of Delta Dynasty

By WENDELL RAWLS Jr.

Special to The New York Times

POINTE A LA HACHE, La., Jan. 6 — For more than 60 years the ardently racist Judge Leander Perez and his sons ran the mineral-rich Plaquemines Parish like a third world dictatorship and injected their influence into state and national politics.

Now the sun 's setting on their control. For the first time in more than two decades, the people here will be allowed to vote for leaders of the parish, which is a political subdivision like a county.

More than 50 candidates are running in an election Jan. 22 for seven available seats on what will be a new nine-member Parish Commission Council. The election is the result of a Federal court consent decree signed by the old five-member council to settle a voter discrimination lawsuit filed in 1975 by a black group.

The settlement provided for the election of councilors from nine districts instead of five members selected at large. The suit had contended that the at-large system diluted blacks' political strength.

In the 21 years since Judge Perez formed the commission council form of government, either he or his son, Chalin, anointed the other four members of the commission; since they faced no opposition, there were no elections. Judge Perez, who died in 1969, was president of the commission for the first six years of its existence and Chalin held the office for the next 15.

The younger Perez insists that he had to face election when he took over the commission in 1967, but the seriousness of that campaign is called into question by the fact that his opponent lived and worked in Mississippi.

The settlement of the lawsuit last fall, which Mr. Perez opposed, was only the latest in a series of political and legal setbacks for the sons of the man who called his fiefdom "the promised land" and ran it as though he were a pharoah.

The first problems emerged almost four years ago when Chalin, who is 59 years old, openly split with his brother, Leander Jr., who is 61 and inherited his father's job as District Attorney, the most powerful position in the parish.

First the commission council refused to allow the District Attorney to use parish funds to buy an airplane for his office. Then Leander impaneled a grand jury to investigate charges of misuse of parish funds and equipment. The grand jury indicted Chalin and a few others, but when it began to investigate Leander, he dismissed it.

Source: Wendell Rawls, Jr., "Louisiana Election Signals End of Delta Dynasty," *New York Times*, January 11, 1983, p. A16.

Request to Move Trial

The indictments against Chalin were later dismissed by the state attorney general, but Leander remains under indictment on charges of malfeasance for dismissing the grand jury.

An indication of the Perez sons' loss of power came last year when Leander said he could not get a fair trial in Plaquemines Parish, which his family had dominated for six decades, and asked to have his trial moved.

In 1981, Chalin Perez's wife, Lynn Perkins Perez, who is also a lawyer, ran for election as a judge on Louisiana's Fourth Circuit Court of Appeals. She was defeated by a 2 to 1 ratio that stretched to 8 to 1 in some areas of the parish.

In another setback last year, three of the five members of the commission council voted to remove Chalin Perez as president. More recently, the commission voted to strip him of most of his responsibilities.

While two of the five council members are running unopposed for seats on the new panel, Chalin has decided not to run for re-election, saying, "I don't want to be a part of what is certain to be a mess."

Rich Deposits of Oil and Gas

The parish the Perezes have dominated, which stretches southeast along the Mississippi River from the New Orleans city limits, virtually floats on oil. It is a flat, wind-blown, sun-baked semi-tropical expanse of sawgrass and cypress, cane and cattle and cottonwood floating above some of the world's richest deposits of oil and gas and sulfur.

Judge Perez controlled the petroleum and the people. In Louisiana politics he was second only to the late Huey Long in power and infuence, and he always helped Long. The extent of his power was such that in the 1930 race for the Senate, St. Bernard Parish, which was part of Judge Perez's 25th District, cast 3,979 votes for Huey Long and 9 for his opponent. St. Bernard Parish had 2,454 registered voters at the time.

Today, Luke Petrovich, the vice chairman of the council, says the Perez dynasty is "not yet dead."

"Chalin is still chairman of the parish Democratic executive committee and still a member of the state central committee of the Democratic Party, and his brother still functions to some extent as District Attorney and has another year or so in office," he said. "I see the end for them politically, but there is still some life left. They still have large financial interests in or claims on parish-owned or held mineral rights."

Chalin Perez contends that there never was a dynasty, "except in the minds of some people," although he acknowledged that he and his father appointed the other members of the council and exercised mineral rights to parish lands on "leases my daddy signed 50 years ago when I was playing marbles."

'Set Back 50 Years'

"We have had an ideal form of government for 21 years," he said, "and now by the stroke of the pen of a Federal judge we have been set back 50 years."

Although he acknowledged that he and his father were "against forced mixing of races," he said racial discrimination was not a problem in the parish, where more than 25 percent of the voters are black. "Ninety percent of the blacks in my area support me, and every black who wants to register to vote has registered," he said.

He added that he thought blacks were not so concerned about integration as in the recent past. "Blacks have had their little fling, so to speak, and now people want to be with their own kind," he said.

Certainly that was the way Judge Perez wanted it.

"There are only two kinds of Negroes," he said. "The good ones are darkies and the bad ones are niggers."

He resisted integration as vigorously as possible and reopened an decaying Spanish fortress for use as a detention camp for civil rights workers and reporters who ventured into his parish.

National Guard Sent as Escort

Judge Perez, who kept the title he gained during a brief stint in state court in the 1920's, was not above hiring gunmen from Texas to support his position or resisting other authority. When an opposition governor appointed a sheriff over his objections, the judge posted deputies at the parish line to turn him back. He acquiesced only after the governor dispatched a National Guard unit with machine guns to escort the new sheriff into office.

While consumed with racism, anti-Communism and state's rights, Judge Perez also made untold millions from his oil and mineral operations on public lands. He ran it all almost as an unopposed monarch, once professing: "Democracy. I hate that word."

When an exasperated Huey Long once told him, "Sometimes I wish I could cut Plaquemines loose and let it drift out into the Gulf," Judge Perez replied, "I wish you could."

But now, almost 14 years after his death, it appears that what is about to be set adrift is the Perez political dynasty.

APPENDIX E
Polyarchy and Path Analysis

While further research may prove otherwise, I drew upon the Providence and Foster research to suggest tentative paths which polyarchies may follow in becoming strong polyarchies.

Figure E.1
Polyarchy and Path Analysis

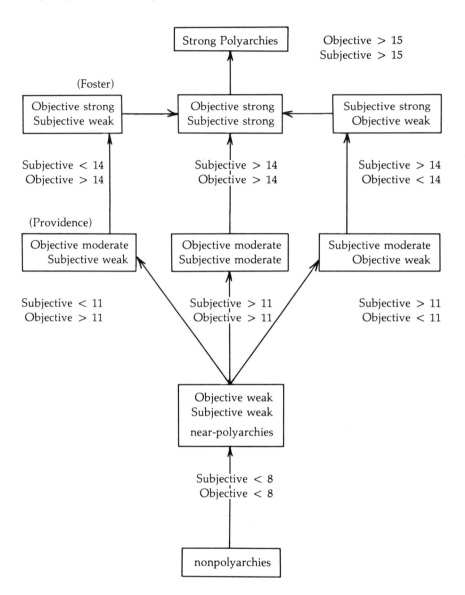

Notes

1. Floyd Hunter, *Community Power Structure* (Chapel Hill: University of North Carolina Press, 1953), and *Community Power Succession* (Chapel Hill: University of North Carolina Press, 1980); G. William Domhoff, *Higher Circles* (New York: Random House, 1970); and Robert A. Dahl, *Who Governs?* (New Haven: Yale University Press, 1961).

2. Robert A. Dahl and Charles E. Lindblom, *Politics, Economics, and Welfare* (New York: Harper & Row, 1953).

3. New Haven is a case in point. See Dahl, *Who Governs?*; Domhoff, *Who Really Rules?: New Haven and Community Power* (Santa Monica, Calif.: Goodyear, 1978); and Dahl's reply, "Who Really Rules?" *Social Science Quarterly* 60 (June 1979): 144-51.

4. David Ricci, *Community Power and Democratic Theory* (New York: Random House, 1971), see especially chapter 11, "The Present Scholarly Impasse," pp. 205-16; and Clarence N. Stone's recent confirmation that the problem continues to plague community power studies. Stone, "Community Power Structure: A Further Look," *Urban Affairs Quarterly* 16 (1981): 505-15. See also Ricci, *The Tragedy of Political Science: Politics, Scholarship, and Democracy* (New Haven: Yale University Press, 1984), see especially chapter 8, "Political Laws, Community Power, and Critical Theory," pp. 249-88.

5. Robert J. Waste (ed.), *Community Power: Directions for Future Research* (Beverly Hills, Calif.: Sage Publications, 1986).

6. For a recent and well-written narrative of how this tone of normative inquiry, of democratic reformism, has gradually been downplayed in urban scholarship since the Progressive era, see Michael H. Frisch, "Urban Theorists, Urban Reform, and American Political Culture," *Political Science Quarterly* 97 (Summer 1982): 295-316.

7. Christian Bay, "Politics and Pseudo-Politics: A Critical Evaluation of Some Behavioral Literature," *American Political Science Review* 59 (March 1965): 39-51; Jack Walker, "A Critique of the Elitist Theory of Democracy," *American Political Science Review* 60 (June 1966): 285-95; and Harvey Mansfield's *ad hominem* review

of Dahl's *After the Revolution* (New Haven: Yale University Press, a Yale Fastback, 1970), reprinted in Mansfield, *The Spirit of Liberalism* (Cambridge, Mass.: Harvard University Press, 1978). See especially page 62, where Mansfield argues that "he who writes a fastback has no time for the fact-value distinction."

8. Dahl, *Who Governs?* pp. 220, 325.

9. C. Wright Mills, *The Power Elite* (New York: Galaxy, 1956). See also, Mills, "The Social Life of Modern Community," in Irving L. Horowitz, *Power, Politics, and People* (New York: Oxford University Press, 1967), pp. 39-52; "The American Business Elite: A Collective Portrait," *Journal of Economic History* 4 (December (1945), Supplement V; "The Middle Class in Middle-Sized Communities," 11 (October 1946): 20-44; and "The Structure of Power in American Society," *British Journal of Sociology* 9 (1958): 29-41. Other adherents of elite explanation include G. William Domhoff, *Who Rules America?* (Englewood Cliffs, N.J.: Prentice-Hall, 1967), and *Who Really Rules? New Haven and Community Power Reexamined* (Santa Monica, Calif.: Goodyear, 1978); Gabriel Kolko, *Wealth and Power in America* (New York: Praeger, 1962); and Floyd Hunter, *Community Power Structure, Top Leadership, USA* (Chapel Hill: University of North Carolina Press, 1959), and *Community Power Succession*.

10. Robert A. Dahl, *Who Governs?* p. 325.

11. Ibid., p. 220.

12. Robert A. Dahl and Charles E. Lindblom, *Politics, Economics, and Welfare* (1953), cited hereafter as *PEW*; 2d ed. (Chicago: University of Chicago Press, 1976); Dahl (ed.), *Political Oppositions in Western Democracies* (New Haven: Yale University Press, 1966); Dahl, *Polyarchy: Participation and Opposition* (New Haven: Yale University Press, 1971); and Dahl (ed.), *Regimes and Oppositions* (New Haven: Yale University Press, 1973).

13. Dahl and Lindblom, *PEW*, p. 275. See also Dahl's discussion of New Haven as a polyarchy in Dahl, "Who Really Rules?" *Social Science Quarterly* 60 (June 1979): 149, n. 2.

14. Floyd Hunter, *Community Power Structure*, 1953. See also his more recent update, *Community Power Succession*, 1980.

15. See C. Wright Mills, *The Power Elite*; G. William Domhoff, *The Higher Circles*; and Paul Sweezy, *The Present as History* (New York: Monthly Review Press, 1953).

16. Domhoff, *Who Really Rules?* p. 8.

17. Notable among these are two participants in the 1960 New Haven study, Nelson Polsby and Raymond Wolfinger. See Polsby, *Community Power and Political Theory* (New Haven: Yale University Press, 1963), and his revised second edition, *Community Power and Political Theory: A Further Look at Problems of Evidence and Inference* (New Haven: Yale University Press, 1980). See also Polsby, " 'Pluralism' in the Study of Community Power: Or *Erklarung* Before *Verklarung* in *Wissenssoziologie*," *The American Sociologist* 4 (May 1969): 118-22; "Community Power: Some Reflections on the Recent Literature," *American Sociological Review* (December 1962): 838-41; "How to Study Community Power: The Pluralist Alternative," *Journal of Politics* (August 1960): 474-84; "Power in Middletown: Fact and Value in Community Research," *Canadian Journal of Economics and Social Science* (November 1960): 592-603; "Community Power Meets Air Pollution,"

Contemporary Sociology 1 (March 1972): 88-91; and "Empirical Investigation of the Mobilization of Bias in Community Power Research," *Political Studies* 27 (December 1979): 527-41. See also Raymond Wolfinger, "Reputation and Reality in the Study of 'Community Power,' " *American Sociological Review* 25 (October 1960): 841-47; "Nondecisions and the Study of Local Politics," *American Political Science Review* 65 (December 1971): 1063-1104; and *The Politics of Progress* (Englewood Cliffs, N.J.: Prentice-Hall, 1974). For a sharp contrast to the defense of Dahl, polyarchy, and the pluralist approach to studying community power, see the oftentimes trenchant criticisms advanced by several members of the Caucus for a New Political Science, including Philip Green and Sanford Levinson (eds.), *Power and Community* (New York: Vintage, 1970); Marvin Surkin and Alan Wolfe, *An End to Political Science* (New York: Basic Books, 1970); and, more recently, Philip Green, *Retrieving Democracy* (Totowa, N.J.: Rowman and Allanheld, 1985).

18. See David Ricci, *Community Power and Democratic Theory: The Logic of Political Analysis* (New York: Random House, 1971), chapter 11, "The Present Scholarly Impasse," pp. 205-16; and Ricci, *The Tragedy of Political Science*, pp. 269-73.

19. A recent step forward in the effort to empirically operationalize community power methodologies is Floyd Hunter's *Community Power Succession: Atlanta's Policy-Makers Revisited*. Hunter offers a numerically weighted interview methodology that makes it possible to rank various members of a community's "power structure." See Hunter, *Power Succession*, pp. 40-65. See also a promising attempt to refine Hunter's method in Philip J. Trounstine and Terry Christensen, *Movers and Shakers: The Study of Community Power* (New York: St. Martin's Press, 1982), pp. 54-77. Note also the tentative pluralist alternative for studying community power sketched by Polsby in *Community Power and Political Theory* (1963), chapter 7, "Notes for a Theory of Community Power," pp. 122-39.

20. Clarence N. Stone, "Community Power Structure: A Further Look," *Urban Affairs Quarterly* 16 (June 1981): 505.

21. Nelson Polsby, *Community Power and Political Theory*, 1980, p. ix.

22. The method for empirically operationalizing polyarchy used in the present study is described in chapter 5. For a brief summary of the methodology and the interview schedule used, see appendices A-C.

23. Two accounts that trace the views of various political philosophers on what moderns would call interest group or "pressure politics" are Robert M. MacIver, "Interests," *Encylopaedia of the Social Sciences*, and Peter Odegard's introduction to Arthur F. Bentley, *The Process of Government* (Cambridge, Mass.: Harvard University Press, 1967), pp. vii-xxvii. At one point, Odegard argues that Bentley's "process-transactionalism" "echos" the writings of Heraclitus and Lucretius, p. xxvii.

24. Mancur Olson, *The Logic of Collective Action* (Cambridge, Mass.: Harvard University Press, 1965); Theodore Lowi, *The End of Liberalism* (New York: W. W. Norton, 1969), and "The Public Philosophy: Interest Group Liberalism," *American Political Science Review* (March 1967): 5-24; Myron Q. Hale, "The Cosmology of Arthur F. Bentley," in William E. Connolly (ed.), *The Bias of Liberalism* (New York: Lieber-Atherton, 1969), pp. 35-50; David Ricci, *Community Power and Democratic Theory* (New York: Random House, 1971); Stanley Rothman, "Systematic Political Theory: Observations on the Group Approach," *American Political Science Review*

(March 1960): 139-45; G. David Garson, *Group Politics* (Beverly Hills, Calif.: Sage Publications, 1978); and William Kelso, *American Democratic Theory: Pluralism and Its Critics* (Westport, Conn.: Greenwood Press, 1978).

25. This definition of pluralism seems adequate for the present work. For a detailed discussion of the difficulties of defining pluralism and a list of "definitions of pluralism," see Nelson W. Polsby, " 'Pluralism' in the Study of Community Power: Or *Erklarung* Before *Verklarung* in *Wissenssoziologie*," *The American Sociologist* 4 (May 1969): 118-22: and Raymond Wolfinger, *The Politics of Progress*, chapter 1. For a more expansive definition of pluralism, including a discussion and definition of four different variants of pluralism applicable to the study of local government, see Robert J. Waste, "Community Power and Pluralist Theory," in Waste (ed.), *Community Power: Future Directions in Urban Research*.

26. James Madison, *Federalist* 10 and 51, in Henry Steele Commager (ed.), *Selections from The Federalist* (New York: Appleton-Century-Crofts, 1949), pp. 9-15, 85-88.

27. See Dahl's criticism of the logic of "Madisonian Democracy" in *A Preface to Democratic Theory* (Chicago: University of Chicago Press, 1956), pp. 4-33.

28. Alexis de Tocqueville, *Democracy in America*, the Henry Reeve text, rev. Francis Bowen (ed.), 2 vols. (New York: Colonial Press, 1900). See also Marvin Zetterbaum, "Alexis de Tocqueville," in Leo Strauss and Joseph Cropsey (eds.), *History of Political Philosophy*, 2d ed. (Chicago: Rand McNally, 1972), pp. 715-36; and Connolly (ed.), *The Bias of Pluralism* (New York: Lieber-Atherton, 1973), pp. 4-8.

29. Tocqueville, *Democracy in America*, 1, chapter 15, p. 274.

30. Tocqueville, *Democracy in America*, 1, chapters 6 and 16.

31. Tocqueville's discussion of the "principle of self-interest rightly understood" is located at vol. 2, chapters 7-9, pp. 129-39. See Zetterbaum's discussion of "SIRU" in "Tocqueville," pp. 726-43; and *Tocqueville and the Problem of Democracy* (Stanford: Stanford University Press, 1967).

32. Tocqueville, *Democracy in America*, the Henry Reeve text, rev. ed. (New York: Vintage-Knopf, 1958), 1, p. 255, cited by Zetterbaum in "Tocqueville," p. 730.

33. Tocqueville, *Democracy in America*, 1, chapters 17 and 18.

34. John C. Calhoun, *Disquisition on Government* (New York: Appleton-Century-Crofts, 1964). Calhoun's full view was set out in a series of three works including the "South Carolina Exposition" (1850), the *Disquisition on Government* (1851), and the *Discourse on the Constitution and Government of the United States* (1851).

35. In fact, Calhoun resigned as Andrew Jackson's vice president in 1832 when Jackson rejected Calhoun's position on tariffs and his adherence to the doctrine of nullification of federal policies by the states.

36. Howard L. Hurwitz, *Encyclopedic Dictionary of American History* (New York: Washington Square Press, 1970), pp. 89-90.

37. See also Tocqueville's discussion of "the most galling tyranny . . . [oppression] by a small faction, or by a single individual, with impunity." *Democracy in America*, 1, chapter 7, p. 195.

38. See Ralph Lerner, "Calhoun's New Science of Politics," *American Political Science Review* (December 1963): 924.

39. Calhoun was not the first American theorist to raise the question of interposition—the doctrine of state legislatures ignoring or nullifying an act of Congress.

Thomas Jefferson in the Kentucky Resolution (1798) and James Madison in the Virginia Resolution (1799) raised similar arguments in response to the Alien and Sedition Acts passed by the Federalists in 1798. It is worth noting that the state interposition doctrine popularly identified with Calhoun's "Negtative," was raised prior to Calhoun and outside of the South. See the discussion of Richard B. Morris (ed.), *Encyclopedia of American History* (New York: Harper, 1953), pp. 153, 166-72, of the Democratic Societies and their role in the Whiskey Insurrection in western Pennsylvania (1794) and the Hartford convention (December 1814) at which angry New England Federalists reacted to the embargo policies enacted by a Republican-dominated Congress. The Morriss discussion is cited in Dahl (ed.), *Political Oppositions in Western Democracies* (New Haven: Yale University Press, 1966); Dahl, "The American Oppositions: Affirmation and Denial," p. 51; and Dahl, *Democracy in the United States: Promise and Performance*, 4th ed. (Boston: Houghton Mifflin, 1981). Although Madison appeared to condone a form of the nullification doctrine, he believed that it should not be made too easy for the states to accomplish. He opposed, for example, a plan in which state action superseded federal action unless overruled by three-fourths of the states. Saul K. Paddover (ed.), *The Complete Madison* (New York: Harper, 1953), pp. 152-58.

40. Arthur F. Bentley, *The Process of Government* (Chicago: University of Chicago Press, 1908), reissued by the Principia Press, Bloomington, Indiana in 1935, 1949 (with an introduction by H. T. Davis), and 1955. It was reissued again, with an introduction by Peter Odegard, in 1967 by Harvard University Press.

41. Mancur Olson, *The Logic of Collective Action* (Cambridge, Mass.: Harvard University Press, 1965), p. 112.

42. Bentley, *Process of Government*, cited in Stanley Rothman, "Systematic Political Theory: Observations on the Group Approach," *American Political Science Review* (March 1960): 139.

43. A quick guide to Bentley's approach and his strident manner can be found in *Process of Government*, p. 222: "There are no political phenomena except group phenomena." Thus, the proper focus of political science is the study of "the political interests and activities of any given group . . . [which] are directed against other activities of men, who appear in groups, political or other." While Bentley and, later, Truman were the major theoretical spokesmen for the emerging study of what Peter Odegard was to label "pressure politics" in 1928, they were not alone in focusing on group or pressure politics. Others involved in the study of groups, their influence, and their role in American politics at about the same time as Bentley and Truman were, as Odegard notes: "Peter Odegard, *Pressure Politics: The Story of the Anti-Saloon League* (New York, 1928) . . . Edward Pendleton Herring, *Group Representation Before Congress* (Baltimore, 1929); Harwood Childs, *Labor and Capital in National Politics* (Columbus, Ohio, 1930); E. E. Schattschneider, *Politics, Pressures and the Tariff* (New York, 1953); M. Louise Rutherford, *The Influence of the American Bar Association on Public Opinion and Legislation* (Philadelphia, 1937); Donald C. Blaisdell, *Economic Power and Political Pressures* (Washington, D.C., 1941); Oliver Garceau, *The Political Life of the American Medical Association* (Cambridge, 1941); and Stephen Bailey, *Congress Makes a Law: The Story Behind the Employment Act of 1946* (New York, 1950). Among other general works are Herman Beyle, *Identification and Analysis of Attribute Cluster-Blocs* (Chicago, 1931); Edward Pendleton Herring, *Public Administration and the Public Interest*

(New York, 1936); Avery Leiserson, *Administrative Regulation: A Study in the Representation of Interests* (Chicago, 1942); . . . and Earl Latham, *The Group Basis of Politics: A Study in Basing Point Legislation* (Ithaca, New York, 1952). Among the many voting studies that owe much to Bentley one might cite Paul F. Lazarsfeld, Bernard Berelson, and Hazel Gaudet, *The People's Choice: How the Voter Makes up His Mind in a Presidential Campaign* (New York, 1948); A. Campbell, G. Gurin, and W. E. Miller, *The Voter Decides* (Evanston, Illinois, 1954); B. R. Berelson, P. F. Lazarsfeld, and W. N. McPhee, *Voting: A Study of Opinion Formation in a Presidential Campaign* (Chicago, 1954); and Angus Campbell, et al., *The American Voter* (New York, 1960). Bentley's emphasis on the need for analysis of small groups and subgroups is reflected in *Group Dynamics: Research on Theory*, ed. Dorwin Cartwright and Alvin Zandler (Evanston, Illinois, 1953); and Herbert Hyman, *Political Socialization: A Study in the Psychology of Political Behavior* (Glencoe, Illinois, 1959); and a brilliant article by Herbert McCloskey and Harold Dahlgren, 'Primary Group Influence on Party Loyalty,' *American Political Science Review*, 52 (September 1959: 757-76)." Odegard, "Introduction" to the 1963 Harvard University Press edition of Bentley's *Process of Government*. Odegard's list is admirably complete. The citation in its entirety includes reference to several additional studies of interest groups in non-American settings, e.g., Samuel Finer, *Autonomous Empire: A Study of the Lobby in Great Britain* (London, 1965). One further addition would seem to make this list complete. Few theoretical studies of the times were as important as Raymond A. Bauer, Ithiel de Sola Pool, and Lewis A. Dexter, *American Business and Public Policy: The Politics of Foreign Trade* (New York: Atherton, 1963); and a celebrated review of the Bauer, Dexter, and Pool book by Theodore Lowi, "Business, Public Policy and Political Theory," *World Politics* 16 (1964): 677-715.

44. Bentley, *Process of Government*, p. 184.

45. Ibid.

46. Garson, *Group Politics*; J. David Greenstone, "Group Theories," in Fred Greenstein and Nelson Polsby (eds.), *The Handbook of Political Science* (Reading, Mass.: Addison-Wesley, 1975), vol. II, pp. 243-318; Hale, "The Cosmology of Arthur F. Bentley"; Kelso, *American Democratic Theory: Pluralism and Its Critics*; Lowi, "The Public Philosophy: Interest Group Liberalism," and *The End of Liberalism*; Olson, *The Logic of Collective Action*.

47. Rothman, "Observations on the Group Approach."

48. Bentley, *Process of Government*, p. 211.

49. Ibid.

50. See the discussion of "brokerage politics" in John C. Livingston and Robert G. Thompson, *The Consent of the Governed*, 3d ed. (New York: Macmillan, 1971), pp. 83-111.

51. Rothman, "Observations on the Group Approach."

52. Bentley, *Process of Government*, p. 220.

53. Ibid., p. 227.

54. David B. Truman, *The Governmental Process* (New York: Knopf, 1951). See also the writings of Truman's contemporary, Earl Latham, "The Group Basis of Politics: Notes for a Theory," *American Political Science Review* 61 (June 1952): 376-97.

55. Truman, *The Governmental Process*, p. 33.

56. Ibid.

57. Ibid., p. 506.

58. David B. Truman, "Groups and Society," excerpts from *The Governmental Process* (New York: Knopf, 1951), pp. 14-17, 33-44, 506-19, in Norman Luttbeg (ed.), *Public Opinion and Public Policy* (Homewood, Ill.: Dorsey Press, 1968), p. 132. Truman's discussion of factors leading to "effective access" is in *The Governmental Process*, p. 506. See also a critical and useful discussion of "effective access" by Harry Eckstein, *Pressure Group Politics* (Stanford: Stanford University Press, 1960), pp. 34-39. See especially Eckstein's criticism of Bentley's account of group formation. Eckstein argues that it is necessary to "stand Bentley on his head. . . . If interaction among politically active groups produces policy, policy in turn creates politically active groups." Eckstein, *Pressure Group Politics*, p. 37.

59. Truman, *The Governmental Process*; Pendleton Herring, *The Politics of Democracy* (New York: W. W. Norton, 1965), p. 32; See also Joseph Schumpeter, *Capitalism, Socialism and Democracy* (New York: Harper & Row, 1942), pp. 232-302, hereafter cited as *CSD*.

60. Truman, *The Governmental Process*, pp. 506-19.

61. David B. Truman, "Groups and Society," p. 133. Truman cites V. O. Key's study of *Southern Politics*, pp. 235-38.

62. Ibid.

63. David Riesman, *The Lonely Crowd* (New Haven: Yale University Press, orig., 1950, 6th printing February 1963 as a Yale Paperbound), p. 206.

64. Riesman, *The Lonely Crowd*, pp. 206-7.

65. Ibid., p. 216.

66. Ibid.

67. Ibid., pp. 213-14.

68. Ibid., pp. 212-14. For the general outlines of Riesman's larger argument, see chapters 8-11, pp. 163-235. See especially his discussion of the differences between the captains of industry system which characterized McKinley's administration and the veto group system which Riesman believed had come to characterize American politics by the time of FDR's administration.

69. *The Governmental Process*, 2d ed., pp. vi-xii.

70. See also David Truman, "Current Trends," *American Political Science Review* (December 1959): 481-97; and "The American System in Crisis," *Political Science Quarterly* (December 1959). See a critique of this shift in Truman's thinking by Peter Bachrach, "Elite Consensus and Democracy," *Journal of Politics* 24 (August 1962): 439-52.

71. Truman, *The Governmental Process*, 2d ed., p. 37.

72. See classic research on this point by James W. Prothro and Charles M. Griggs, "Fundamental Principles of Democracy: Bases of Agreement and Disagreement," *Journal of Politics* 22 (May 1960): 276-94.

73. Schumpeter, *CSD*, pp. 232-302.

74. Truman, *The Governmental Process*, 2d ed., p. 37.

75. Rothman, "Systematic Political Theory."

76. B. R. Berelson, P. F. Lazarsfeld, and H. Gaudet, *The People's Choice* (New York: Duell, Sloan and Pearce, 1944). In addition to the Berelson study, there was a

large body of literature presumably available to Truman, including Sigmund Freud, *Group Psychology and the Analysis of the Ego* (London: Hogarth, 1945); Leon Festinger, Stanley Schachter, and Kurt W. Black, *Social Pressures in Informal Groups* (New York: Harper, 1950); Alvin Gouldner, *Studies in Leadership: Leadership in Democratic Action* (New York: Harper, 1950); George Hormans, *The Human Group* (New York: Harcourt, Brace, 1950); Muzafer Sherif and Hadley Cantril, *The Psychology of Ego-Involvements: Social Attitudes and Identifications* (New York: John Wiley, 1947); Edward Shils, "Primary Groups in the American Army," in Robert K. Merton and Paul Lazarsfeld (eds.), *Studies in the Scope and Method of "The American Soldier"* (Glencoe, Ill.: Free Press, 1950).

77. Olson, *Logic of Collective Action*.

78. Edward Banfield, *Political Influence* (Glencoe, Ill.: Free Press, 1961); and James Q. Wilson, *Political Organizations* (New York: Basic Books, 1973). Wilson's study includes a criticism of Olson's theory of group formation.

79. Olson, *Logic of Collective Action*. See also Barbara and John Ehrenreich, *The American Health Empire: Power, Profits, and Politics* (New York: Vintage Books, 1971); and Robert R. Alford, *Health Care Politics: Ideological Groups Barriers to Reform* (Chicago: Unviersity of Chicago Press, 1975).

80. Robert Michels, *Political Parties* (orig., 1915, New York: Free Press, 1966), pp. 342-56.

81. Grant McConnell, *Private Power and American Democracy* (New York: Knopf, 1966).

82. Lowi, *End of Liberalism*. See also Lowi, "The Public Philosophy: Interest Group Liberalism," *American Political Science Review* 61 (March 1967): 5-24; and Robert Grady, "Distributive Justice and Hard Choices," a paper delivered at the American Political Science Association Annual Meeting, New York City, September 3-6, 1981.

83. Rothman, "Observations on Systematic Political Science."

84. Olson, *Logic of Collective Action*.

85. Rothman, "Observations on Systematic Political Science," p. 139; Lowi, *End of Liberalism* and "Interest Group Liberalism."

86. McConnell, *Private Power and American Democracy*.

87. John Kenneth Galbraith, *Economics and the Public Purpose* (New York: Houghton Mifflin, 1973).

88. E. E. Schattschneider, *The Semi-Sovereign People* (New York: Holt, Rinehart & Winston, 1960), p. 35.

89. John Kenneth Galbraith, *American Capitalism: The Concept of Countervailing Powers* (Boston: Houghton Mifflin, 1952). See also Galbraith, *The New Industrial State* (Boston: Houghton Mifflin, 1967).

90. Talcott Parsons, "The Distribution of Power in American Society, *World Politics* (October 1967): 123-43. See also Daniel Bell, "The Power Elite—Reconsidered," *American Journal of Sociology* (November 1958): 238-50; Robert A. Dahl, "A Critique of the Ruling Elite Model," *American Political Science Review* (June 1958): 463-69, and "The Concept of Power," *Behavioral Science* (July 1957): 201-15; and Suzanne Keller, *Beyond the Ruling Class: Strategic Elites in Modern Society* (New York: Arno Press, 1963).

91. Dahl and Lindblom, *Politics, Economics, and Welfare* (1953). Despite their many differences, C. Wright Mills reviewed *PEW* quite favorably in the *American*

Sociological Review 19 (August 1954): 495-96. Von Der Muhll cites this review and notes that Mills regarded the Dahl and Lindblom study as "a welcome break from the fact-bound descriptiveness of status quo political science." Von Der Muhll, "Dahl and the Study of Contemporary Democracy," *American Political Science Review* 71 (September 1977): 1076, n. 18; Dahl, *Preface to Democratic Theory* (1956); and Giovanni Sartori, *Democrazia e definizione* (Bologna: Il Mulino, 1958), 2d ed., translated by Sartori and published as *Democratic Theory* (Detroit: Wayne State University Press, 1962).

92. See also the pioneering study by Harry Eckstein, who sought to extend Truman's pluralist model by describing pressure group politics as "a function of three main variables: the pattern of policy, the structure of decision-making both in the government and voluntary associations, and the attitudes—broadly speaking, the 'political culture'—of the society concerned." Eckstein, *Pressure Group Politics* (Stanford: Stanford University Press, 1960), p. 38.

93. Or, more precisely, they reinvented the term. The term was known to the Greeks and Romans. Early English usage includes: "1609 C. BUTLER *Fem. Mon* (1643) 5 The bees abhor as well Polyarchy as Anarchy. 1868 J. SCOTT *Chr. Life* (1696) 56 Any Government . . . whether it be a Monarchy or Polyarchy," *Compact Edition of the Oxford English Dictionary*, vol. II (New York: Oxford University Press, 1979), p. 1086.

94. Sartori, *Democratic Theory*, pp. 124-25.

95. Ibid., p. 461.

96. Dahl and Lindblom, *PEW*, p. 270.

97. The institutional pluralists and their work should be distinguished from a related but separate development in political theory. Pendleton Herring in *Politics of Democracy* (New York: W. W. Norton, 1940); Joseph Schumpeter in *CSD*; Bernard Berelson in "Democratic Theory and Public Opinion," *Public Opinion Quarterly* (Fall 1952): 313-30; and William Kornhauser in *The Politics of Mass Society* (Glencoe, Ill.: Free Press, 1959) developed the competitive or "democratic elite" explanation of democracy. In contrast to the institutional pluralists, the democratic elitists sought both to describe the common political institutions in the West *and* to label these institutions and practices as democratic. Dahl, Lindblom, and Sartori sought to distinguish between the concrete practices and institutions of the West (polyarchy) and the earlier Greek and Enlightenment conceptions of democracy. A third group of theorists sought both to define democracy and to test it empirically. These founders of empirical democratic theory include Anthony Downs, *An Economic Theory of Democracy* (New York: Harper, 1957); Seymour M. Lipset, *Political Man* (Garden City, N.Y.: Doubleday, 1960); James W. Prothro and Charles M. Grigg, "Fundamental Principles of Democracy: Bases of Agreement and Disagreement," *Journal of Politics* 22: 227-29; Gabriel Almond and Sidney Verba, *The Civic Culture* (Princeton: Princeton University Press, 1963); Mostafa Rejai, *Democracy: The Contemporary Theories* (New York: Atherton, 1967); Deane E. Neubauer, "Some Conditions of Democracy," *American Political Science Review* 61 (December 1967): 1002-9; David Braybrooke, *Three Tests for Democracy* (New York: Random House, 1968); Charles F. Cnudde and Deane E. Neubauer, *Empirical Democratic Theory* (Chicago: Markham, 1969). See also Douglas W. Rae and Michael Taylor, *The Analysis of Political Cleavages* (New Haven: Yale University Press, 1970). For an effective critique of the work of empirical democratic theorists,

see John D. May, *Of the Conditions and Measures of Democracy* (Morristown, N.J.: General Learning Press, 1973); and "Defining Democracy: A Bid for Coherence and Consensus," *Political Studies* 26 (March 1978): 1-14. Two of Dahl's books—*A Preface to Democratic Theory* (1956) and *Polyarchy* (1971)—fall within the broad scope of the empirical democratic theory approach. In sum, three approaches temporarily shared the stage: democratic elitists seeking to define the status quo in the West as democratic, institutional pluralists seeking to describe the status quo and distinguish it from democracy per se, and empirical democratic theorists who sought both to define democracy in terms of scientifically testable propositions and, then, to subject status quo political relationships in the West to such testing. Dahl and polyarchy, we shall argue in subsequent chapters, are incompatible with democratic elitism. Dahl is primarily an institutional pluralist, although, as mentioned earlier, *Preface* and *Polyarchy* share interests and links with the studies conducted by the empirical democratic theorists (see chapters 2, 3, and 5, as well as note 49).

98. Ricci, *Community Power and Democratic Theory*, p. 74.

99. Dahl and Lindblom, *PEW*, p. 270.

100. Christian Bay, "Politics and Pseudo-Politics."

101. Ibid.; Walker, "A Critique of the Elitist Theory of Democracy"; Kariel, *Frontiers of Democratic Theory*; Connolly, *The Bias of Pluralism*; Ricci, *Community Power and Democratic Theory*; McCoy and Playford, *Apolitical Politics*.

102. Henry M. Oliver, Jr., review of *Politics, Economics, and Welfare*, in *Journal of Political Economy* 62 (1954): 71.

103. Dahl and Lindblom, *PEW*, pp. 275-76.

104. Ibid., pp. 277-78.

105. Ibid., p. 278.

106. Ibid., p. 277.

107. Ibid. More recently, in an interview (January 14, 1980), Dahl suggested that Mexico with its increasingly strong party system might be more closely a near-polyarchy than a full polyarchy.

108. Dahl and Lindblom, *PEW*, p. 279.

109. Ibid., p. 292.

110. Ibid., p. 289.

111. Ibid., p. 294.

112. Ibid., p. 296.

113. Ibid., p. 302.

114. Ibid., p. 304.

115. Ibid.

116. Ibid., p. 309.

117. Ibid., p. 313.

118. Ibid., p. 315.

119. Ibid., p. 314.

120. Ibid., p. 317.

121. Ibid., p. 319.

122. David Apter, *Introduction to Political Analysis* (Cambridge, Mass.: Winthrop Publishers, 1977), pp. 329-30.

123. Robert A. Dahl, interview (March 31, 1980).

124. For two particularly misguided reviews, see Christian Bay's discussion of

Preface in Bay, "Politics and Pseudo-Politics," *American Political Science Review* 59 (March 1965): 39-51; and Harvey Mansfield's review of *After the Revolution*, reprinted in a collection entitled *The Spirit of Liberalism* (Cambridge, Mass.: Harvard University Press, 1978).

125. See Dahl, *Preface to Democratic Theory* (Chicago: University of Chicago Press, 1956), appendix to chapter 3, pp. 84-90.

126. Dahl, *Polyarchy*, p. 3.

127. See George Von Der Muhll, "Robert A. Dahl and the Study of Contemporary Democracy: A Review Essay," *American Political Science Review* 71 (September 1977): 1070-96; David Ricci, *Community Power and Democratic Theory*, chapter 10, "Pluralism Opposed: The Critique of Tolerance," pp. 161-82; Jack Walker, "A Critique of the Elitist Theory of Democracy," *American Political Science Review* 60 (June 1966); and Henry Kariel (ed.), *Frontiers of Democratic Theory*. See also the criticisms of Dahl's alleged "value-free" methodology in Christian Bay, "Politics and Pseudo-Politics"; George Graham, Jr., "Latent Madisonianism: Before and After *A Preface to Democratic Theory*," *Political Science Reviewer* (Fall 1972): 66-89; Ronald M. Peters, Jr., "Political Theory, Political Science, and the *Preface*: A Review of Robert A. Dahl: *A Preface to Democratic Theory*," *Political Science Reviewer* (Fall 1978): 145-80.

128. Von Der Muhll, "Dahl," p. 1071.

129. Ibid.

130. Robert A. Dahl, *Congress and Foreign Policy* (New York: Harcourt, Brace and Co., 1950).

131. Robert A. Dahl, *Who Governs? Democracy and Power in an American City* (New Haven: Yale University Press, 1961).

132. Robert A. Dahl, *Pluralist Democracy in the United States: Conflict and Consent* (Chicago: Rand McNally, 1st ed., 1967), 2d ed., *Democracy in the United States: Promise and Performance*, 1972; 3d ed., 1980.

133. Robert A. Dahl (ed.), *Political Oppositions in Western Democracies* (New Haven: Yale University Press, 1966); and Dahl (ed.) *Regimes and Oppositions* (New Haven: Yale University Press, 1973).

134. Robert A. Dahl and Ralph S. Brown, *Domestic Control of Atomic Energy* (New York: Social Science Research Council, 1951).

135. Dahl and Lindblom, *PEW*.

136. Robert A. Dahl, *After the Revolution* (New Haven: Yale University Press, 1970).

137. Robert A. Dahl, "The City in the Future of Democracy," *American Political Science Review* 61 (December 1967): 953-70; Dahl and Edward R. Tufte, *Size and Democracy* (Stanford: Stanford University Press, 1973).

138. Robert A. Dahl, *Dilemmas of Pluralist Democracy: Autonomy and Control* (New Haven: Yale University Press, 1984).

139. Stanley W. Moore, "The Political Science of Robert A. Dahl," unpub. Ph.D. diss., Claremont Graduate School, 1971.

140. Dahl and Lindblom, *PEW*, p. 275.

141. Ibid., p. 276.

142. Ibid.

143. Robert A. Dahl, "Atomic Energy and the Democratic Process," *Annals of the American Academy of Political Science* 29 (November 1953): 1.

144. Robert A. Dahl, "Hierarchy, Democracy and Bargaining in Politics and Economics," in *Research Frontiers in Political Science and Government* (Washington, D.C.: Brookings Institute, 1955), p. 45, cited in S. W. Moore, "Robert Dahl," p. viii.

145. Both Etzioni and Sartori regarded Dahl's work as seminal though Etzioni has important value differences with Dahl; Amitai Etzioni, *The Active Society* (New York: Free Press, 1968); Giovanni Sartori, *Democratic Theory* (Detroit: Wayne State University Press, 1961).

146. Dahl, *Preface*, p. 1.

147. See also Daniel Bell, "The Power Elite Reconsidered," *American Sociological Review* (November 1958): 238-50; Raymond Wolfinger, "A Plea for a Decent Burial," *American Sociological Review* (December 1962): 841-47; Talcott Parsons, "The Distribution of Power in American Society," *World Politics* (October 1957); and Nelson Polsby, *Community Power and Political Theory* (New Haven: Yale University Press, 1963), 2d ed., 1980.

148. Robert Dahl, *Polyarchy: Participation and Opposition* (New Haven: Yale University Press, 1971). Primarily theoretical works include *PEW* (1953); *Preface* (1956); "A Critique of the Ruling Elite Model," *American Political Science Review* 52 (June 1958): 462-69; *Modern Political Analysis* (1963); "The City in the Future of Democracy" (1967); *After the Revolution* (1970); *Size and Democracy* (1973); and *Dilemmas of Pluralist Democracy* (1983). Primarily descriptive or empirical works include *Congress and Foreign Policy* (1950); *Who Governs?* (1961); *Political Oppositions* (1966); *Pluralist Democracy in the United States* (1972); and *Regimes and Oppositions* (1973). *Polyarchy* (New Haven: Yale University Press, 1971) is an admixture of both theory construction and attempts at validation.

149. Four recent books are notable exceptions: David Ricci, *The Tragedy of Political Science* (New Haven: Yale University Press, 1984); G. William Domhoff, *Who Really Rules?*; (Santa Monica, Calif.: Goodyear, 1978), and *Who Rules America Now: A View for the 1980's* (Englewood Cliffs, N.J.: Prentice-Hall, 1983); and William Kelso, *American Democratic Theory: Pluralism and Its Critics* (Westport, Conn.: Greenwood Press, 1979). The bulk of the criticism on Dahl and polyarchy came in a one-shot, decade-long avalanche following the publication of *Who Governs?* in 1961 and culminating in the publication of William Connolly (ed.), *The Bias of Pluralism* (1969), and David Ricci, *Community Power and Democratic Theory* (1971). See also Charles A. McCoy and John Playford (eds.), *Apolitical Politics* (New York: Thomas Y. Crowell, 1967); Philip Green and Sanford Levinson, *Power and Community* (New York: Vintage, 1970): Henry Kariel (ed.), *Frontiers of Democratic Theory* (New York: Random House, 1970); Philip Green and Alan Wolfe (eds.), *An End to Political Science* (New York: Basic Books, 1970); and a recent exchange between Dahl and Philip Green in *Dissent* (Summer 1979): 351-68, reprinted in part as chapter 8, "What Is Political Equality?" in Green, *Retrieving Democracy*, p. 174. Green was responding to Dahl's article "On Removing Certain Impediments to Democracy in the United States," which first appeared in *Political Science Quarterly* 92 (Spring 1977): 1-20, and was reprinted in *Dissent* 25 (Summer 1978): 320-24. The argument in greatly expanded form was published by Yale University Press as *Dilemmas of Pluralist Democracy* (1982).

150. Joseph Schumpeter, *Capitalism, Socialism, and Democracy* (New York: Harper, 1961), pp. 232-302; Carole Pateman, *Participation and Democratic Theory* (Cambridge: Cambridge University Press, 1970), pp. 1-21.

151. Ricci, *Community Power*, pp. 184-85.

152. Ibid., pp. 188-91.

153. William Connolly, *Bias*; Theodore Lowi, *End of Liberalism* (New York: W. W. Norton, 1969), and "Interest Group Liberalism," *American Political Science Review* (March 1967): 5-24; and Ricci, *Community Power*.

154. Lowi, "Interest Group Liberalism."

155. Ricci, *Community Power*, pp. 184-85.

156. Ibid., p. 184.

157. Ibid., p. 187.

158. Ibid., p. 190.

159. Arnold S. Kaufman, "Human Nature and Participatory Democracy: Ten Years Later," in Connolly (ed.), *Bias*, pp. 178, 212. Also see Lane Davis, "The Cost of the New Realism," Graeme Duncan and Stephen Lukes, "Democracy Restated," and Henry Kariel, "The Pluralist Norm," in Kariel (ed.), *Frontiers of Democratic Theory*. See also Robert Pranger, *The Eclipse of Citizenship* (New York: Holt, Rinehart & Winston, 1968).

160. Connolly, *Bias*, p. 9; see also the discussion of the "conditions of pluralism" in Robert Presthus, *Men at the Top: A Study in Community Power* (New York: Oxford University Press, 1964), pp. 3-27, 29-41, 430-33.

161. Robert Dahl, "Equality and Power," in William D'Antonio and Howard J. Ehrlich (eds.), *Power and Democracy in America* (Notre Dame, Ind.: Notre Dame University Press, 1961), p. 83.

162. Dahl, *Pluralist Democracy*, p. 38.

163. Dahl, *Who Governs?* and *Pluralist Democracy*, p. 38.

164. See Michael Parenti, "Power and Pluralism: A View from the Bottom," *American Political Science Review*, 32 (1970): 501-30; Jacobus Ten Broek (ed.), *The Law of the Poor* (San Francisco: Chandler, 1966); and Gunnar Myrdal, *Beyond the Welfare State* (New Haven: Yale University Press, 1960).

165. Michael Harrington, *The Other America* (New York: Macmillan, 1960). See also Harrington's recent update, in which he argues persuasively that the twin problems of poverty and invisibility are still very active in American society. Harrington, *The New American Poverty* (New York: Viking-Penguin, 1985).

166. Kariel, *Frontiers*, and *The Decline of American Pluralism* (Stanford: Stanford University Press, 1961); Lowi, *End of Liberalism*, and "Interest Group Politics"; Grant McConnell, *Private Power and American Democracy* (New York: Knopf, 1966). For a recent update, see the collection of essays exploring McConnell's thesis edited by J. David Greenstone, *Public Values, Private Power, and Politics in America* (Chicago: University of Chicago Press, 1983).

167. McConnell, *Private Power*.

168. C. Wright Mills, *The Power Elite*; Suzanne Keller, *Beyond the Ruling Class: Strategic Elites in Modern Society* (New York: Random House, 1963); and G. William Domhoff, *Who Rules America?* (Englewood Cliffs, N.J.: Prentice-Hall, 1967). See also Gabriel Kolko, *Wealth and Power in America* (New York: Praeger, 1962); Floyd Hunter, *Community Power Structure* (Chapel Hill: University of North Carolina Press, 1953); Robert Presthus, *The Organizational Society* (New York: Vintage Books, 1962), and *Men at the Top: A Study in Community Power*; Peter Bachrach and Morton Baratz, "Decisions and Nondecisions: An Analytical Framework," *American Political Science Review* (September 1963): 632-42, and "Two Faces of Power," *American Political Science Review* (December 1967): 947-52.

169. Domhoff, *Who Really Rules?* p. 7.

170. Ibid., p. 4.

171. See Mills, *The Power Elite*; G. William Domhoff, *The Higher Circles* (New York: Random House, 1970), *The Bohemian Grove and Other Retreats: A Study in Ruling Class Cohesiveness* (New York: Harper & Row, 1974), and "Social Clubs, Policy-Planning Groups and Corporations: A Network of Ruling Class Cohesiveness," *The Insurgent Sociologist* (Spring 1975): 179. See also Robert O. Schulze and Leonard V. Blumberg, "The Determination of Local Power Elites," *American Journal of Sociology* (November 1957): 293-96; Harry R. Dick, "A Method for Ranking Community Influentials," *American Sociological Review* (June 1960); and Thomas R. Day and Harmon Zeigler, *The Irony of Democracy*, 4th ed. (North Scituate, Mass.: Duxbury Press, 1978).

172. Jack Walker, "A Critique of the Elitist Theory of Democracy," *American Political Science Review* 60 (June 1966): 285-95; Graeme Duncan and Steven Lukes, "The New Democracy"; Bachrach, *The Theory of Democratic Elitism* (Boston: Little, Brown, 1967); Christian Bay, "Politics and Pseudo-Politics"; Lane Davis, "The Cost of Realism"; J. Farganis and S. W. Rousseaus, "American Politics and the End of Ideology," *British Journal of Sociology* 14 (1964): 347-62.

173. Schumpeter, *Capitalism, Socialism, and Democracy*.

174. Walker, "Critique."

175. The phrase is that of Seymour Martin Lipset. See his introduction to the Collier Books paperback edition of Robert Michels, *Political Parties* (New York: Collier, 1962), p. 33.

176. See Jack Walker, "Critique," p. 285, n. 1. See also the definition of democracy in Lane Davis, "The Cost of Realism," cited in Kariel (ed.), *Frontiers of Democratic Theory*, p. 214, n. 2. Davis notes: "Classical democracy refers to the mainstream of the democratic tradition which includes such diverse figures as the seventeenth-century Levellers, Jean-Jacques Rousseau, Jeremy Bentham, James Mill, and the Jacksonian Democrats. Among its many twentieth-century spokesmen may be mentioned Ernest Barker, John Dewey, A. D. Lindsay and Roland Pennock. Two recent statements which agree on classical democracy though perhaps little else, are Joseph Tussman, *Obligation and the Body Politic* (New York: Oxford University Press, 1960), and Raymond Williams, *The Long Revolution* (New York: Columbia University Press, 1961). See also J. Roland Pennock, *Democratic Theory* (Princeton: Princeton University Press, 1979).

177. Exponents of modern theory are alleged to be Schumpeter, *Capitalism, Socialism, and Democracy*; Bernard Berelson et al., *Voting* (Chicago: University of Chicago Press, 1954), chapter 14; articles by Louis Hartz and Samuel Beer in W. N. Chambers and R. H. Salisbury (eds.), *Democracy in the Mid-20th Century*; S. M. Lipset, *Political Man* (New York: Doubleday, 1960); Robert Dahl, *Preface*, and *Who Governs?* especially pp. 223-325; V. O. Key, Jr., *Public Opinion and American Democracy* (New York: Knopf, 1961), especially part VI; Lester Milbrath, *Political Participation* (Chicago: Rand McNally, 1965). For a general summary of the position see Henry Mayo, *An Introduction to Democratic Theory* New York: Oxford University Press, 1960), cited in Walker, "Critique," p. 285, n. 2. See also Harry Eckstein, "A Stable Theory of Democracy," appendix B, *Division and Cohesion in Democracy* (Princeton: Princeton University Press, 1966). Several writers have strenuously objected to the claim that a single unified classical democratic theory

exists. See Giovanni Sartori, *Democratic Theory*; Carole Pateman, *Participation and Democratic Theory*, especially chapter 1, pp. 1-21; Robert Dahl, *Preface*, p. 87, and "Hierarchy, Democracy and Bargaining in Politics and Economics," in *Research Frontiers*, pp. 138-41.

178. Walker, "Critique," p. 287.

179. V. O. Key, *Public Opinion*; S. M. Lipset, *Political Man*; Robert Lane, *Political Man* (New York: Free Press, 1972); L. W. Milbrath, *Political Participation*; R. Dahl, *Who Governs?* pp. 223-325.

180. See Sidney Verba and Norman Nie for a discussion of current participation levels, *Participation in America* (New York: Harper, 1972). See also Nie, Sidney Verba, and John Petrocik, *The Changing American Voter* (Cambridge, Mass.: Harvard University Press, 1976); and Raymond Wolfinger and Steven Rosenstone, *Who Votes?* (New Haven: Yale University Press, 1980).

181. Kariel, *Decline of American Pluralism*, p. 4.

182. Ibid.

183. See Ricci, *Community Power*, p. 153. See also Pateman, *Participation*; and Walker, "Critique."

184. Pateman, *Participation*, p. 18.

185. Ibid., p. 9.

186. Ricci, *Community Power*, p. 153.

187. Dahl, *Who Governs?* p. 220.

188. Dahl, "Hierarchy," cited in Ricci, *Community Power*, p. 153.

189. Ricci, *Comunity Power*, p. 153.

190. Pateman, *Participation*; Walker, "Critique"; Kariel, *Frontiers of Democratic Theory*; Pranger, *Eclipse*; Lane Davis, "The 'New Democracy.' " The argument is usually made by focusing on a small portion of Dahl's published writings—typically *Preface* (1956), "Hierarchy" (1956), or *Who Governs?* (1961). Walker's study, for example, focuses on one book, *PEW*, pp. 272-314, in his essay in *Frontiers of Democratic Theory*; Bay considers only *Modern Political Analysis*, pp. 1, 6, 63; Duncan and Lukes concentrate on "Hierarchy," pp. 83-90, and *Preface*, p. 86. Lane Davis' criticisms of the "new realism" in democratic theory include a study of *Preface*; Bachrach and Baratz in their "Two Faces" article concentrate on *Who Governs?* and "Critique of the Ruling Elite Model" (1958).

191. Walker, "Critique," p. 286.

192. See Dahl's rejoinder to Walker's critique, "Further Reflections on 'The Elitist Theory of Democracy' "; see also Richard Merlman, "On the Neo-Elitist Critique of Community Power," *American Political Science Review* 60 (1966): 451-60.

193. John Dewey, *Democracy and Education* (New York: Macmillan, 1916), *The Public and Its Problems* (New York: Henry Holt, 1927), and *Human Nature and Conduct* (New York: Henry Holt, 1922). For an interesting and recent critical account of workplace democracy, see John Witte, *Democracy, Alienation and Authority in Work: Worker's Participation in an American Corporation* (Chicago: University of Chicago Press, 1982).

194. Walker, "Critique," p. 287.

195. Ibid.

196. Ibid., p. 295. See also Bachrach, *The Theory of Democratic Elitism*; and McCoy and Playford, *Apolitical Politics*.

197. Walker, "Critique," p. 289.

198. Ibid., p. 295. See also Lowi, *End of Liberalism*.

199. Ibid.

200. Ibid.

201. See H. H. Gerth and C. Wright Mills (ed.), *From Max Weber* (New York: Oxford University Press, 1946).

202. Rousseaus and Farganis, "Equilibrium Rationalized," in Kariel (ed.), *Frontiers*, p. 312.

203. Ibid.

204. See Eugene Miller, "Positivism, Historicism and Political Inquiry," *American Political Science Review* 66 (September 1973): 796-874. For a rejection of the conventional view of Weber as an advocate of "value-free" social science, see Edward B. Partis, "Political Action and Social Science: Max Weber's Two Arguments for Objectivity," *Polity* 12 (Spring 1980): 407-27.

205. George Graham, Jr., "Latent Madisonianism"; Ronald M. Peters, Jr., "Political Theory, Political Science and *The Preface*"; and Christian Bay, "Pseudo-Politics."

206. Graham, "Latent Madisonianism"; and Peters, "Political Theory." See also a review of *A Preface to Democratic Theory*, Douglas N. Morgan, *American Political Science Review* 51 (December 1957): 1040.

207. Peters, "Political Theory," p. 176.

208. Ibid., p. 177.

209. Graham, "Latent Madisonianism," pp. 88-89.

210. Rousseaus and Farganis, "Equilibrium Rationalized," p. 311.

211. Ibid. See also Miller, "Historicism"; Peter L. Berger and Thomas Luckmann, *The Social Construction of Reality* (New York: Anchor, 1967); and Marjorie Grene, *The Knower and the Known* (Berkeley: University of California Press, 1974).

212. Rousseaus and Farganis, "Equilibrium Rationalized," p. 311.

213. Bay, "Pseudo-Politics," p. 44.

214. R. Dahl, closing paragraph of *Preface*, p. 151, cited in Bay, "Pseudo-Politics," p. 44.

215. Ibid.

216. The phrase is David Ricci's. This selection draws heavily from Ricci's excellent study of Dahl's methodological critics. See Ricci, *Community Power and Democratic Theory*, chapter 9, "Pluralism Opposed: The Critique of Method," pp. 161-82.

217. Thomas J. Anton, "Power and Pluralism and Local Politics," *Administrative Science Quarterly* (March 1963): 449-51; Herbert Danzger, "Community Power Structure: Problems and Continuities," *American Sociological Review* (October 1964): 714-16; and Bachrach and Baratz, "Two Faces of Power."

218. Delbert C. Miller in D'Antonio and Ehrlich (eds.), *Power and Democracy in America*, pp. 105-7.

219. Ricci, *Community Power*, p. 163.

220. Ibid.

221. Miller, in *Power and Democracy*, p. 106.

222. Danzger, "Community Power," pp. 714-16; Bachrach and Baratz, "Two Faces of Power," pp. 950-51.

223. Ricci, *Community Power*, p. 153.

224. Bachrach and Baratz, "Nondecisions," p. 632. See also "Two Faces of Power"; Anton, "Power," p. 453. For a more recent statement of this argument, see

Frederick W. Frey, "Comment: On Issues and Nonissues in the Study of Power," *American Political Science Review* 65 (December 1971): 1081-1101. See also Richard L. Simpson, "Comment by a Sociologist," *Southwest Social Science Quarterly* (December 1967): 287-91. For a precursor to the nondecisions argument, see Carl Friedrich, *Constitutional Government and Politics* (New York, 1939), pp. 17-19, wherein Friedrich discusses what he calls the "rule of anticipated reactions." Two recent nondecision-making case studies include John Gaventa, *Power and Powerlessness* (Chicago: University of Illinois Press, 1980); and Matthew A. Crenson, *The Unpolitics of Air Pollution: A Study of Non-Decisionmaking in the Cities* (Baltimore: Johns Hopkins University Press, 1971). See also Green and Levinson (eds.), *Power and Community*; and Surkin and Wolfe, (eds.), *An End to Political Science*.

225. David Easton, *Systems Analysis of Political Life* (New York: John Wiley, 1965), chapter 8 on "gatekeeping activities."

226. C. Wright Mills, in I. L. Horowitz (ed.), *Power, Politics and People: The Collected Papers of C. Wright Mills* (New York: Ballantine Books, 1961), p. 253, cited in Connolly (ed.), *The Bias of Pluralism*, p. 14.

227. Anton, "Letter"; Howard J. Ehrlich, "Power and Democracy: A Critical Discussion," in D'Antonio and Ehrlich, *Power*, p. 92. Andrew Hacker, "Liberal Democracy and Social Control," *American Political Science Review* (December 1957): 1009-26; Walker, "Critique"; Presthus, *Men at the Top*. For a more extensive treatment of the potential power critics, see Ricci, *Community Power*, pp. 170-75.

228. Ricci, *Community Power*, p. 171.

229. Ibid. See C. Wright Mills, *Power Elite*; Domhoff, *Who Really Rules?* and *Bohemian Grove*; Hacker, "Liberal Democracy and Social Control"; Presthus, *Men at the Top*; and Shin'ya Ona, "The Limits of Bourgeois Pluralism," *Studies on the Left* 5 (1965): 46-72; and Todd Gitlin, "Local Pluralism as Theory and Ideology," *Studies on the Left* 5 (1965): 21-45.

230. Bachrach and Baratz, "Nondecisions," and "Two Faces of Power"; Ehrlich in D'Antonio and Ehrlich, *Power and Democracy in America*. The most recent and most persuasive restatement of this position is that of Clarence N. Stone, "Systemic Power in Community Decisionmaking: A Restatement of Stratification Theory," *American Political Science Review* 74 (December 1980): 978-90.

231. Ricci, *Community Power*, p. 180. For a rejoinder to Ricci's criticism, see Dahl, "Rethinking *Who Governs?*: New Haven, Revisited," in Waste (ed.), *Community Power: Future Directions in Urban Research*.

232. The phrase is Ricci's. See his discussion in *Community Power*, pp. 133-35.

233. Dahl, *Who Governs?* p. 1.

234. Robert Dahl, in D'Antonio and Ehrlich, *Power and Pluralism in America*, pp. 83-85.

235. Ibid., p. 84.

236. For a less sanguine view of mobilization by low-resource groups, see John Mollenkopf, "On the Causes and Consequences of Political Mobilization," a paper presented to the Annual Meeting of the American Political Science Association, New Orleans, 1973; and a related study, Mollenkopf, *The Contested City* (Princeton: Princeton University Press, 1983). See also Mollenkopf, "Neighborhood Political Development and the Politics of Urban Growth: Boston and San Francisco, 1958-78," *International Journal of Urban and Regional Research* 5 (1981): 17-38.

237. Dahl, in D'Antonio and Ehrlich, *Power and Democracy in America*, p. 84.

238. The list of resources is that of Dahl and Polsby, cited in Ricci, *Community Power*, p. 133.

239. McCoy and Playford, *Apolitical Politics*, "Introduction," p. 7.

240. Ibid., p. 25.

241. Leo Strauss, "Epilogue," in Herbert J. Storing (ed.), *Essays on the Scientific Study of Politics* (New York: Holt, Rinehart & Winston, 1962), p. 327.

242. Von Der Muhll, "Robert A. Dahl and the Study of Contemporary Democracy," p. 1074.

243. Strauss, "Epilogue," p. 317.

244. Walker, "Critique," p. 295. See Dahl's rejoinder, "Further Reflections," pp. 296-305; and Walker's reply, "A Reply to 'Further Reflections on the Elitist Theory of Democracy,' " *American Political Science Review* (June 1966): 391-92.

245. Bay, "Politics and Pseudo-Politics," p. 45.

246. Three anthologies adhering to this perspective are McCoy and Playford (eds.), *Apolitical Politics*; Kariel (ed.), *Frontiers of Democratic Theory*; and Connolly (ed.), *The Bias of Pluralism*. See also Ricci, *Community Power and Democratic Theory*, chapter 9, "The Critique of Tolerance," pp. 183-204, and *The Tragedy of Political Science*.

247. Dahl, *Preface*, chapter 5, "American Hybrid," pp. 124-51.

248. Dahl, *After the Revolution*, pp. 104-66; "On Removing Certain Impediments to Democracy in the United States"; "What Is Political Equality?" *Dissent* (Summer 1979); 363-68; "Fundamental Rights in a Democratic Order," a paper presented to the International Congress of Political Science, Moscow, Summer 1979, reprinted as "The Moscow Discourse: Fundamental Rights in a Democratic Order," *Government and Opposition* (Winter 1980): 3-30; and "Procedural Democracy," in Peter Laslett and James Fishkin (eds.), *Philosophy, Politics and Society*, Fifth Series (New Haven: Yale University Press, 1979), pp. 97-103. See also Dahl, *Dilemmas of Pluralist Democracy: Autonomy and Control* (New Haven: Yale University Press, 1981); and *Controlling Nuclear Weapons: Democracy versus Guardianship* (Syracuse: Syracuse University Press, 1985).

249. Kariel, *Frontiers of Democratic Theory*; Connolly, *The Bias of Pluralism*.

250. Kariel, *Frontiers of Democratic Theory*, p. 35.

251. Ibid., p. 32.

252. Connolly, *The Bias of Pluralism*, p. 30, n. 18. The most recent exposition of the "two Dahls" thesis is Richard W. Krouse, "Polyarchy and Participation: The Changing Democratic Theory of Robert Dahl," *Polity* 14 (Spring 1982): 441-63.

253. New Haven, Connecticut, February 18, 1980; March 31, 1980. See also Robert Dahl, "Rethinking *Who Governs?*: New Haven, Revisited," in Waste (ed.), *Community Power: Future Directions in Urban Research*.

254. The charge that Dahl is an apologist with regard to racial discrimination is especially ironic given Dahl's participation (with James Tobin) in the 1964 "Mississippi summer" civil rights crusade.

255. Dahl and Lindblom, *PEW*, p. 279.

256. Dahl, "Procedural Democracy," p. 101.

257. Ibid. Although a full demonstration of this argument is well beyond the scope of the present chapter, we shall have occasion to suggest several pre-1967

passages that would lead a careful reader to reject the Pateman et al. view of Dahl as a democratic-elitist.

258. Dahl, *Preface*, p. 138.

259. Dahl, *Who Governs?* pp. 220, 290. Studies appearing after *Who Governs?* have been even less sanguine in their analysis of black voting patterns in New Haven. See Fred Powledge, *Model City* (New York: Simon & Schuster, 1970). Powledge argues that the high electoral turnout by blacks was, at best, an organizational and coalition-building device by Fred Harris and other black community organizers. Elections in New Haven, for blacks, were limited linkage institutions because there was only one real choice—Mayor Lee—for the black community *to link to*. As Powledge describes it (pp. 325-26), "Lee kept running and getting re-elected, and even for those who disliked him, he was always the lesser of two evils." Powledge quotes Harris as saying: "the only good I see coming out of elections and stuff like that is that campaigns can bring people together—people who have never been involved before." If, then, black electoral overparticipation was a reaction to being locked out in other spheres of urban community activity, it was in effect their best collective shot at political activity and community representation. It was, however, not a very good shot, nor a truly effective linkage institution. Lee, after all, was their only real choice and the choice of Lee presented, as Powledge notes, a cruel paradox. Powledge notes: "Lee and the handful of people like him were successful in at least starting something—in creating expectations" (p. 335). But as the expectations of the early 1960s led to the dashed hopes of the late 1960s, New Haven blacks turned to a different use of slack resources. Thus, in the summer of 1967, New Haven blacks turned to extralegal protests and urban rioting to communicate their alienation and disappointment.

260. Dahl, *Democracy in the United States: Promise and Performance*, 2d ed. (Chicago: Rand McNally, 1971), p. 432.

261. Ibid., p. 431.

262. Ibid., pp. 423-33.

263. Dahl, *Congress and Foreign Policy*; Dahl and Ralph S. Brown, *Domestic Control of Atomic Energy* (New York: Social Science Research Council, 1951).

264. Dahl and Tufte, *Size and Democracy*.

265. Dahl, *Congress and Foreign Policy*, pp. 63-65, 263-65.

266. Von Der Muhll, "Dahl and Study of Contemporary Democracy," pp. 1074-75.

267. Ibid., p. 1075.

268. Dahl, *Congress and Foreign Policy*, p. 89.

269. Ibid.

270. Ibid., pp. 90-91.

271. Dahl, "On Removing Certain Impediments to Democracy," p. 5.

272. Ibid., p. 6.

273. Ibid., p. 5.

274. Ibid., p. 17.

275. Robert Dahl, interview, March 31, 1980. For a less optimistic estimate of the impact that less restrictive registration laws might have, see Raymond E. Wolfinger and Steven J. Rosenstone, *Who Votes?* (New Haven: Yale University Press, 1980), especially chapter 4, "The Effect of Registration Laws on Turnout," pp. 61-68. See

also Douglas Rae, *The Political Consequences of Electoral Laws* (New Haven: Yale University Press, 1967).

276. Dahl and Lindblom, *PEW*, p. 278.

277. Ibid., 2d ed., p. xxvi.

278. Ibid., p. xxvii.

279. Ibid.

280. Ibid., p. xxix.

281. Dahl, "What Is Political Equality?: Reply," p. 365.

282. Dahl, "On Removing Certain Impediments to Democracy," p. 8.

283. Ibid. p. 15.

284. Dahl, *Preface*, pp. 84-90, 124-51; Dahl and Lindblom, *PEW*, pp. 227-324; and Dahl, *Polyarchy*, pp. 3, 203-49.

285. Dahl, *Who Governs?* p. 220.

286. Dahl and Lindblom, *PEW*, p. 313. Although it may come as a surprise to some observers, there are similarities between the "strategic positions" argument in *PEW* and the "strategic elites" argument of Suzanne Keller. See Suzanne Keller, *Beyond the Ruling Class: Strategic Elites in Modern Society* (New York: Arno Press, 1963).

287. Dahl and Lindblom, *PEW*, p. 318.

288. Ibid., p. 315.

289. Ibid.

290. Ibid., p. 314.

291. Dahl, *Who Governs?* p. 293.

292. Carole Pateman, *Participation and Democratic Theory* (Cambridge: Cambridge University Press, 1970), p. 9.

293. Dahl, *Democracy in the United States*, 2d ed., pp. 431-33.

294. Ibid., pp. 432-33.

295. Dahl, *After the Revolution*, p. 106. Readers may wish to read in its entirety Dahl's selection entitled "First Problems: Inequality of Resources" (pp. 105-16) and judge for themselves the merit of Harvey Mansfield's characterization of *After the Revolution* as a Yale Fastback with "no time for the fact-value distinction." Mansfield's review is reprinted in Mansfield, *The Spirit of Liberalism* (Cambridge, Mass.: Harvard University Press, 1978), especially p. 62.

296. Philip Green, "What Is Political Equality?" *Dissent* (Summer 1979): 351-62; and Robert A. Dahl, "II: A Reply," *Dissent* (Summer 1979): 363-68.

297. Green, "What Is Political Equality?" p. 360.

298. Robert Dahl, "Workers Control of Industry and the British Labor Party," *American Political Science Review* 41 (October 1947): 875-900.

299. Robert Dahl, interview, March 31, 1980.

300. Dahl, "Procedural Democracy," pp. 97-133; "The Moscow Discourses: Fundamental Rights in a Democratic Order"; "Egoism, Altruism and the Public Good" (Department of Political Science, University of Illinois at Urbana-Champaign), the Edmund James Lecture, delivered on February 4, 1980; *Dilemmas of Pluralist Democracy: Autonomy and Control*; and *A Preface to Economic Democracy* (Berkeley: University of California Press, 1985). Dahl is also currently working on a book-length study of "democracy and its critics" which will, no doubt, bear on the questions raised at this point in our study.

301. Nelson Polsby, *Community Power and Political Theory*; see also

" 'Pluralism' in the Study of Community Power: Or *Erklarung* Before *Verklarung* in *Wissenssoziologie*"; "Community Power: Some Reflections on the Recent Literature," *American Sociological Review* (December 1962): 838-41; "How to Study Community Power: The Pluralist Alternative," *Journal of Politics* (August 1960): 474-84; "Power in Middletown: Fact and Value in Community Research," *Canadian Journal of Economics and Social Science* (November 1960): 592-603; "Community Power Meets Air Pollution"; and "Empirical Investigation of the Mobilization of Bias in Community Power Research," *Political Studies* 27 (December 1979): 527-41. See also Raymond Wolfinger, "Reputation and Reality in the Study of Community Power"; "A Plea for a Decent Burial"; "Nondecisions and the Study of Local Politics"; and *The Politics of Progress*. See also Aaron Wildavsky, *Leadership in a Small Town* (Totowa, N.J.: Bedminster Press, 1964). The collateral literature surrounding the New Haven literature and its defenders and detractors is extensive. Several texts and readers trace this topic and the larger debate between the pluralist and elitist approaches to the study of community power. Readers and articles summarizing the literature in question include Terry N. Clark (ed.), *Community Power Structure and Decisionmaking: Comparative Analysis* (San Francisco: Chandler, 1968); Thomas R. Dye, "Community Power Studies," in James A. Robinson (ed.), *Political Science Annual*, vol. 2 (New York: Bobbs-Merrill, 1970); Edward Keynes and David Ricci, *Political Power, Community and Democracy* (1970); Robert E. Agger, Daniel Goldrich, and Bert S. Swanson, *The Rulers and the Ruled* (New York: John Wiley, 1964); C. Bonjean and M. Grimes (ed.), *Social Stratification: A Reader* (1974); Willis D. Hawley and Frederick M. Wirt (eds.), *The Search for Community Power*, 2d ed. (Englewood Cliffs, N.J.: Prentice-Hall, 1974); and G. William Domhoff (ed.), *Power Structure Research*, Sage Focus Editions, vol. 17 (Beverly Hills: Sage Publications, 1980). Two lengthy bibliographies include Willis D. Hawley and James H. Svara, *The Study of Community Power* (Santa Barbara, Calif.: ABC Clio, 1972); and Irving P. Leif, *Community Power and Decision-Making* (Metuchen, N.J.: Scarecrow Press, 1974).

302. Anton, "Power, Pluralism and Local Politics"; Peter Bachrach and Morton Baratz, "Decisions and Nondecisions"; and "Two Faces of Power." See also Herbert Danzger, "Community Power Structure: Problems and Continuities," *American Sociological Review* (October 1964): 714-16; Delbert Miller in D'Antonio and Ehrlich (eds.), *Power and Democracy in America*, pp. 105-7; and David Ricci, *Community Power and Democratic Theory*.

303. The recent book by J. Anthony Lukas analyzing desegregation in Boston public schools is a case in point. J. Anthony Lukas, *Common Ground: A Turbulent Decade on the Lives of Three American Families* (New York: Knopf, 1985).

304. More, however, is not always better. While the inclusion of more issues seems desirable in the abstract, including more issues in the concrete does not necessarily mean the study would have been improved or the conclusions any different. The New Haven study did include an extensive analysis of another issue—the 1958 defeat of a new city charter. Not much is done with the issue in the *Who Governs?* study. The issue, although well researched, did not add materially to the overall study. In this specific case, at least, adding another issue would have done little to clarify or strengthen the study.

305. Floyd Hunter, *Community Power Structure*; Robert Schulze, "The Role of Economic Dominants in Community Power Structure," *American Sociological*

Review 23 (February 1958): 3-9; See also Roland J. Pelligrini and Charles H. Coates, "Absentee-owned Corporations and Community Power Structure," *American Journal of Sociology* (March 1956): 413-19; and Delbert Miller, "Industry and Community Power Structure," *American Sociological Review* 23 (February 1958): 9-15.

306. See Polsby's discussion of issue selection in *Community Power and Political Theory*, p. 96.

307. It should be noted, however, that at least among elite or stratification theorists, one city and one issue may still be enough to prove one's point. Such seems to be the thrust of Floyd Hunter's *Community Power Succession* (1980), which focuses exclusively on Atlanta and primarily on urban redevelopment. Hunter deals in much less detail with the collateral issues of race, election law changes, education, political reform, welfare, and police action against the black community in a closing chapter of his study. See especially chapter 9, "Other Projects, Issues and Policies," pp. 144-56. See also Domhoff's restudy of New Haven, *Who Really Rules?* and Philip Trounstine and Terry Christensen, *Movers and Shakers: The Study of Community Power*, a single-city study of San Jose, California.

308. Polsby, *Community Power and Political Theory*, p. 113; Wolfinger, "Nondecisions and the Study of Local Politics," pp. 1064-65; and Dahl, *Who Governs?* p. 333.

309. The quotation is from Polsby, *Community Power and Political Theory*, p. 113. See also Wolfinger, "Reputation and Reality in the Study of Community Power."

310. Polsby, *Community Power and Political Theory*, p. 96.

311. See, however, Polsby, *Community Power and Political Theory*, p. 88, n. 16. What may have been more disturbing to the power elite school of Dahl's critics is not that the suburban "economic notables" were uninterested in local politics as that they seemed in many respects *uninterested in New Haven politics*. As Polsby notes: "Several Republican economic leaders whom we interviewed mentioned that they were active in politics in one or another of the suburban towns surrounding New Haven." Such a finding, of course, squares poorly with a Hunter-Domhoff view of "economic notables" pulling the strings of urban politics form the comfort of their suburban enclaves.

The best-known rejection of the "wrong question" argument is in Wolfinger, "Nondecisions and the Study of Local Politics," pp. 1064-65. It should be noted that elitists proposed alternative ways of determining which issues should be studied in a community. Jan Deutsch suggested in 1968 that the "primary difficulty with *Who Governs?* as an analysis of the existing distribution of power is the assumption that the decisions canvassed represented conflicts sufficiently serious to force *all potentially affected powerholders to mobilize their resources* in hopes of obtaining a favorable outcome." Deutsch, "Neutrality, Legitimacy, and the Supreme Court: Some Intersections Between Law and Political Science," *Stanford Law Review* 20 (January 1968): 251 (emphasis added), cited in Wolfinger, "Nondecisions," p. 1064. However, as Wolfinger observed: "This seems to be an excessively stringent criterion for 'distinguishing between important and unimportant issues arising in the political arena.' If taken literally, this standard would relegate all issues to the unimportant category, for when in history have 'all potentially affected powerholders' mobilized their resources? Certainly not in, say, the Russian Revolution and the Civil War [which] were fought with most potential participants on the sidelines. If earthshaking events like these fail to meet Deutsch's standards, what hope can we have of ever finding an important decision in local politics?" Wolfinger, "Nondecisions and the Study of Local Politics," p. 1064.

In *Power and Poverty* (New York: Oxford University Press, 1970), pp. 47-48, Bachrach and Baratz offer a less stringent but—because of its inherent ideological bias—an equally problematic measure for important or key issues. "A key issue, in our terms, is one that involves a genuine challenge to the resources of power or authority of those who currently dominate the process by which policy outputs in the system are determined." As Wolfinger notes, in discussing the pros and cons of this approach: "Recognizing that the consequences of decisions may not be immediately apparent, they suggest that this difficulty may be eased by choosing several issue areas to study, thus giving the researcher a fuller perspective on outcomes and their implications, and increasing his chances of picking a 'key issue.' Interestingly, they do not discuss another drawback to their proposal: It involves a conclusion about who dominates politics before data have been collected." Wolfinger, "Nondecisions and the Study of Local Politics," p. 1064. For an approach that is sympathetic to the elitist perspective, but considerably more evenhanded, see the discussion of new proposals to research "nondecision-making" in Gunnar Falkemark, *Power, Theory and Value* (Lund, Sweden: Lieber-Gleerup, 1982).

312. For a recent restatement of the elitist position, see the discussion of the "growth machine" thesis in Thomas R. Dye, "Community Power and Public Policy"; and G. William Domhoff, "The Growth Machine and the Power Elite: A Challenge to Marxists and Pluralists Alike," in Waste (ed.), *Community Power: Future Directions in Urban Research.*

313. Bachrach and Baratz, *Power and Poverty*, p. 10, cited in Polsby, *Community Power and Political Theory*, p. 192.

314. Polsby, *Community Power and Political Theory*, p. 114; see also p. 70 and Dahl, *Who Governs?* pp. 330-43.

315. Polsby, *Community Power and Political Theory*, pp. 70-71. See also Dahl, *Who Governs?* pp. 121-33, especially Figure 10-1; and Wolfinger, *The Politics of Progress.*

316. Ibid.

317. Polsby, *Community Power and Political Theory*, p. 81.

318. Dahl, *Who Governs?* p. 333.

319. Nor does a nondecisions focus seem superior to the issue selection method outlined by Polsby in *Community Power and Political Theory*, p. 96. For an analysis that illustrates both the strengths and weaknesses of the nondecisions approach, see Matthew Crenson, "Nonissues in City Politics: The Case of Air Pollution," in Surkin and Wolfe (eds.), *An End to Political Science*, pp. 144-66. For a more recent and novel—if ultimately unconvincing—attempt to unravel the Gordian knot associated with nondecision-making, see Gunnar Falkemark, *Power, Theory and Value*. See also a review of Falkemark's book by this author in the *American Political Science Review* (December 1984): 1197-98.

320. John Gaventa's prize-winning study of "quiescence and rebellion in an Appalachian valley," suggests a promising way out of the two faces of power standoff. The first face is pluralist competition and bargaining for policy outcomes in the public and formal arenas; the second is Bachrach and Baratz's conspiratorial, deliberate manipulation of values by a community elite to control the issues on the

public agenda; the third is a political culture face—the deliberate manipulation of symbolism and values that are dominant in a given community. The control of local elites hinged on the use of the second and third faces to control activity in the first; for example, "as brokers of political resources such as jobs or votes, as mediators of values and policies, and as 'gatekeepers' of information between the 'outside' and 'inside' worlds." Gaventa, *Power and Powerlessness* (Chicago: University of Illinois Press, 1980), p. 259. Unlike the second face of power which is, almost by definition, impossible to confirm, the third face of power more readily lends itself to empirical study and measurement. In addition to Gaventa's case studies of the influence of a regulatory agency and a multinational, see Matthew Crenson's study of the influence of industrial concerns in the air pollution issue in Gary and East Chicago. Crenson, *The Unpolitics of Air Pollution: A Study of Nondecisionmaking in the Cities* (Baltimore: Johns Hopkins University Press, 1971). Clarence Stone has also proposed a research methodology superior to the Bachrach and Baratz focus on nondecision-making's second face. Stone argues for a study of "the flow of decisions over time" to determine net winners and losers, and, second, to build a composite picture of the structure of influence within each community that conditions and influences the exercise of power by elected decision-makers. Stone, "Community Power Structure: A Further Look," *Urban Affairs Quarterly* 16 (1981): 514-15. See also Stone, "Systemic Power in Community Decision Making." Another development which seems promising in both pluralist and elitist approaches to the study of power in community politics is the discussion of "containers" and gatekeepers and their role in slowing and preventing issues from reaching the public or formal agenda of community politics, in Roger Cobb and Charles Elder, *Participation in American Politics: The Dynamics of Agenda Building*, 2d ed. (Baltimore: Johns Hopkins University Press, 1983). The second edition contains a valuable discussion of the role of "policy entrepreneurs" that lends itself well to an analysis of politics at the local level.

321. For an argument to the contrary, see Jan G. Deutsch, "Neutrality, Legitimacy and the Supreme Court."

322. See Polsby's discussion of organizing "a community power study around the perspective of putative big shots, defined as such in advance of empirical investigation." *Community Power and Democratic Theory*, p. 201.

323. For a more detailed and, in all probability, a definitive rejection of the nondecisions approach, see Wolfinger, "Nondecisions and the Study of Local Politics," p. 1079.

324. C. Wright Mills, in I. L. Horowitz (ed.), *Power, Politics and People: The Collected Writings of C. Wright Mills* (New York: Ballantine Books, 1961), p. 253.

325. Ibid.

326. See Von Der Muhll, "Robert A. Dahl and the Study of Contemporary Democracy."

327. Dahl, *Congress and Foreign Policy*; "On Removing Certain Impediments to Democracy"; and "What Is Political Equality: Reply."

328. Howard Ehrlich, "Power and Democracy," in D'Antonio and Ehrlich, *Power*, p. 92; Andrew Hacker (ed.), *The Corporation Take-Over* (New York: Oxford University Press, 1964); and Jack Walker, "A Critique of the Elitist Theory of Democracy."

329. The precursor to this argument is Carl Friedrich's celebrated "rule of antici-

pated reactions," outlined by Friedrich in his *Constitutional Government and Democracy* (Boston: Ginn, 1946), pp. 589-91.

330. David Ricci, *Community Power and Democratic Theory*, p. 172.

331. Polsby, *Community Power and Political Theory*, pp. 60-67, 207-9; and Wolfinger's discussion of how to measure influence in which he makes "a plea for modesty," in "Nondecisions and the Study of Local Politics," pp. 1079-80.

332. Consider, for example, the situation of black repression in the South. When our examination was revised to focus upon public issues (e.g., black codes, election laws), it demonstrated repression of blacks by whites in the South. This is hardly, we would suggest, a "pluralist" finding "necessitated" as Ricci suggests by a "pluralist method."

333. Robert Dahl, interviews, New Haven, January 14 and March 31, 1980.

334. See Polsby, *Community Power and Political Theory*, for a full discussion of "competence differentials" and the problem of respondent ignorance.

335. Polsby, *Community Power and Political Theory*, p. 113.

336. Ibid., p. 207. See also Wolfinger, "Nondecisions and the Study of Local Politics," p. 1079, where he rejects the potential power methodology on the grounds that the data required would not only be difficult but, in some cases, probably "unobtainable." He offers the following examples of data implicitly measurable by the potential power approach: "(1) measuring politicians' anticipations of responses to alternative courses of action; (2) defining abstention in such a way as to distinguish it from apathy or unwillingness to participate; (3) assessing the impact on partici- pation and on the distribution of governmental benefits of alternative values, proce- dures, and institutions; (4) identifying those responsible for contemporary values, procedures and institutions." Wolfinger continues: "Equally formidable objections concern how one draws sensible conclusions about the distribution of political power from the sorts of data described in the preceding paragraph. In part this reflects contradictory criteria; (1) those who are responsible for a particular institution or procedure may not be its beneficiaries; (2) factors that increase participation in politics may not necessarily also help equalize the distribution of public goods. More important, there seems to be no way to develop a common currency of power from all the nondecisions that researchers would turn up. For example, how does one deduce power from a politician's sensitivity to the electorate and then express the result in terms that can be aggregated with the power deduced from, say, an understanding of the etiology and consequences of the nonpartisan ballot?" Wolfinger, "Nondecisions and the Study of Local Politics," p. 1079. See also James L. Payne, "The Oligarchy Muddle," *World Politics* 20 (April 1968): 452.

337. See, for example, Dahl, *Who Governs?* p. 220. See also Dahl's discussion of "certain tacit understandings in the local political culture that sophisticated partici- pants can hope to rely on." *Who Governs?* pp. 80-81. More recently, Dahl has reemphasized this point in "Rethinking *Who Governs?*: New Haven, Revisited," in Waste (ed.), *Community Power: Future Directions in Urban Research*.

338. Ricci, *Community Power and Democratic Theory*, p. 180.

339. See also Wolfinger's discussion of the need for a "common currency of units of power," in n. 336 above and in "Nondecisions and the Study of Local Politics," pp. 1079-80.

340. *Baker v. Carr* 369 U.S. 186 (1962), and *Reynolds v. Sims* 377 U.S. 533 (1964).

341. Dahl, in D'Antonio and Ehrlich, *Power and Democracy in America*, pp. 83-85.

342. Robert Dahl, interviews, New Haven, January 14 and March 31, 1980.

343. See chapter 3.

344. For a general discussion of the use and, in at least one case, the gratuitous interpolation of Dahl's discussion of cumulative inequalities, see the example cited in Polsby, *Community Power and Political Theory*, pp. 193-96. See also Kenneth Newton, *Second City Politics* (Oxford: Clarendon Press, 1976), pp. 242-44.

345. Dahl, *A Preface to Democratic Theory*.

346. See especially Ricci, *Community Power and Political Theory*, pp. 133-35.

347. Ricci, *Community Power and Democratic Theory*, pp. 125-204.

348. Ibid.; and Dahl, *Polyarchy*, pp. 206-7.

349. Dahl, *Polyarchy*, p. 207.

350. For an argument to the contrary, see Wolfinger, "Nondecisions and the Study of Local Politics," p. 1079. See also Polsby, *Community Power and Political Theory*, p. 207; and Fred Frey, "Comment: On Issues and Nonissues in the Study of Power," *American Political Science Review* 65 (December 1971): 1081-1101; and Wolfinger's "Rejoinder," in the same issue, pp. 1102-5. See also James L. Payne, "The Oligarchy Muddle."

351. One problem with determining such weights is that the assigned weights may be subject to shifts in environmental or extramural forces. See the discussion of the "ideology of the times" and the impact that a shift in this "ideology" can have upon the influence and resources of various intramural bargainers in a tariff bargaining arena, in Bauer, Pool, and Dexter, *American Business and Public Poilcy* (New York: Atherton Press, 1963), which describes the congressional battle over renewing the Reciprocal Trade Act in 1955. Also, as the authors of *American Business* and Suzanne Keller have noted, elites may be "weighty" or "strategic" in one context and relatively powerless in another. How, then, are we to test for this sometimes powerfulness, sometimes powerlessness—or, even to distinguish between these two sets of arena, in Bauer, Pool, and Dexter, *American Business and Public Policy* (New York: *Strategic Elites in Modern Society*.

352. Wolfinger, "Nondecisions and the Study of Local Politics," pp. 1070-80.

353. Robert Dahl, interview, New Haven, March 31, 1980.

354. See chapter 1 for a full description of the polyarchal model and its eight process requirements.

355. See appendix A, "Contemporary Polyarchies, circa 1969," in Dahl, *Polyarchy*, pp. 246-49.

356. I am grateful to Professor L. L. Wade of the University of California at Davis for repeatedly raising this question, to which, admittedly, I, along with pluralist writers generally, have no easily defended or well-developed answer.

357. See Robert Dahl, *A Preface to Democratic Theory*, appendix to chapter 3, "Polyarchal Democracy," pp. 84-89; and Dahl, *Polyarchy*, pp. 206-7. See also Deane Neubauer, "Some Conditions of Democracy," *American Political Science Review* 61 (1967): 1002-9; John May, "Defining Democracy," *Political Studies* (March 1978): 1-14; and Dahl, interview, New Haven, January 14 and March 31, 1980.

358. For a full discussion of the differences between ordinary or "working" polyarchies and egalitarian polyarchies (ideal democracies), see chapter 1.

359. It can, however, show the probable routes that lead to a polyarchy, and the conditions necessary to facilitate the movement away from hegemonic rule, as Dahl notes in *Polyarchy*.

360. This is especially so within urban areas in the United States, where most cities would probably be regarded as polyarchies. Nuances and differences become especially important in such cases. Otherwise, we are left with the not entirely helpful observation that most U.S. cities are polyarchies. Comparative urban study and prescriptive research would seem to call for an ability to distinguish between urban regimes, both for purposes of description and prescription.

361. This does not mean, however, that all U.S. cities are *necessarily* polyarchies (see Appendix D).

362. Michael Lipsky, *Street-Level Bureaucracy*. Much the same argument can be made for the decentralized amateur bureaucrats generated by the citizen participation requirements of various federal-urban programs dating from the community action programs of the early 1960s to the present. The Housing and Community Development Act (the now-defunct CDBG program) is a case in point. See Dale Rogers Marshall and Robert Waste, *Large Cities and the Community Development Act* (Davis, Calif.: University of California, Davis-Institute of Governmental Affairs, 1977).

363. See the discussion of TWO by John Fish in *Black Power/White Control* (Princeton: Princeton University Press, 1973); and the discussion of the role of the UMW in Appalachia by John Gaventa, *Power and Powerlessness*. See also Tom Wolfe, *Radical Chic and Mau Mauing the Flak Catchers* (New York: Farrar, Straus & Giroux, 1970); and Frederick Wirt, *Power in the City: Decision Making in San Francisco* (Berkeley: University of California Press, 1975). As Crenson has pointed out, however, the relationship between close-knit neighborhood or village friendship networks and community associations may be paradoxical, especially in urban neighborhoods. See Matthew Crenson, "Social Networks and Political Processes in Urban Neighborhoods," *American Journal of Political Science* 22 (August 1978): 578-94. For a more recent use of network analysis, see Eulau, "From Labyrinths to Networks: Political Representation in Urban Settings," in Waste (ed.), *Community Power: Future Directions in Urban Research*.

A second area important to explore includes the representative role played by secondary groups, such as the League of Women Voters, which, while such linkage is not their primary function, occasionally serve as effective ad hoc linkages between government officials and neighborhood interests. See especially Michael Lipsky, "Protest as a Political Resource." The "Radical Chic" essay by Tom Wolfe, which describes a party thrown by Leonard Bernstein to raise money for the Black Panthers, speaks to the ironies involved in some of the linkages between community groups and government officials. For a less ironic account which offers a careful typology of community linkage mechanisms in general see Rufus Browning, Dale Rogers Marshall, and David Tabb, "Responsiveness to Minorities: A Theory of Political Change in Cities," a paper prepared for the Annual Meeting of the American Political Science Association, August 1978.

364. Jack Walker, "A Critique of the Elitist Theory of Democracy," p. 295.

365. The interviews were conducted in two Rhode Island cities, Providence and Foster. A total of 322 respondents were polled in Providence (1980 pop. 156,804) and

292 respondents were polled in Foster (1980 pop. 3,370). In theory, it can be said that, in 95 cases out of 100, the results of the entire sample are no more than 5 percentage points above or below what would have been obtained by interviewing all adult Providence and Foster adults. The theoretical limitation on errors does not take into account a margin of additional error resulting from various practical difficulties in taking any survey of public opinion. See Herbert Arkin and Raymond B. Golton, *Tables for Statisticians* (New York: Barnes and Noble, 1963), pp. 151-52; and H. P. Hill, J. L. Roth, and H. Arkin, *Sampling in Auditing* (New York: The Ronald Press, 1962). See also Charles S. Backstrom and Gerald Hursh-Cesar, *Survey Research*, 2d ed. (New York: John Wiley, 1981), pp. 72-73; and Earl R. Babbie, *The Practice of Social Research* (Belmont, Calif.: Wadsworth, 1979), pp. 169-75.

366. Dahl, *Who Governs?* pp. 1-63.

367. Michael Barone, Grant Ujifusa, and Douglas Matthews, *The Almanac of American Politics* (Washington, D.C.: Barone and Co., 1981), p. 989. See also Chilton Williamson, "Rhode Island Suffrage Since the Dorr War," *New England Quarterly* (March 1955): 34-50.

368. Ibid. See also John Sitely, "Rhode Island Voting Patterns, 1940-1964," (Kingston, R.I.: University of Rhode Island, Bureau of Government Research, 1966); and Richard Gabriel, "Ethnic Voting in Primary Elections: The Irish and Italians of Providence, Rhode Island" (Kingston, R.I.: University of Rhode Island, Bureau of Government Research, 1969).

369. Elmer Cornwell, "Ethnic Group Representation: The Case of the Portuguese," *Polity* 13 (Fall 1980): 5-22. See also Murray and Susan Stedman, "The Rise of the Democratic party in Rhode Island," *New England Quarterly* (September 1951): 173-77.

370. Richard Gabriel, "The Political Machine in Rhode Island," (Kingston, R.I.: University of Rhode Island, Bureau of Government Research, 1969).

371. For a brief history of Foster, see Sandra Alson, Marcia Bowden, Margery Matthews, and Elizabeth Olausen, *Foster and the Patriot's Dream* (North Scituate, R.I.: Cardinal Press, Foster Preservation Society, 1976).

372. The state House of Representatives minority leader, a Republican, is the long-term representative from Foster. Foster's Republicanism is as ubiquitous as electoral adherence to the Democratic party is in most of the rest of Rhode Island. The state has, for example, "gone Republican for president only three times in the last 50 years, twice for Eisenhower and once for Nixon; it has elected only one Republican to the U.S. Senate since 1930; and it elected no Republicans to the House of Representatives between 1938 and 1980. In 1980, when most of the nation was going for Ronald Reagan, Rhode Island gave him only 37% of its votes—his worst showing outside the District of Columbia." *Almanac of American Politics*, p. 989.

373. This was to be financed with the aid of a 4 percent loan from the federal government, but the thrifty New Englanders voted the loan down on the grounds that, as one local wag described it, the interest was unacceptably high.

374. The figure was 15 percent for Providence.

375. For a recent and promising use of network analysis, see Heinz Eulau, "From Labyrinths to Networks: Political Representation in Urban Settings," in Waste (ed.), *Community Power: Future Directions in Urban Research*.

376. This is also the case of Foster. Possible reasons for the relatively close scores of Foster and Providence may include the possibility that much of the intuitive view

of Foster is in need of change. Leading possibilities include: (1) the possibility that the social/ideological sameness of Foster may be as stifling as the strong party system of Providence; (2) the grasp and hold of the old families in Foster may affect would-be candidates; (3) the small size of Foster may actually work against openness and accessibility—no doubt, in Foster a political activist or dissident is instantly visible, much more so than in Providence; and/or (4) it may be that one needs to have roots in the community to have influence. Because so many people in the community either are politicians or have a close friend or relative who is, to "know someone" in local politics becomes not simply an asset but *the minimum cost of political entry/effectiveness*. If you are a new resident or an old resident without such connections, it may be that you are below the minimum threshold for political efficacy in Foster.

377. Elmer Cornwell, "Rhode Island: The Long Count and Its Aftermath," in *Party Politics in the New England States* (New Hampshire: New England Center for Continuing Education, 1968), pp. 21-30; and "Bosses, Machines, and Ethnic Groups," *The Annals of Political Science* (May 1964): 29-34. See also Cornwell, "Party Absorption of Ethnic Groups: The Case of Providence, Rhode Island," *Social Forces* 38 (March 1960): 205-10. For a well-written, although indirect, counter-argument, see David R. Mayhew, *Two Party Competition in the New England States* (Amherst, Mass.: University of Massachusetts, Bureau of Government Research, 1967). The classic treatment of urban political machines, Tammany Hall style, is William Riordan, *Plunkitt of Tammany Hall* (New York: E. P. Dutton, 1962).

378. Gabriel, "Ethnic Voting in Primary Elections: The Irish and Italians of Providence, Rhode Island," p. 11.

379. Richard Gabriel, "The Political Machine in Rhode Island," pp. 13-16. See also the late V. O. Key's dated but still persuasive discussion of the tendency for party factions to compete in areas where one party dominates a city's electoral scene. V. O. Key, Jr., *American State Politics* (New York: Knopf, 1965), pp. 104-5. Two theoretical discussions of political machines which might be applied to the Providence case include Wolfinger, *The Politics of Progress*, chapter 4, "Machine Politics," pp. 74-129; and Martin Shefter's revision of the traditional view of the origins of municipal machines in Willis Hawley et al., *Theoretical Perspectives on Urban Politics* (Englewood Cliffs, N.J.: Prentice-Hall, 1976), pp. 14-44.

380. This has been true over time in Providence. According to Gabriel and Paul Savage in a 1969 study of Providence voters: "Our data appear to support the premise that Providence voters see themselves as participants in the game of politics rather than as observers and that they appear to perceive a clear connection between political action and the benefits to be derived therefrom." Gabriel and Savage, "Political Ethos: What Providence Voters Think About Politics and Why" (University of Rhode Island, unpublished paper, 1972). See also Richard Gabriel, "Political Ecology and Voting Behavior: A Case Study of Rhode Island," unpub. Ph.D. diss., University of Massachusetts, 1969.

381. Providence has a law on the books prohibiting passing out political pamphlets in the city parks. This law has gone unenforced for some time. Of more immediate interest has been the irregular procedure by which some groups have been denied parade permits while others have been granted and the city's penchant for frequently arresting one Fred Fratiello, leader of a group calling itself the Proletarian

Warriors, whenever Mr. Fratiello takes to leafletting in front of city hall or speaking on street corners or in public parks.

382. Here I would defer to the issue selection criteria described by Polsby in *Community Power and Political Theory*, pp. 95-97. See also Wolfinger, "Nondecisions and the Study of Local Politics," pp. 1064-65, and "Reputation and Reality in the Study of Community Power," pp. 636-44; and Dahl, *Who Governs?* p. 333.

383. See, however, Clarence Stone's discussion of "the activities that precede the formulation of official proposals." These include: (1) "to take into account the substantive content of decisions"; (2) to "give more attention to the constraints surrounding the flow of decisions"; and (3) to focus more explicitly on "the capacity to mobilize politically." Stone's agenda for examining "closely the activities that precede the formulation of official proposals" seems promising. Stone, "Community Power Structure: A Further Look," pp. 514-15.

384. See the "Voting: Providence Style" series in the *Providence Journal* written by Bruce De Silva, Katherine Gregg, Deane Hulick, and Alan Rosenberg. *Providence Journal*, February 13-15, 1983. See especially "Cianci Supporters Abused Mail Ballot System in Providence Campaign," *Providence Journal*, Sunday, February 13, 1983, p. 1; "Cianci Supporters Pressed Students to Vote by Mail," *Providence Journal*, February 14, 1983, p. 1; and John Kiffney, "Darrigan Says Ballot Probe Could Dictate New Election," *Providence Journal*, February 15, 1983, p. 1.

385. *Arbitron* and *Nielsen* are the best available sources, and they rely on journals and spot surveys.

386. As well as research on such related topics as paths associated with various polyarchal types. See appendix E.

387. See Edward C. Banfield and James Q. Wilson, *City Politics* (Cambridge, Mass.: Harvard University Press, 1967); Banfield, *Big City Politics* (New York: Random House, 1965); and Agger, Goldrich, and Swanson, *The Rulers and the Ruled* (1964). More recent studies include J. David Greenstone and Paul Peterson, *Race and Authority in Urban Politics: Community Participation and the War on Poverty* (New York: Russell Sage, 1973); Laura Morlock, "Business Interests, Countervailing Groups and the Balance of Influence in 91 Cities," in Hawley and Wirt (eds.), *The Search for Community Power* (Englewood Cliffs, N.J.: Prentice-Hall, 1974); and Rufus Browning, Dale Rogers Marshall and David Tabb, *Protest Is Not Enough: The Struggle for Black and Hispanic Equality in Cities* (Berkeley: University of California Press, 1984). See also the argument by Willis Hawley and Michael Lipsky: "Indeed, it seems that interest in conceptualizing urban systems as a whole and in specifying critical dimensions of urban political systems has significantly declined since the work of Edward Banfield and James Wilson, Robert Dahl, Robert Agger and his associates, Norton Long, and Wallace Sayre and Herbert Kaufman in the late 50's and early 1960's focused attention on the urban polity as a whole." Hawley et al., *Theoretical Perspectives on Urban Politics* (Englewood Cliffs, N.J.: Prentice-Hall, 19765), pp. 2-3. See also Norton Long, *The Polity* (Chicago: Rand McNally, 1962); and Wallace Sayre and Herbert Kaufman, *Governing New York City* (New York: Russell Sage, 1960).

388. See, for example, R. Waste and Glen W. Sparrow, "Democracy Through the Mail: A Call for Municipal Mail Ballots," *Social Policy* (Fall 1985): 58-59.

389. Some exceptions, however, do spring to mind. The Louisiana parish described in appendix D is a case in point.

390. Deane Neubauer, "Some Conditions of Democracy," pp. 1002-9. See also Neubauer, *On the Theory of Polyarchy: An Empirical Study of Democracy in Ten Countries*, unpub. Ph.D. diss., Yale University, 1965; Neubauer and Charles F. Cnudde (eds.), *Empirical Democratic Theory* (Chicago: Markham Publishing Co., 1966); and Anthony Downs, *An Economic Theory of Democracy* (New York: Harper & Row, 1957), pp. 23-24.

391. Neubauer, "Some Conditions of Democracy," p. 1005.

392. Ibid., p. 1006.

393. Ibid.

394. Ibid.

395. Backstrom and Hursh-Cesar, *Survey Research*, pp. 72-73, 113-114; and Earl R. Babbie, *The Practice of Social Research*, pp. 169-175.

396. Theodore Caplow, "Decades of Public Opinion: Comparing NORC and Middletown Data," *Public Opinion* 5 (October/November 1982): 30-31.

Bibliography

BOOKS

The following books are a combination of classic pluralist writings and more recent attempts to confront contemporary problems in pluralist theory and community power research.

Bentley, Arthur F. 1967. *The Process of Government*. Cambridge, Mass.: Harvard University Press, orig. ed., 1908.

Connolly, William E. (ed.). 1969. *The Bias of Pluralism*. New York: Lieber-Atherton.

Crenson, Matthew. 1971. *The Un-Politics of Air Pollution*. Baltimore: Johns-Hopkins University Press.

Dahl, Robert A. 1961. *Who Governs?* New Haven: Yale University Press.

_____. 1971. *Polyarchy*. New Haven: Yale University Press.

_____. 1982. *Dilemmas of Pluralist Democracy: Autonomy vs. Control*. New Haven: Yale University Press.

Dahl, Robert A., and Charles E. Lindblom. 1953. *Politics, Economics, and Welfare*. New York: Harper & Row, 2d. ed., 1976, Chicago: University of Chicago Press.

Domhoff, G. William. 1978. *Who Really Rules? New Haven and Community Power Reexamined*. Santa Monica, Calif.: Goodyear Publishing Company.

_____. 1983. *Who Rules America Now?: A View for the 1980's*. Englewood Cliffs, N.J.: Prentice-Hall.

Falkemark, Gunnar. 1982. *Power, Theory and Value*. Lund, Sweden: Lieber-Gleerup.

Garson, G. David. 1978. *Group Politics*. Beverly Hills, Calif.: Sage Social Research Series, Vol. 61.

Gaventa, John. 1980. *Power and Powerlessness: Quiescence and Rebellion in an Appalachian Valley*. Urbana: University of Illinois Press.

Green, Philip, and Sanford Levinson (eds.). 1970. *Power and Community: Dissenting Essays in Political Science*. New York: Vintage Books.

Greenstone, J. David (ed.). 1983. *Public Values and Private Power in American Politics*. Chicago: University of Chicago Press.

Kariel, Henry S. 1961. *The Decline of American Pluralism*. Stanford: Stanford Univ_.   174   Name Index

———— (ed.). 1970. *Frontiers of Democratic Theory*. New York: Random House.

Keller, Suzanne. 1979. *Beyond the Ruling Class: Strategic Elites in Modern Society*. New York: Random House, orig. ed., 1963.

Kelso, William. 1978. *American Democratic Theory: Pluralism and Its Critics*. Westport, Conn.: Greenwood Press.

Lindblom, Charles E. 1977. *Politics and Markets*. New York: Basic Books.

Lowi, Theodore. 1969. *The End of Liberalism: Ideology, Policy and the Crisis of Public Authority*. New York: W. W. Norton.

McConnell, Grant. 1966. *Private Power and American Democracy*. New York: Vintage Books.

Mills, C. Wright. 1956. *The Power Elite*. New York: Oxford University Press.

Nagel, Jack H. 1975. *The Descriptive Analysis of Power*. New Haven: Yale University Press.

Olson, Mancur. 1965. *The Logic of Collective Action*. Cambridge, Mass.: Harvard University Press.

Polsby, Nelson W. 1963. *Community Power and Political Theory*. New Haven: Yale University Press, rev. 2d. ed. 1980.

Ricci, David M. 1971. *Community Power and Democratic Theory*. New York: Random House.

————. 1984. *The Tragedy of Political Science: Politics, Scholarship, and Democracy*. New Haven: Yale University Press.

Riesman, David. 1967. *The Lonely Crowd*. New Haven: Yale University Press.

Truman, David B. 1951. *The Governmental Process*. New York: Alfred A. Knopf, 2d ed. with new introd., 1971.

Waste, Robert J. (ed.). 1986. *Community Power: Future Directions in Urban Research*. Beverly Hills, Calif.: Sage Publications.

Wildavsky, Aaron. 1964. *Leadership in a Small Town*. Totowa, N.J.: Bedminister Press.

Wirt, Frederick M. 1974. *Power in the City: Decision Making in San Francisco*. Berkeley: University of California Press.

Wolfinger, Raymond E. 1974. *The Politics of Progress*. Englewood Cliffs, N.J.: Prentice-Hall.

Yates, Douglas. 1977. *The Ungovernable City: The Politics of Urban Problems and Policy Making*. Cambridge: MIT Press.

ARTICLES

The following articles are excellent summaries of the pluralist-elitist debate or criticisms of the various approaches to studying community power.

Dahl, Robert A. 1977. "On Removing Certain Impediments to Democracy," *Political Science Quarterly* Vol. 92, Spring (1-20).

————. 1978. "Pluralism Revisited," *Comparative Politics* Vol. 10, January (191-204).

————. 1979. "Who Really Rules?" *Social Science Quarterly* Vol. 60, June (144-51).

Greenstone, J. David. 1975. "Group Theories," in Fred Greenstein and Nelson W.

Polsby (eds.), *The Handbook of Political Science*, Vol. 2. Reading, Mass.: Addison-Wesley, (243-318).

Lowi, Theodore. 1964. "American Business, Public Policy, and Political Theory," *World Politics* Vol. 16 (677-715).

_____. 1967. "The Public Philosophy: Interest-Group Liberalism," *American Political Science Review* Vol. 61, March (5-24).

Manley, John F. 1983. "Neo-Pluralism: A Class Analysis of Pluralism I and Pluralism II," *American Political Science Review* Vol. 77, June (368-83).

Polsby, Nelson, W. 1960a. "How to Study Community Power: The Pluralist Alternative," *Journal of Politics*, August (474-84).

_____. 1960b. "Power in Middletown: Fact and Value in Community Research," *Canadian Journal of Economics and Social Science*, November (592-603).

_____. 1969. " 'Pluralism' in the Study of Community Power: Or *Erklarung* Before *Verklarung* in *Wissenssoziologie*," *The American Sociologist* Vol. 4, May (118-22).

_____. 1972. "Community Power Meets Air Pollution," *Contemporary Sociology* Vol. 1, March (88-91).

_____. 1979. "Empirical Investigation of the Mobilization of Bias in Community Power Research," *Political Studies* Vol. 27, December (527-41).

Rothman, Stanley. 1960. "Systematic Political Theory: Observations on the Group Approach," *American Political Science Review* Vol. 54, March (15-33).

Stone, Clarence N. 1981. "Community Power Structure: A Further Look," *Urban Affairs Quarterly* Vol. 16, June (505-15).

Wolfinger, Raymond E. 1960. "Reputation and Reality in the Study of 'Community Power,' " *American Sociological Review* Vol. 25, October (634-44).

_____. 1971. "Nondecisions and the Study of Local Politics," *American Political Science Review* Vol. 65, December (1063-1104).

Name Index

Calhoun, John C., 3, 5, 6
Clay, Henry, 5
Connolly, William, 22, 39, 41, 42, 61, 62, 72, 78

Dahl, Robert A., xiii, xiv, xv, 1, 2, 3, 18, 19, 20, 21, 24, 27, 30, 32, 40, 45, 137; on active and legitimate groups, 87-88; and the American hybrid, 61; and arena theory of pluralism, 42-44, 48; and classical democratic theory, 47, 49; corporate influence, 70-72; criticism of polyarchal theory, 89-91; and the critique of method, 55-58, 77-88; the cycles of success and defeat, 74-75; Dahl's task, 37; as democratic apologist, 22, 39-46, 59, 61, 63-76; as democratic elitist, 47-51, 59, 63-76; as democratic theorist, 35-39, 59, 77; and egalitarian polyarchies, 26; the essential Dahl, 36, 62; as failed scientist, 51-55, 77-88; and industrial democracy, 75; as institutional pluralist, 15-17, 77; and institutional prescriptions, 69; and noncumulative resources, 58-59, 87-88; political impacts of wealth and status, 72-76; and the political stratum, 12; and racial discrimination, 63-66; the two

Dahls thesis, 62; and the *wertlos-wertfrei* critique, 51-55
Danzger, Herbert, 55, 56, 78
Davis, Lane, 41
Dewey, John, 50, 67
Domhoff, G. William, xii, xiv, 1, 2, 44-46, 80, 137
Duncan, Graeme, 41, 48-49
Dye, Thomas R., 80

Easton, David, 56
Eckstein, Harry, 49
Ehrlich, Howard, 57, 84
Etzoni, Amitai, 37-38, 49

Farganis, James, 53

Galbraith, John K., 15
Gaudet, Helen, 13
Graham, George, 53
Green, Philip, 75-76

Hacker, Andrew, 57, 84
Harrington, Michael, 43
Herring, Pendleton, 9
Hunter, Floyd, xii, xiv, 1, 44, 46, 79, 137

Jefferson, Thomas, 4

Subject Index

American Farm Bureau, 14, 44
American Legion, 9, 13
American Medical Association, 13
Analytical pluralists, 6-8, 13-15
Anarchistic fallacy, 13
Atlanta, xiv, 46, 91
Australia, 21

Baker v. Carr (1962), 86
Black Panthers, 85
Boston, 16, 74
Business Council, 44

Canada, 21
Chicago, 82, 91, 102
Chronic nonparticipants, 9, 50, 69-70
Civil Rights Acts of 1964 and 1965, 65
Cleveland, 79
Congress, 23, 43, 69, 93; and foreign policymaking, 36
Council on Foreign Relations, 68
Countervailing power, 15

Democracy: classical democratic theory, 47, 62; democratic theory, 47; empirical democratic theory, 111; at the limits of human realization, 31-32; neoclassical democratic theory, 47
Denmark, 21

East Germany, 93
Eastern Europe, 16
English Parliament, 69
Equilibrium, 7, 8

Foster, 97-98, 100-110
France, 21, 91

Great Britain, 21, 27, 91, 93
Groups, 7, 9; overlapping groups, 9, 11-12; potential groups, 7, 9; veto groups, 10

Homo civicus, 40-43, 49, 51
Homo politicus, 40, 43, 49, 86

Indianapolis, 79
Inner-directedness versus other-directedness, 10-11
Institutional pluralists, 15-17
Interest groups, 13-14; potential groups, 12-13; underlying groups, 14
Iron law of oligarchy, 13-14
Israel, 21

Los Angeles, 79

Mexico, 21, 91
Miami, 79

About the Author

ROBERT J. WASTE, Associate Professor of Urban Studies and Director of the Institute of Public and Urban Affairs, San Diego State University, is the editor of *Community Power: Future Directions in Urban Research.* His articles have appeared in *Urban Studies, Administration and Society,* and other journals.